Data Insights
New Ways to Visualize and Make Sense of Data

Hunter Whitney

ELSEVIER

AMSTERDAM • BOSTON • HEIDELBERG • LONDON
NEW YORK • OXFORD • PARIS • SAN DIEGO
SAN FRANCISCO • SYDNEY • TOKYO
Morgan Kaufmann is an imprint of Elsevier

Acquiring Editor: Meg Dunkerley
Editorial Project Manager Heather Scherer
Project Manager: Marilyn E. Rash
Designer: Joanne Blank

Morgan Kaufmann is an imprint of Elsevier
225 Wyman Street, Waltham, MA 02451, USA

Notices
Knowledge and best practice in this field are constantly changing. As new research and experience
broaden our understanding, changes in research methods or professional practices, may become
necessary.

Practitioners and researchers must always rely on their own experience and knowledge in evaluating
and using any information or methods described herein. In using such information or methods they
should be mindful of their own safety and the safety of others, including parties for whom they have a
professional responsibility.

To the fullest extent of the law, neither the Publisher nor the authors, contributors, or editors, assume
any liability for any injury and/or damage to persons or property as a matter of products liability,
negligence or otherwise, or from any use or operation of any methods, products, instructions, or ideas
contained in the material herein.

Library of Congress Cataloging-in-Publication Data
Application submitted.

British Library Cataloguing-in-Publication Data
A catalogue record for this book is available from the British Library.

ISBN: 978-0-12-387793-2

Author image on back cover courtesy of Charles Wharton. Copyright © 2012, Hunter Whitney.

For information on all Morgan Kaufmann publications
visit our website at *http://store.elsevier.com*.

Printed in China
12 13 14 15 16   10 9 8 7 6 5 4 3 2 1

Working together to grow
libraries in developing countries

www.elsevier.com | www.bookaid.org | www.sabre.org

ELSEVIER   BOOK AID
International   Sabre Foundation

To my mother, Rachel, for her sense of humor
To my grandmother, Esse, for her sense of wonder
To my grandfather, Doug, for his sense of determination
To my mentor, Don, for his sense of grace

Contents

Preface

SANDBOXES AND MUSEUM CASES

We don't receive wisdom; we must discover it for ourselves.

– MARCEL PROUST

This book is not a set of specifications but, rather, a collection of ideas, observations, juxtapositions, and conversations. Think of it more like a sandbox than a museum case. It's not a hermetically sealed bit of perfection but instead a place where we can take out some ideas, turn them around, and view them from different angles. Don't get me wrong, I love going to museums and looking into cases containing collections of truly cutting-edge advances in technologies such as arrowheads and astrolabes, but *hands off*! In these pages, you'll find some beautiful examples of work to spark your imagination, and places to play with ideas. I hope this book encourages a spirited, relaxed, interactive mindset.

A broad range of skills, abilities, and knowledge is needed to fully realize the far-reaching potential of data visualization. I've included observations in this book from a number of people with different backgrounds and perspectives, ranging from data scientists and statisticians to painters and writers. I would hope that my audience is just as diverse. Many perspectives are needed.

I'm a participant, along with you, in the daily process of making sense of the world, and that process increasingly involves understanding certain kinds of data and putting them to use. Ambiguity, contradictions, and uncertainty are the attributes that often go into making a great story. Double meanings can sometimes be a feature, not a bug, in the code of language. In the realm of science, for example, some of the greatest insights and discoveries have come in unanticipated ways. I would venture to guess that the last word on making sense of data has not been written and won't be for a long time.

I don't intend to suggest every view about the subject offered here is an absolute or meant to answer every possible criticism. Quite the contrary. The opinions and observations of the interviewees that appear in the book may not necessarily align with all of mine. The goal is to spark your own ideas and imagination about the topic and encourage conversation. Some debate is a useful aspect of collaboration. My approach to this subject may be relaxed and offbeat, but I tried to be thoughtful at the same time. Whatever flaws you may perceive in this book, I hope they are offset by a spirit of adventure and willingness to engage in the discussion. I'm dogmatic about being open-minded.

Acknowledgments

Good design begins with honesty, asks tough questions, comes from collaboration and from trusting your intuition.

– FREEMAN THOMAS

Gaining insights from data requires drawing on the skills, knowledge, and craft of many disciplines. The same is true for writing a book about this topic. To provide you with a sense of the expansiveness involved, I've collaborated with a number of people and interviewed many more. Writing this book has made me step out of my comfort zone, as I think it should, and I couldn't have ventured out alone. For the people most involved, creating it has been a significant experience.

For those who've put in long hours and late nights and given a part of themselves to this project, thank you:

John Bosley, Veena Kumar, Maria DiLisio, Valerie Demos, and Carl Quesnel

I appreciate the efforts of others who have made important contributions to this book:

Editors, reviewers, researchers, content contributors: Austin Rotondo, Becky Ebenkamp, Todd Holloway, Nicolas di Tada, Jon Duke, Barbara Tversky, and Quynh Nguyen

Graphic designers: Allison Bruce, Jo Bangphraxay, Mana Nahavandian, Sepideh Vahidi, Elaine Wilson, Mia Temple Medeiros, Marya Villarin, Axel Schmitzberger, Gavin Pledger, Adam Katz, and George Casino

Those who helped guide the process: Ben Shneiderman, Rachel Roumeliotis, Meg Dunkerley, and Heather Scherer

Writing a book is really difficult, and moral support is essential, so, thank you:

Jann Hoffman and Michael Aratow

To all the interviewees in the book, I've done my best to highlight some of your great work. Thank you.

About the Author

Hunter Whitney is a user experience (UX) designer who has helped create useful and usable interface designs for clients in areas ranging from bioscience and medicine to information technology and marine biology. In addition to his UX work, he has written numerous articles about a range of subjects, including data visualization, for various online and print publications. His aim is to encourage conversations among people with diverse skills and perspectives about presenting data in ways that are more widely accessible and engaging. Hunter received dual bachelor's degrees—one in english literature from UCLA and the other in biology from UCSC—and has completed postgraduate neuropsychology research at UCLA. The combination of these multidisciplinary studies reflects his long-standing interest in the intersection between the humanities and the sciences; you can contact him at *www.hunterwhitney.com*.

From Terabytes to Insights

The real voyage of discovery consists not in seeking new landscapes, but in having new eyes.

— MARCEL PROUST

FIGURE 1.1A

"Wanderer Above a Sea of Fog," Caspar David Friedrich, 1817. *Source: bpk, Berlin/Hamburger Kunsthalle/Elke Walford/Art Resource, New York.*

FIGURE 1.1B

Viewer looking at a 3D representation of a protein structure from the Protein Data Bank inside UCSD's Calit2 StarCAVE. *Source: Hunter Whitney.*

Note: One terabyte is 1,000,000,000,000 bytes. There are many more byte sizes, large and small, to derive insights from, as well.

INTRODUCTION: A GRANDER VIEW

Where the telescope ends, the microscope begins. Which of the two has the grander view?

— VICTOR HUGO

From our latest purchase decisions to global population trends, data of all kinds are increasingly swept up and carried along into ever-expanding streams. These surging flows are often so fast, and the volume so massive, they can overwhelm people's capacities to distill the essential elements, derive meanings, and gain insights. We invent tools to solve problems, accomplish tasks, and augment our abilities. We've devised instruments to see distant stars and view subatomic particles; now, people are creating new ways to peer at[1] multiple layers of data that otherwise would be invisible to us. Visualizations offer a way to extend and enhance our innate powers of perception and cognition and get a "grander view" of the world around us.

However, no matter how necessary these visual representations might be or how reliant we've become on them, they don't tell the complete story. The processes that go into making the visualization, the parts you don't typically see, are still key components of the picture. The more you know about what goes into making a visualization, as well as its relative strengths and weaknesses, the more effective a tool it can be. Technology enables us to interact with data on more levels to accomplish objectives ranging from completing simple day-to-day tasks to solving long-term, seemingly intractable problems. Visualizations help us transcend the jumbles of data, allowing us to see more of the stories life has to tell.

THINGS THAT MAKE US SMARTER: HOW THOUGHTFUL VISUALIZATIONS CAN MAKE OUR LIVES BETTER

How have we increased memory, thought and reasoning? By the invention of external aids: it is things that make us smart.

— DONALD NORMAN

For all of the things you care about most, do you ever wonder whether your decisions are well informed, uninformed, or even misinformed? Digital data of all kinds has the potential to provide us with deeper, more useful insights into many aspects of life. However, the elements we may need or want are typically not delivered to us in convenient little packages; they are heaped before us, strewn around, or stored away in vast repositories. The people who regularly work with data hold some of the keys and codes to unlocking the value held in countless databases. But the tools of access, the things that help make us smarter, don't all have to belong to the relative few. With the help of well-designed visualizations, and an awareness of their strengths and limitations, the doors can be thrown open to far greater numbers of people. Doors can be opened in different ways—from a blunt implement

---

[1]For more about "peering at" data, see later in this chapter.

like a battering ram to the precision instruments used by a locksmith. Each approach requires a different level of skill and applies in a different range of instances.

If all the data being collected, distilled, and disseminated about our lives were physical, it would create vast heaps that we would have to step over, sift through, trip on, or walk around. Imagine your computer as a vast storage locker, filling with ever-increasing stuff. There may be crucial items in there, but if you can barely remember, or keep track of, what you have, what good are they to you? Take the analogy a step further, and think of all the boxes in this locker as representing categories of your life: health, finance, work, family, social life, and so on. How do you find, filter, and fact-check all the information to have a clearer understanding and make good choices? Complicating the picture further, we live in a world of flux; depending on the timing and context, we may have a greater or lesser ability to make good decisions. And for some, the ability to rapidly and effectively make decisions from fast-flowing streams of data is an integral part of their work. From emergency rooms to operational command centers, a clear understanding, rapid assessment, and decisive actions based on data can make the difference between life and death.

An amazing quantity and variety of data is theoretically available at our fingertips through smart phones, tablets, and various other devices. It's a veritable "Neurvana" for inquisitive minds. However, the true value is often totally out of reach. We could all be better informed about what matters to us, but the catch is that all the data[2] is useless, or misleading, if we don't know what it means.

The remainder of this section examines some of the ways that data visualization and other emerging approaches can help fill this gap.

Your "peripheral brain"

For many of us, it's not natural to think in purely numerical and mathematical terms. Because of this, it can be difficult to make assessments and decisions as quickly and confidently as we might need to in the moment. However, if we can distribute some of the mental workload required to perform tasks, such as making comparisons between data elements, to various areas of our brains, we can redeploy our overall effort to solve higher order problems. For example, we can engage our visual systems' capacity for sensing difference rather than relying solely on contemplating abstract numbers.

Expanded vision

Different types of visualizations can reveal distinct aspects of the world that otherwise would be invisible to us. Although the terminology is not always entirely clear-cut, here's one way to think about two broad categories of technology-enhanced vision: *data visualizations* provide concrete visual representations of the nonphysical and the abstract such as a

---

[2]Although the word "data" is the plural form of "datum," as I'll discuss later, colloquially "data" usually is used as a singular noun. I take a little poetic license with the word and use it as plural or singular as needed to avoid awkward sentences and have a more natural, conversational feel to the writing. To the sticklers and purists, I appreciate your understanding in advance.

statistical trend; *scientific visualizations* allow people to see hidden physical forms and processes, such as a positron emission tomography (PET) scan that shows the level of metabolic activity in various regions of the brain when performing certain tasks.

Filtering out the noise

It doesn't take much time or effort to open floodgates of information, only to soon need to stem the flow and start dumping the excess—sometimes throwing out the essential along with the marginal in the process. That said, what we consider to be essential and marginal can vary depending on the context and circumstances. It can be a challenge to make easy distinctions and reorder priorities on the fly. Well-executed interfaces and visualizations can help by presenting simple, clear cues that allow us to easily identify and differentiate different kinds of data and information and rearrange them rapidly.

Many kinds of data only matter when they matter. For example, when I drive on the highway, I barely look at my gas gauge, but I'll keep an eye on the speedometer to ensure my speed is in a good range. However, I want my gas gauge in my peripheral vision, and only want it to call attention to itself when I'm low on fuel and need to address it. Even if I'm deep in thought about other things, my little yellow warning light has something important to communicate, and I pay attention when it comes on. For various kinds of purposes, visualizations can apply these basic concepts of threshold detection and peripheral vision to let us know to attend to something when it really matters and not bother us when it doesn't.

Finding needles, haystacks, and things you should look for but didn't realize you wanted

I know there is information available out there that could be very useful and interesting to me, I just don't know where it is or how to find it. It would be nice to be able to scan the "big picture" of a topic or interest and see if there are areas I might want to dive into more deeply.

Pattern recognition

Our brains are wired to recognize patterns of many varieties. However, as good as humans may be at this form of perception and cognition, some of the most important and useful patterns are not directly available to our senses. For example, aspects of an individual's physiological profile, or a big public health problem, can only be seen and fully understood with the help of data, devices, and displays. Sometimes, even the patterns that are relatively available to our senses can fade from our consciousness and their meanings can disappear. For all us creatures of habit, it might be useful to be able to see patterns in our lives that we are so accustomed to that we actually forget they're there. Maybe our spending or sleeping habits are worse—or better—than we think, if we look at them in aggregate. Again, visualizations can help mirror or "re-present" facets of our lives in compact form and cast them in a useful new light.

Sometimes, seeing patterns is only half the equation. The key is to figure out if they are meaningful and, if so, what to do next. We may want to explore certain patterns of interest further. If we start out with too many details, we could get lost in them. We need to reduce the details to see the larger patterns and relationships, but we also should be able to dissect those patterns to see what they mean and what we might do about them.

Lines of thought

Problem solving and discovery with data have a number of potential departure points and pathways. Here are just a few lines of approach:

- *Horizon lines.* Begin by surveying a broad expanse of data with overviews to search for larger contours, features, and patterns. Data visualizations can be indispensible for being able to view truly immense data sets, such as maps of very large digital networks. However, to be fully useful, they should be highly interactive, responsive, and reasonably easy to use to allow users to navigate to any areas that might suggest a closer look.
- *Interconnecting lines.* Instead of starting with the big picture, an investigation can open with a minute detail. The challenge then becomes seeing how it connects to the bigger picture. The same attributes of interactivity and ease-of-use that are important for starting from the overview, and being able to dive in, are just as necessary, if not more so, for going from the particular to the larger framework in which it resides.
- *Storylines.* Start with a story (theory, thesis, hypothesis) and look for data to confirm or reject it. If individuals do this honestly and persistently, refusing to accept "first impressions," perhaps they've got the temperament of a scientist. When people do it just enough to "make their case," maybe they're more sales-minded, have a political bent, or are simply trying to close a deal. In that case, they might stop looking when they feel they've made their point and might start building the support to defend this point of view.

DON'T BE AFRAID OF THE CHART

Visualizations can help foster a clearer, deeper understanding of a data set and make it easier to communicate that insight to others. In many cases, they can greatly expand the range of people with different perspectives, skills, and expertise, who are able to effectively participate in problem solving. Ironically, despite the potential for visualizations to make data more accessible, many examples can convey a strong impression of inaccessibility. Highly intricate and abstract visualizations reinforce the sense that the data are impenetrable and entirely beyond our grasp. They can make us feel more dependent on others to decrypt the tangled masses of lines and dots, or mosaics of multicolored rectangles in a range of sizes. However, is the complexity of the data always the barrier—or is it sometimes the form and amount that's represented at a given time that is making it seem opaque?

Most of us are very familiar with aspects of data visualization—even though we don't realize it—and we are capable of gaining insights and meaning with just a little context and drawing on our own knowledge and experience. Simple and familiar images will not always be sufficient but, sometimes, less can be more. There are representations that use only a few elements but still pack a meaningful punch. Think about it: you're already familiar with a number of devices that monitor and display dynamic data, as shown in Figures 1.2 and 1.3. You can understand the essential message and the stories their displays convey almost immediately; notice the Code Blue in Figure 1.3 or how about what's shown in Figure 1.4.

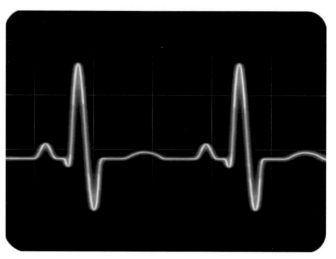

FIGURE 1.2
Heart monitor: looks good.

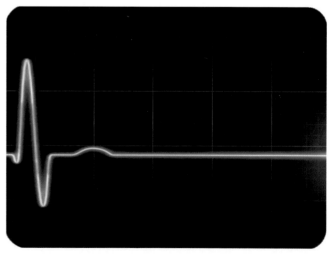

FIGURE 1.3
Heart monitor: Code Blue!

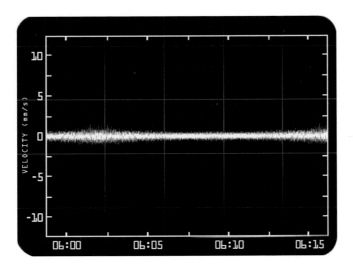

FIGURE 1.4
Seismograph: just another day.

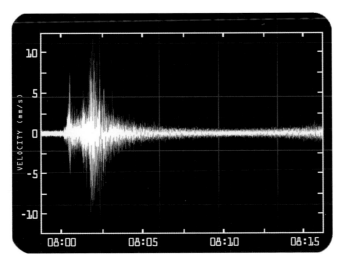

FIGURE 1.5
Seismograph: Red Cross on the way!

Of course, there are many details that we might want to know, such as the magnitude and duration of the earthquake that was measured in Figure 1.5. That's where additional context and interactivity come into play.

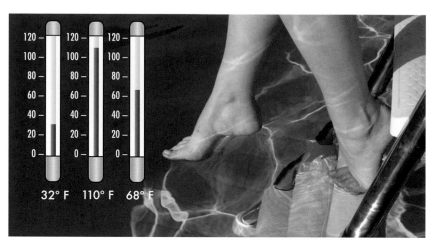

FIGURE 1.6
Okay to dive in?

Information visualization pioneer Ben Shneiderman's mantra "Overview first, zoom and filter, then details-on-demand" is a great summary of what these interactive visualizations should be able to do. The main point is that important real-time data can be captured and displayed in ways that are, if not intuitive, relatively easily perceived and understood. (See Figure 1.6.) From social graphs that show how people relate in groups to heat maps that graphically represent dynamic patterns of activity such as crime in a specific region to "treemaps" of actively traded areas of the stock market and hypertrees that look at a complex network system with a fisheye lens, there are many different kinds of data visualizations. Figures 1.7 through 1.9 show typical examples.

This book will help you see the basic stories these images are telling you nearly as easily as the story told by the heart monitor, the seismograph, or the pool thermometer.

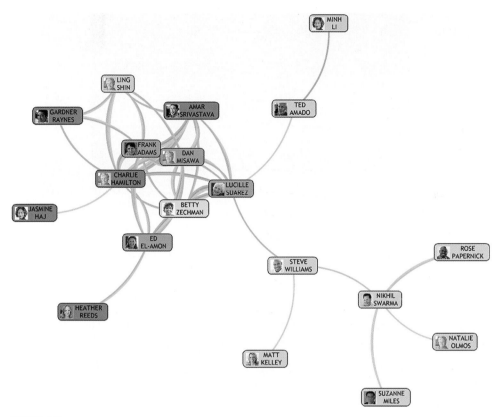

Thumbnail example of a social graph.

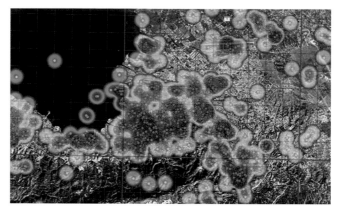

FIGURE 1.8

Heat map of SMS messages sent to the "4636" emergency aid number after the 2010 Haitian earthquake.

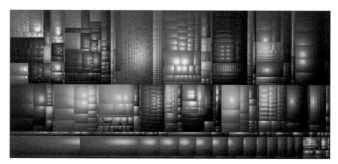

FIGURE 1.9

Tree map of a computer hard drive contents.

PEER AT THE WORLD OF DATA

To get useful insights from data, you first need to be able to perceive what's there in some form. In this book, I will focus primarily on visual representations, but any other representations that make data perceptible by elements, such as sound or touch, also apply. They help us make intellectual sense of data by making the data available to our sense of perception. The tools that help us perceive and work with representations of data come in many varieties and offer many possibilities. Figure 1.10 lists a few important data visualization methods encapsulated in the acronym "PEER AT." (You won't see many acronyms in this book, but this is one that I coined and I find useful.) Although the list is not comprehensive, it captures some primary roles for those looking to represent data.

Prompt people to attention and, sometimes, action—"The reactor core is rapidly overheating, Jim...."

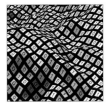

Explore patterns, trends, and anomalies in the data that are noteworthy and important, if not always easy to anticipate—"Let's see if we find any interesting outliers in the clinical studies' data we have on this diabetes treatment...."

Explain interesting features in the data to others using visual indicators—"As you can see in this diagram, the high network traffic between this set of nodes is causing the sluggish performance...."

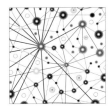

Relate data using various kinds of techniques to help connect the dots—"When Alice tweets about a product, sales of that product skyrocket...."

Analyze the structure of data, and examine key aspects—"When we lowered the price of 'Pineapple Palooza' by 1.5%, sales increased by 12.4% in Eastern Region stores but remained stable in all other regions...."

Track the pathways and predict trajectories that are captured in data—"According to the server logs, the majority of first-time users leave the site after they reach this page, and the rest visit an average of four pages...."

FIGURE 1.10
PEER AT: Prompt, Explore, Explain, Relate, Analyze, Track.

FROM DATA TO WISDOM

Before you become too entranced with gorgeous gadgets and mesmerizing video displays, let me remind you that information is not knowledge, knowledge is not wisdom, and wisdom is not foresight. Each grows out of the other and we need them all.

— ATTRIBUTED TO ARTHUR C. CLARKE (LATHROP, 2004)

Data are the basic building blocks that, when arranged in different ways, become information that, in turn, can become practical knowledge and, ideally, even wisdom. Looking at the sequence as a whole, insights are possible at every step. This is not the kind of journey where you never look back. Instead, looking back and ahead at every phase can make the entire process more effective and meaningful. It's also important to consider where you may have veered off a good path because of some errors or misinformation. Figure 1.11 shows a shorthand version of that pathway.

Many questions arise along that pathway, such as:

- Is the data accurate?
- Is it sufficient to answer the question?
- Where did the data come from?
- Who interpreted it?
- How was it interpreted?
- Are the conclusions correct?
- Are the conclusions applicable in any instance?
- Can any other conclusions be drawn?

Data visualization can help address as well as spark new insight in this process.

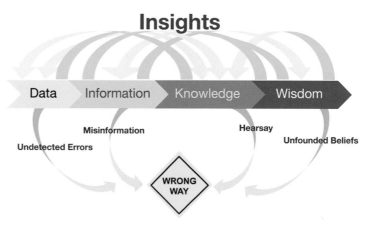

FIGURE 1.11

From data to wisdom.

A DAY WITH DATA

7:45 A.M.: It's only the first coffee of the day, and already two screens are making demands on my barely caffeinated powers of attention and thought. My mobile phone and laptop both have fresh accumulations of data and information—some personal, others business, and a few offering small previews into what I might expect from the day ahead (Figure 1.12). When I glance out my window this morning, the sky's a bright, cloudless blue. When I look at my weather app, it appears there may be rain on the horizon.

The National Weather Service measures current conditions with an array of land, ocean, and airborne sensors and combines this data with historical models and satellite data to predict that it will rain later on today—better bring an umbrella.

I probably shouldn't check, but I still wonder how my stock in Flying Vehicles, Inc. has been doing. The stock is down 8% this week, but with the slider control that allows me to expand the time scale I can see, I note the stock is still trading higher than it was a month ago. The best thing for me to do is probably ignore these kinds of short-term gyrations in the numbers, but these little charts can be all too seductive (Figure 1.13).

An icon is alerting me that there's an update available for one of my applications (Figure 1.14). Should I get it now or wait to see if there are any glitches in the new release?

Before I walk out the door, I do a search with the parcel tracking number for my new pair of running shoes. The automatic tracking system handles millions of packages a day and can completely automate the process of sending a parcel across the United States. This complex system knows exactly where each and every item is at any given moment, whether it's in the air, on a truck, or sitting at a distribution point. My shoes are already on the local delivery truck and will be delivered to my doorstep by the time I'm home from work. The minute my order gets delivered, I should receive an email telling me the delivery is complete.

FIGURE 1.12
Rain in the picture.

FIGURE 1.13
Stock swings.

FIGURE 1.14
Application update available.

8:30 A.M.: "Traffic congestion reported ahead in 1.6 miles," my phone warns me. While I'm driving to work, 24 satellites, each containing four independent atomic clocks, hurtle through space, continually blanketing the earth with GPS signals. An inexpensive chip in my cell phone picks up these signals, does some complicated math, and tells me my geographic position to within a few yards.

Meanwhile, a network of sensors underneath the highway detects a slowdown in traffic. This traffic data travels to a central bank of servers at close to 186,282 miles per second—the speed of light. Billions of microscopic switches flip back and forth as these servers send data across the United States to yet more servers, which automatically calculate how this new data will ultimately end up impacting me. After a brief journey through the atmosphere, the information alert arrives at my cell phone with disappointing news. The regular route to work is going to be a bear today, so with the help of more data, I look for a good alternative (Figure 1.15).

9:03 A.M.: It's the first meeting of the day at work, and the attendees are discussing different technical approaches for managing *really* big data sets with complex interrelationships, contained in millions of rows held in a giant database. Their livelihoods involve grappling with these vast collections and helping to turn them to practical use.

5:40 P.M.: On my drive home, my phone lets me know there's yet more traffic to confront. I think for a minute and take an alternate route, wondering how many other people are getting the same real-time data and doing their own quick recalculations.

Our relationship with data is a two-way street: We contribute to the data at the same time we use it. I'm personally just one tiny data point, a small blue dot on a map, and there are many other blue dots all heading in the same direction at the same time. Some blue dots are combining to create red lines designating traffic congestion on my GPS display. Others are reacting, rerouting, and creating new patterns in the map (Figure 1.16).

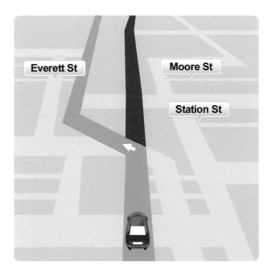

FIGURE 1.15
Traffic ahead.

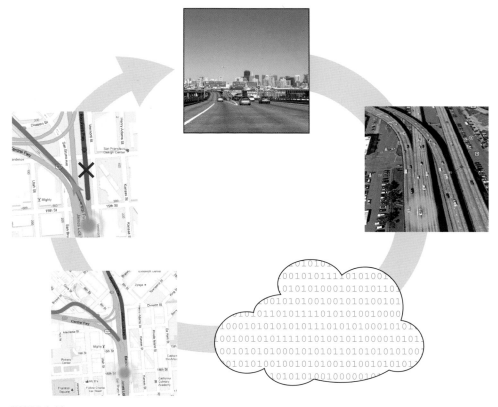

FIGURE 1.16
Data-driven decisions.

My daily life may be inconsequential, but when my decisions are aggregated with other people's data, useful and interesting trends can emerge. These data interactions create a ripple effect, unimaginably large and always in flux.

Catching the drops

Many drops make a bucket, many buckets make a pond, many ponds make a lake, and many lakes make an ocean.

– PERCY ROSS

Sure enough, the rain predicted on my phone's app in the morning came down while I was at work. The sky is clear again now, but there's a telltale pattern of raindrops spattered across the sliding glass doors at home, each drop lit by the late afternoon sun (Figure 1.17). It's a visual record, in water and glass, of the brisk wind and slanting rain that passed

FIGURE 1.17
Catch as catch can.

through earlier. A few observations of the windows suggest many things—the pattern and location of the drops hint the strength and direction of the wind. If I wanted to dig deeper, I could find out about the weather system—where it came from and where it's going.

Just as the sun draws up countless water molecules from sources all over the earth and leaves them suspended in clouds, all the human and machine collection systems take up data and deposit some of it in virtual "clouds." Given the right conditions, clouds release the water back down in forms ranging from a fine mist to rain to snow to hail. Of all the water that's pulled from the earth's surface, only a tiny fraction will reach us. One thing is certain, whether we are drenched by rain or rarely see a drop, we are nevertheless affected by the process in various ways.

The same is true for data: the weather forecasts checked; stock prices monitored; route suggestions requested; emails and texts sent; phone calls, purchases, and recommendations made; searches done; blogs, statuses, and tweets posted; opinions stated; photos shared; videos uploaded and viewed; online games played; event invitations sent; RSVPs confirmed; packages shipped and tracked. Many more kinds of interactions create oceans of data that can be sucked up into the electronic clouds. That enormous daily uptake, the condensation that happens in clouds of data, and the eventual diffusion of some of it back into the world have an impact on what we see around us, even if it's not apparent.

Along with the data we access and generate purposely, automatic processes generate massive quantities of data every day. Nearly every website on the Internet stores information about the computer or device that visits the page. Automatic sensors track temperature and humidity at various points across the globe. Every credit card transaction is logged. Cell phones transmit location data for a variety of purposes. Any single one of these data points is a trivially small amount of data to store, but in aggregate they represent an enormous number of data points that requires an equally vast amount of data storage capacity.

Fortunately, data storage is so inexpensive now that most of us never have to worry about deleting anything—and it's getting cheaper every day.

THE TORRENTS AND TRICKLES OF DATA: OBSERVATIONS FROM STATISTICIAN JOHN BOSLEY

The purpose of computing is insight, not numbers.

— RICHARD HAMMING

For good reasons, many people are spending their time and attention on the challenges of managing torrents of what is often called *big data* (a term offering evocative understatement, if not much precision or clarity). However, certain types of data can trickle in only at substantially lower flows (Figure 1.18). Sometimes, people have no choice but to rely on the scarce supplies of *small data* that are available about a particular area of interest.

Statistician and Usability Consultant John Bosley spent many years with the U.S. Bureau of Labor Statistics working with data sets of many different sizes about various aspects of the United States economy, such as employment and unemployment, wages, prices, and productivity. Not all important data sets are big data—Bosley notes the tiny amount of raw data associated with the origins and evolution of human beings. The fossil record that constitutes our sum total of many millions of years of hominid evolution, he says, can essentially be "stored in the back of a pickup truck." With a data collection that

FIGURE 1.18
The reign of data.

small, an important part of our understanding of how we came to be *Homo sapiens* could conceivably be revised by a single new discovery.

Other small data sets may be at the center of policy decisions, such as endangered species protection. In these cases, effective sampling is often a crucial component of the process. There's also an element of "luck of the draw"; that is, the collection consists of what happened to be found at the time. Any data set, large or small, can have crucial gaps that computational power alone cannot address. A lone paleontologist walking through a river gully who spots a fossilized bone jutting out from the dirt and rocks still may be the only way to connect a full set of dots.

Many kinds of data are difficult and expensive to collect. For example, putting together a clinical trial to obtain data for a new medical treatment can take many years and millions of dollars. Bosley takes an example from his own life: "A specialist I saw considered putting me on a 'new, improved' drug, but first, she determined it was not covered by insurance. Second, she checked the retail cost to me—then said, 'No, it's only been tried on 200 patients; it's not worth switching you.'" Bosley thinks "thousands of decision points like that come up every day in this country." In the example involving the decision to take a medication, Bosley, a professional statistician, agreed with the specialist's reasoning. However, he acknowledges that many patients would not appreciate that kind of thinking and decision making: "Small numbers can spark big disagreements," he notes.

Sometimes, the clearest picture only arises from a combination of "big" and "small" data. For example, government intelligence analysts may draw on the massive amounts of data netted every day by electronic trawlers, but other kinds of key data can only come from human interactions. Those data can be very hard-won and may be collected only in rare, unpredictable moments in time. Then too, there's the issue of what decisions and actions are to be made—or not be made—based on the totality of the evidence from all of these disparate kinds of sources.

Perhaps because of the increasing power of computing and growing interest in such things as data mining, big data can have a greater allure in the tech community because it can be more readily addressed by technological approaches. However, certain kinds of data depend on humans going out and collecting it. There is a concept known as "the law of the instrument" that was popularized by Abraham Maslow in his saying, "If all you have is a hammer, everything looks like a nail." In the world of powerful computing, the natural inclination may be to make all the discussions about big data and the tools to work with it while overlooking essential, complementary small data that can be obtained only with the human touch.

Drops and oceans

The basic unit of digital storage is the *bit*. A single bit has two possible values, commonly notated as "1" and "0." Think of a single bit like a light switch that can be either "off" or "on." One bit isn't a lot of storage, but it can be used to store things like the value of a "yes/no" statement (see Figure 1.19).

FIGURE 1.19
Kerplunk!

8 bits = 1 byte
1000 bytes = 1 kilobyte
1,000,000 bytes = 1 megabyte
1,000,000,000 bytes = 1 gigabyte
1,000,000,000,000 bytes = 1 terabyte
1,000,000,000,000,000 bytes = 1 petabyte
1,000,000,000,000,000,000 bytes =1 exabyte

On their own, these numbers seem fairly meaningless. Although it's possible to picture in your mind's eye having five of something (five jelly beans easily fit in the palm of your hand) or even 100 of something (the number of tiles in a Scrabble® game), we can't picture a trillion of something.

The flow of data

The process by which data is collected, transmitted, and stored varies widely between types of data and storage methods used, but the basic process is always the same. Digital data is collected through electronic sensors or through human input. This data is then transmitted across some distance that can be as short as the few centimeters between the keyboard on a laptop and its hard drive or as far away as the Voyager 1 Spacecraft, more than 11 billion miles from Earth. Once the data reaches its destination, it is stored on magnetic, optical, or solid-state media.

"Big Data" collections are stored in data centers or data warehouses. A data center is a special room or building with rows and rows of computers stacked on top of each other in a *rack*. The computers used in data centers, *servers*, are generally much more powerful than standard desktop or laptop computers, with significantly more storage space, processing power, and random-access memory (RAM). The servers talk to each other on a high-performance network that allows data to be transferred at very high speeds. Data is stored in memory, which is expensive but allows almost instant data recall, or on a disk, which is slower to access but stores lots of data per dollar.

Well-designed data centers use a mix of technologies to provide the best performance at reasonable costs.

A very small proportion of this stored data eventually becomes the material that is transformed into charts, infographics, and visualizations.

Data as a "social commodity"

The most erroneous stories are those we think we know best—and therefore never scrutinize or question.

— STEPHEN JAY GOULD

Although sophisticated technology and polished charts can sometimes obscure it, the fact is that working with data is a deeply human and context-dependent process. Being mindful of some of the main undercurrents that move data from initial collection to presentation can help to drive more honest, effective, and useful displays. "Data are not just numbers," John Bosley says. They are, he believes, "a social commodity fundamentally shaped by human interactions and social negotiations." We need to pay attention to these dynamics to truly understand and make the most of what finally gets collected, stored, analyzed, and presented. As data sets, and the tools to work with them, become more accessible to a broader range of people, opportunities will expand for sharing, interpretation, and collaborative problem solving. In addition, there will also be more places for messages and meanings to get garbled. Ideally, potential group and individual biases about what data to collect, analyze, and present would be regularly explored and discussed in ongoing conversations.

CASCADES OF CONFUSION

At times, words can create a cascade of confusion by deforming the meaning of the sentences used by one person as interpreted by another. Just for fun, consider this excerpt from a classic literal comedy of unforced error. Lou Costello plays a hapless peanut vendor who asks Bud Abbott, in the role of the manager of the St. Louis Wolves, about the surnames of the players on his team, which happen to be both proper nouns and pronouns (e.g., "Who").

> **Costello:** Look, you got a first baseman?
> **Abbott:** Certainly.
> **Costello:** Who's playing first?
> **Abbott:** That's right.
> **Costello:** When you pay off the first baseman every month, who gets the money?
> **Abbott:** Every dollar of it.
> **Costello:** All I'm trying to find out is the fellow's name on first base.
> **Abbott:** Who.
> **Costello:** The guy that gets…

Abbott: That's it.
Costello: Who gets the money...
Abbott: He does, every dollar. Sometimes his wife comes down and collects it.
Costello: Whose wife?
Abbott: Yes.
PAUSE
Abbott: What's wrong with that?
Costello: Look, all I wanna know is when you sign up the first baseman, how does he sign his name?
Abbott: Who.
Costello: The guy.
Abbott: Who.
Costello: How does he sign...
Abbott: That's how he signs it.
Costello: Who?
Abbott: Yes.

The disconnect in the scene stems from the clash of mindsets between the person asking the question and the person answering. The peanut vendor is making a perfectly reasonable mistake, and it's easy to excuse him for his inability to understand what's going on. Costello could not break out of the mindset that "Who" is only a word that signifies a question and not a person's name. Let's leave out the comic device aspect of this for a moment. Given the fact that the names of the players are so clear and concrete to the manager, he can't understand the natural misinterpretation of the questioner.

So, what does this have to do with asking questions of data? Simply that the meanings of even the most basic words can get lost in their transmission from one person to another in ways that are not obvious to the direct participants. The more intermediaries there are in the chain of communication, the greater the likelihood of losing something in translation. Data visualizations can help address this issue in a few ways. They can shrink the feedback loops required to ask big questions of complex data and reduce the chance of miscommunication. They can also provide additional ways to answer questions without the need to strictly rely on the vagaries of language or the occasionally impenetrable stories told by numbers. In the case above, a simple visual, such as a team roster or baseball cards with the players' names on their uniforms, could have solved the disconnect.

Let's say that Costello is a data visualization user and Abbott is the interface—how could their miscommunication be addressed? If the interface is good, it might be able to detect a problem and guess about the source of it (names with double meanings). In the conversation above, the user, Costello, made the effort of asking the question in a different way—"When you pay off the first baseman every month, who gets the money?" The problem is, it wasn't different enough. Nevertheless, it seems easier to blame the manager/interface than the peanut vendor. The manager should have had more insight about the confusion. Now, if the person asking a question were an advanced researcher using a data analysis tool, he might be in the same quandary as Costello, but, in this case, the tool would be even less likely than Abbott to correct the confusion. As this chapter proceeds, we will look further at the interplay of questions and answers in data visualizations.

THE DATA LIFECYCLE

Information is to data what wine is to a vineyard: the delicious extract and distillate.

— DAVID WEINBERGER

You may be familiar with the saying, popularized by Mark Twain, "There are three kinds of lies: lies, damned lies, and statistics." To me, what is especially interesting is not that people can deceive with data and statistics or mislead with messy visualizations of clean stats, rather, it is how profoundly human decisions, interactions, and negotiations affect every step of the data lifecycle, phases of which could be roughly broken out as shown in Figure 1.20.

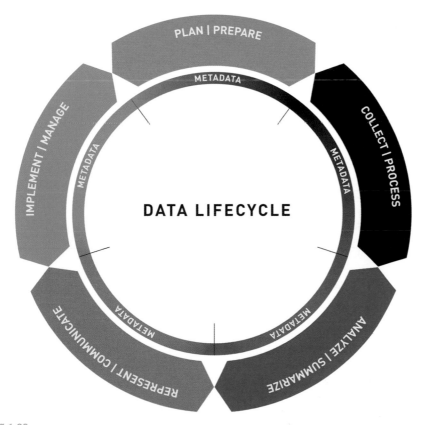

FIGURE 1.20
Data lifecycle infographic.

Data are not necessarily "just numbers" but instead are shaped at various points in various ways by human interactions and social negotiations. We should never lose sight of how much we have our handprints on the raw materials that underpin the information on which we rely.

Data visualization is only one aspect of a long, complex process that can be repeated from every nanosecond to every X number of years. Data collection sometimes continues until someone tells somebody else to stop, or the sensors die, or the batteries run out, or Hubble de-orbits.

Every step of the data lifecycle has a basic storyline. Someone comes forward and says we need some type of data for some reason—social or economic policy, scientific model testing, and so on. Every stage, from data gathering to display, involves human decisions and interventions. They are an integral, fascinating, and essential part of "the data story." We don't even know what data we're going to end up with unless we take part in, or at least pay attention to, these social arguments and negotiations that determine what finally gets collected, stored, analyzed, and presented. There are, of course, contingencies at every one of those stages.

The rest of this section examines some fundamental ideas and basic questions in the data lifecycle.

Planning and preparing

First things first: why might you want to collect data about something, and how wide a net should you—and can you—cast to get what's needed? For this net, how fine or coarse should you make the filtering mesh? At some level, there's a certain cost in time, effort, and money to obtain data, so what will it take, and who cares enough to do what's necessary to get the job done? This can range from voluntary, privately funded efforts, such as counting bird species, to the billions of dollars spent on each Decennial Census in the United States.

Collecting and processing

The kinds of measures and methods used to collect data set the course for the subsequent steps in the process. For example, person-to-person in the case of the Census, telephone polling for surveys, sensors for environmental data, seismic detectors for geologic data, satellites for weather and ocean data, the Hubble Telescope for deep space—all of this has to be thought through, planned, and implemented.

All the data that's collected has to go somewhere. How is the data stored? Boxes of papers? Computer files? What are the formats? Is it "cleaned" or "preprocessed" before storage? How is it organized, indexed, and arranged? (For example, longitude goes here; latitude goes there; elevation above sea level goes somewhere else. Now you have a geo database.) How easy is it to retrieve? These questions bring up the importance of metadata (to be discussed shortly in more detail) and the idea that "all data is good data."

Flip Kromer, cofounder of the data marketplace Infochimps, says, "Making minimally useable data computable is ferociously expensive, and deeply frustrating." Yet, he says, people often discount this. "What's so insidious here is a process that seems mechanical—

transform a semi-structured data set—in fact always requires domain-specific knowledge." The solution his company sees is to provide "pure incentives for people to gather, refine, and analyze data, and an open platform to connect commercial and public data sets with people who want to consume them."

Analyzing and summarizing

How much processing, quality assurance, and statistical analysis does all the raw data undergo? Will it be necessary to perform complex and extensive analyses or just take a more basic approach? The steps taken could involve a substantial statistical inquiry, but that isn't always necessary. Such work can be costly, and there may not be a compelling reason to perform it. It's important to determine and apply the level of analysis and summarization that's appropriate for the data in question.

Representing and communicating

How are the products of the planning, collection, analysis, and so on, displayed and otherwise disseminated? Who disseminates them? And to whom are they disseminated? Do the producers disseminate them, or do third parties? Do the third parties perform additional data analyses or massaging, and, if so, do they make it clear that they're going further? Does all the necessary metadata get packaged along with the data products? How are the products formatted and displayed?

Implementing and managing

After all the work from the prior steps has been done, how are the results put to use? Do you make changes to the marketing plan or reroute parts of the supply chain? Although the data has answered certain questions, a whole new set of interesting questions have come up based on the previous results.

These new questions are important and may warrant planning and preparation for a new round of the data lifecycle. At the same time, all the data that already has been collected may not have yielded all the important insights that it contains. There often needs to be a plan to manage what's done with a very large data set; some of the data might be good to keep close at hand, but it's more cost-effective to store some of it away in the proverbial back closet of cheap servers.

Making the data lifecycle even more interesting and complex is the often constantly renewing stream of updates. Very little of the data we deal with is "new" in the sense of "never been seen before." Most of it, or almost all, is just the latest version of data that has been flowing for years or even centuries and will keep flowing. For instance, the total global human population numbers have been of interest for a long, long time.

Although we need to filter out unnecessary data to create useful visualizations, we also need to keep in mind that the filtering process itself can lead to, and reinforce, false conclusions and bad decisions, as well as good ones. There is an infinite supply of data out there but a finite capacity to work with it. That said, the ability to collect, store, and analyze data is expanding rapidly, and that should help address the problem of what to keep and what to toss. If more is captured and saved in retrievable forms, then we have the possibility of going back to data that once might have looked like trash but, in retrospect, is actually a treasure trove of vital metadata. From this perspective, all data is "good" data.

"JUST THE FACTS": WHAT ARE DATA AND METADATA?

Just the facts, ma'am.

> *— A FAMOUS LINE FROM THE JACK WEBB 1950S TV SERIES DRAGNET THAT*
> *WAS NEVER ACTUALLY UTTERED BY HIS CHARACTER, SGT. JOE FRIDAY*

When I started thinking about a title for this section, the phrase "Just the facts, ma'am" came to mind. This famous quote, associated with the old syndicated TV series featuring a no-nonsense Los Angeles police detective, has taken on a life of its own. I researched it and found that it was never actually used in the original. It's a misquote. According to Wikiquote, and other sources, the original, correct versions are "All we want are the facts, ma'am" and "All we know are the facts, ma'am."

This little episode describes one of the most important points of this section. It's not "just the facts" or data that are important, but also the data about the data—where did it come from, and how valid is it? In this case, the quote is so well established that it's almost a "given." The metadata put the quote in a new light. So what? Well, in this case, it may be no big deal, if you're not a purist. But what if someone were going to do some kind of visualization on the origination, use, and spread of phrases from TV shows? In this imaginary visualization, the raw data would be incorrect and result in a potentially misleading visualization.

Here are some rough definitions: *Data* is the plural of *datum*, "a piece of information." It comes from the Latin word *dare*—to give (as in data are things that are "given or granted"). They are facts that can be used for thinking, communicating, and discussing. "Metadata"[3] are the data *about* data, including such things as the origin and context of the individual datum. Without this metadata, the context and authenticity of the data we want to use can be hard to assess and, consequently, might make them less useful and valuable. If a datum were a bottle of fine old wine, let's call it MetaReserva, the metadata would be the descriptions and details on the label (Figure 1.21). That is, it would be the information about the wine's attributes, such as the variety, vintage, and vineyard, as well as its alcohol content and whether it contains sulfites. The ultimate value we might find in our bottle of MetaReserva can depend on many factors that may not be evident on the bottle—for example, the way it was stored before it was purchased.

---

[3]There are many details, and some disagreements, about usage of the word "metadata." Some argue for the use of terms such as "entities," "relations," and "attributes" to more precisely describe data and its characteristics. Let's leave that level of semantic granularity to others.

NAME: MetaReserva

VARIETY: Cabernet Sauvignon

VINTAGE: 2012

VINEYARD: Server Farms, California

ALCOHOL CONTENT: 13% by volume

FIGURE 1.21
MetaReserva.

Speaking of storage, the bottle of MetaReserva could be placed in a specific location in a meticulously organized wine rack that is arranged so that it's easy to locate the bottle later on, even in the midst of a large wine collection. This is akin to *structured data*, such as lists of customer email addresses and telephone numbers that reside in fixed, predefined places such as spreadsheet cells or relational database fields.

Or it could be stashed in a cupboard among a variety of other unarranged wine bottles. Of course, it's not as easy to find the bottle in this context, but that's often how we have to deal with the things we want or need. This scenario represents *unstructured data*, which would be typified by freeform text. In my small kitchen, there's a combination of organized and unorganized bottles. Likewise, in the realm of information, there are combinations of structured and semi-structured data.

Returning to the topic of metadata, John Bosley says:

Good accurate metadata are essential for separating wheat from chaff quickly and efficiently. Nobody should have to wonder if they've landed on the right data set. If I find data that doesn't adequately self-describe, I disregard it as useless and make a note to never visit it again. Metadata are neglected because they're expensive and nobody wants to generate them. But without them data are literally meaningless. Just numbers. And that goes for visualization—without the metadata, they're just pretty pictures, abstract art.

Of course, having good data and metadata is only part of the story. It's not always clear what data matter and what their uses might be (Figures 1.22 and 1.23).

FIGURE 1.22
Between Five Bells, 2010 Geelong Red Wine. *Label design credit: Nicholas Felton.*

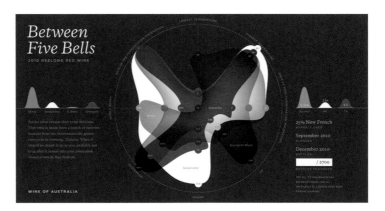

FIGURE 1.23
Between Five Bells label close-up, 2010 Geelong Red Wine. *Label design credit: Nicholas Felton.*

WHAT TO LEAVE IN AND WHAT TO LEAVE OUT: A CONVERSATION WITH JOURNALISM PROFESSOR AND TECH ENTREPRENEUR, LEN SELLERS

What kinds of skills and practices can people use to pull together disparate facts and assemble them into forms that reveal accurate, interesting, and important aspects of the world? There are many answers to that question, but one field that has long grappled with such issues is journalism. Although traditional journalism's future may be cloudy, the journalistic skills required to turn data into engaging stories have relevance for data visualization.

Len Sellers, Professor of Journalism, Statistician, and Tech Entrepreneur, has considered this question for years while working in both print and digital media. He says one of the central challenges for reporters and editors is to address the question captured in the Bob Seger song lyric, "what to leave in and what to leave out." Sellers says, "The best of editors can instinctively put themselves into the minds of readers and can ask the questions readers would ask." This ability comes from talent, training, and experience. Journalists try to figure out, "What do I need to be told so I can see this in its entirety?"

When he managed the digital design agency Razorfish in San Francisco, Sellers says, his designers told him the same thing, which is to put everything together, look at it, and then remove an element and see if it still holds up. However, that doesn't mean writers, editors, and designers can, or should, anticipate everything or completely control the presentation of the content. "If you are doing your job, you let the readers and viewers reach their own conclusions." To illustrate the point, Sellers says a reporter covering local politics doesn't introduce editorializing qualifiers to the content: "The city council, in a truly stupid decision, changed the zoning laws today." Even without overt editorializing, the act of including, excluding, prioritizing, and arranging the details from a story often can be a significant editorial act in its own right.

Seeing patterns and finding stories

Part of Sellers' academic training included statistics, which he says served him well in his work as a journalist. "Good journalists can tell you the margin of error for the data in their stories, and I'm one of those people who reads the bottom of the chart." Sellers says he would comb through data looking for patterns of correlation that might provide the groundwork of an article. "Patterns can be the schematics for stories." Although many correlations can be meaningless in themselves, sometimes patterns can suggest correlations that lead you to interesting relationships among a set of facts (Figure 1.24). "Taking the time to sit back and analyze is crucial—it is in the analysis that you find the meaning."

FIGURE 1.24

All Over Coffee #513, DUMBO, Brooklyn, New York, by Paul Madonna.

WHAT COUNTS?

We demand rigidly defined areas of doubt and uncertainty!

– DOUGLAS ADAMS, THE HITCHHIKER'S GUIDE TO THE GALAXY

What is the significance of the word "significant"? Depending on who you are and what you're doing, the answer to that question can have very different meanings, implications, and outcomes. When it comes to divining meaning from data and taking actions accordingly, there's an immense amount of power, sometimes on a truly life-and-death level, contained in that word. It can decide what makes the cut, and what doesn't, for a new medication or environmental regulation.

The difference between the numbers 0.05 and 0.06, despite being only a hundredth of a percent, is vast in its real-world implications and has far more impact than the difference between 0.04 and 0.05. The figure 0.05 is a commonly used *critical p-value*, or benchmark probability level, that is calculated to decide whether it's sufficiently unlikely that a set of observations may have occurred by chance, that they can be considered "significant." Calculating a p-value depends on (a) being sure the observations truly represent some population characteristic in an unbiased way, and (b) the characteristic occurring with a known probability distribution that's specified in advance. An everyday example of such a distribution is the bell-shaped *normal curve*, but others are used as well. A full definition of p-value is much more subtle, nuanced, and intricate than I've alluded to, but there's a lot of other ground to cover here.

The people who use statistical summarizations of data and make decisions based on considerations such as significance are, in part, relying on the judgment of others who have made prior decisions about how to slice the numbers. When it comes to seeing the patterns and stories in the data, not only do we have to be aware of compelling but misleading false narratives, we also need to keep in mind that the stories we do accept as true and valid can have their own set of artificially drawn contours and boundaries. The lines we trace and the patterns we see, even with the most rigorous analysis of "hard data," can be subject to informed but nevertheless subjective human interpretation. That's simply the reality.

To get a good handle on how to understand and describe the world, it's necessary to draw some lines in the sand. Perhaps one of the services emerging types of data visualization can offer is to remind us about the gray areas and make them more visible rather than simply being forgotten (Figure 1.25). The line of "significance" is, to me at least, not a sharp one, although by necessity it becomes one in action. A new drug, for example, may or may not enter the marketplace based on which side of the line it lands. For many clinicians and the public, these occurrences are invisible—but do they need to be?

With all that important data at our fingertips, how do we recognize what counts and what doesn't, what is "significant" in more than just the statistical sense? What are the cues and contours that tell us exactly where we stand in relation to the information we're seeing? Perhaps at times the boundaries between "significant" and "not significant" could be visually represented not only as crisp numbers and lines on displays, but also as gray zones to convey a sense of the limitations of statistical modeling.

Statistical significance depends on looking at the data in light of an explicit mathematical model of how the world works. In theory, this model represents a probabilistic pattern suggesting something may be important—or at least interesting. Although data can be statistically significant (the recorded observations were probably determined by something other than chance), the findings may still have no practical meaning or utility in a given set of circumstances. For example, as John Bosley mentioned previously, researchers obtained "significant" results for a drug used in a 200-person clinical trial. However, because of the small sample size, and the fact that his physician had seen only one study that showed some drug efficacy, she didn't believe the findings were sufficiently "proven" to warrant him starting to use the medication. Bosley recalls an old proverb that, in a lyrical kind of way, is relevant here: "One swallow doesn't make a summer." In other words, before coming to a conclusion about something, build up a little weight of evidence. He suggests it's generally a good idea in the world of statistics to wait for some corroboration before acting, and he's certainly had many years of observations to back up that statement.

Even a tiny effect can, in a sense, be "forced" into the "statistically significant" column simply by inflating the size of the study sample. Without going into details, the

FIGURE 1.25
When Numbers Lie, by Paul Madonna.

size of the difference required to have a low probability of occurring by chance goes down as the size of the study sample goes up (they are *inversely related*). Some of the important medical findings about the causes of diseases, such as cancer, were only confirmed after it became possible to conduct large studies over a long period of time, because the relationship, while real, is not terribly strong.

In medicine, even a weak relationship will affect the health and longevity of enough people to make its detection worth the time and expense of a large study. In many areas, though, it's foolish to pay for a large study to detect a small but statistically significant difference. Is it really of any lasting importance that one keyboard layout for a copier allows users to perform a task 0.002 seconds faster than another? And yet, with a large enough sample, this puny and inconsequential difference could be found to be reliable. What's important is that this "fact" has no practical consequence, except in a surrealistic work environment where the bosses really care about time savings of fractions of a second. There's no *practical* difference between the keyboard layouts.

FIGURE 1.26

Chew on this . . . *Source: CALVIN AND HOBBES ©1992 Watterson. Distributed by UNIVERSAL UCLICK. Reprinted with permission. All rights reserved.*

Sometimes, the things that people think "count" become the data that are more likely counted and that, in turn, show up in various kinds of representations, visual and otherwise. Those visualizations may then reinforce our ideas of what matters and what doesn't. It's essential to have a sharp focus so we don't develop tunnel vision. Given that, we should always keep asking what "significant" means in all senses of the word (Figure 1.26).

Seeing dinner versus being dinner (pattern recognition and narrative fallacies)

We will now discuss in a little more detail the Struggle for Existence...

– CHARLES DARWIN

"What just moved over there? ...There...in that rustling tuft of reeds by the river?" The sun was nearly down, and the rocky bank was turning black against a pale orange sky. The plants were swaying in the breeze, but something seemed different—it didn't look like the movement of the wind. Tired and thirsty as this ancient human ancestor may have been, she sensed something barely detectable that told her to drink water at another spot.

Although the actual scenarios involving this kind of scene are lost to time, it's clear our ability to perceive and process visual patterns, and to detect slight differences, is strong and was forged from our basic survival needs. Was that faint shadow over there something looking for its next meal or something that could feed a small family? What was that shifting shadow? A predator or something to catch and eat? Maybe it was nothing at all. Yes, that deeper analysis is important. Sometimes, however, it's better to consider those questions after making sure you're on safer ground. Maybe it will prove to be nothing at all, but then again, your preattentive mind is potentially giving you some very important information upon which you can take action. It's giving you options.

We've evolved to have some very powerful perceptual capabilities to help us avoid becoming dinner...and to help us find our own (Figure 1.27).

Fortunately for us, those particular concerns have changed, but the fundamental issues are the same: we want to maximize our choices and opportunities to improve our lives (in

FIGURE 1.27
Crouching lion, hidden danger.

areas such as health, safety, and finance) and minimize risks. We can redeploy some of the same capabilities that we've developed over the eons to take on the challenges of our time.

We live in an age of data and visualizations can give us unprecedented perspectives into the world and ourselves. We inhabit a world of invisible data that we can transform, and are transforming, into something that connects to our senses so that we can "make sense of it." That involves making some parts of reality more palpable so we can work with it. As we interact with that data, though, some of the powers we use to help avoid harm and find sustenance in the visible world could work against us.

In the very old days, a false positive may not have hurt us as much as a false negative. For example, maybe that rustling in the reeds was just the wind. Our ancestor may have made a mistake by going elsewhere and been a little inconvenienced, but if she was—in the scheme of things—that's a pretty small price to pay for a false positive. Now, let's say that she discounted her subtle pattern detections and went ahead and took that sip of water by the reeds...and there really was a hungry alligator biding his time. That is a costly false negative that might well have been the last mistake she ever made.

These days, that balance may be changing in a big way. The same remarkable powers of pattern recognition that we have developed to survive may be leading us toward bad decisions for ourselves and our loved ones.

Our deeply rooted tendency to construct stories from apparent patterns in unrelated bits of data is called the *narrative fallacy*. The ability of stories to capture our hearts and minds is double-edged—there's always the danger of creating, reinforcing, and proliferating misguided ideas about, for example, our physical and financial lives. Then again, without stories, we can lose the ability to fully connect with important narratives the data gives us. The scientific method is based on collecting, interpreting, and understanding valid data but is fueled by proving and disproving hypotheses (which are simply a particular genre of story). Darwin's observations about the variations in sizes and shapes of finch beaks is interesting, but the story those birds tell about evolution is what makes the data truly powerful (see Figure 1.28).

Later, I'll discuss the characteristics of great films, books, and games and how they might apply to data visualization. That is, can visualizations engage people as active

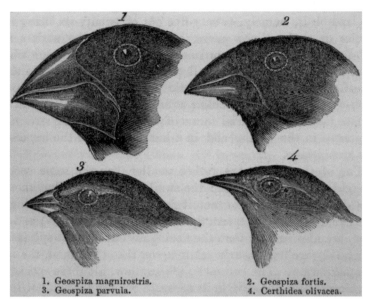

FIGURE 1.28

Darwin's Galapagos finches, from Darwin's account of his voyage on the HMS Beagle (Stevens, 2009).

participants and help them, to some extent, co-create valuable stories embedded within the data? It's a touchy subject, but one that I want to address for several reasons. I tend to think the more aware of a concern you are, the less capacity it might have to cause trouble. Also, data-sense-making tools can offer a wide range of people many benefits.

The reality is, though, if these data points can't be described in a manner that tells a story in some way, they are less likely to be useful, to be motivating, or to be remembered. There is a necessary but fine line to walk. Many times I've heard the expression—"Humans are a story-telling species." Why not strive to present data not only responsibly, but also in a manner that people can best see the meaning for themselves?

THE RIPPLE EFFECT

Some circumstantial evidence is very strong, as when you find a trout in the milk.

– HENRY DAVID THOREAU

There's a ripple effect that starts the moment plans are made to collect data and carries through to all the eventual uses (Figure 1.29). It begins with decisions about what is gathered and ends with the ways the data are displayed in tables, charts, and visualizations. Then there's a secondary ripple that flows out from the people who view these representations and make decisions based on what they see (Figure 1.30). Every interaction in the process has effects downstream.

FIGURE 1.29
Milkshape.

FIGURE 1.30
Making waves.

http://goo.gl/Aa6er

Note: A QR code is a type of barcode that can be read by smart phones equipped with cameras. Nearly all smart phones are capable of reading QR codes with the right software. Look on your phone's mobile app store for the latest QR code reader, install the software, and point the camera at the code. QR codes will be used occasionally throughout the book to quickly link you to web content and interactive examples.

Whether they are simple or complex, colorful or muted, visual representations of data can sometimes be so compelling—or complicated—that they can obscure the origins and processes that give them shape. It's understandable to take things for granted, but sometimes taking a look at the ripple effects that come with making sense of data is a good idea.

Imagine there's a tall, cold glass of milk next to some warm chocolate chip cookies on the table in front of you. It was poured from an unlabeled carton and offered to you by a stranger. Would you drink it? Perhaps you might typically glance at one or two things on the carton, but now all the labeling you generally ignore might seem uncomfortably absent (Figure 1.31).

Without the labels—the "metadata"—about this beverage, many kinds of questions might occur to you that start from the moment when the first drop hit the proverbial milk pail: How fresh is this? Was it collected in accordance with standard health codes? Was it consistently refrigerated for the entire trip? Did this beverage come from a cow, a goat, or a vat of soybeans? Could it have been transported in a tank that was used to also haul gasoline? Just by looking at the full glass, you might not be able to tell. However, if even a single answer to any one of those questions is problematic, it could completely change your attitude about consuming the milk. For example, if it was first collected two months ago, you might not want to drink it, even if all the other steps were perfectly fine; or, if it was collected three days ago, but only refrigerated on the last day, that would be concerning, as well. You may not typically look closely at labels, but they signify a process that you basically know and trust at some level and offer an easy way to verify if you feel unsure (Figure 1.32).

With all the metadata present and a basic trust in the process, you can feel okay—or not—about taking that sip. By the way, I believe the Henry David Thoreau quote that starts off this section refers to a practice in his time by some unscrupulous people of watering down milk. Back in those days, it may not always have been easy to tell, but finding a trout in the milk pail would have been a pretty good clue that something fishy occurred.

Nutrition Facts

Serving Size 6.7 fl oz (200ml)
Servings Per Container 1

Amount Per Serving

Calories 110	Calories from Fat 45

	% Daily Value*
Total Fat 5g	8%
Saturated Fat 4g	20%
Cholesterol 35mg	12%
Sodium 80mg	3%
Total Carbohydrate 11g	4%
Dietary Fiber 0g	0%
Sugars 6g	
Protein 6g	

Vitamin A	4%	Vitamin C	0%
Calcium	20%	Iron	8%

Percent Daily Values are based on a 2,000 calories diet

FIGURE 1.31

Missing: Metadata.

FIGURE 1.32

100% of recommended information.

Consider how much you pay attention to the ripple effects involving the data in charts and visualizations that you use. Ask yourself—do any of these visual representations ever significantly affect your decisions and actions? If so, should you think about them in the same way you'd think about consuming the mystery milk? Because of the explosion of data involving complex relationships, increasingly many of us have little choice but to rely on a host of unknown participants and processes we largely don't understand. We all get the basics of refrigeration, pasteurization, and nutritional labeling, but even people who work with visualizations may not all have the same grounding in statistics, algorithms, graphic design, or the particular subject matter of interest, to name a few.

Although no one can be an expert in everything, a more general awareness of everything that's involved can't hurt. Sometimes it doesn't really matter how the data reach us, but, as with the glass of milk described above, in many instances it matters a great deal. Perhaps it's better to not always take the things we consume for granted, whether they're dairy-based or data-based.

How else are visualizations like a glass of milk?

Like a glass of milk:

- The methods of collection, processing, storage, and delivery are extremely important factors in the final consumption of milk...as well as many kinds of data.

Not like a glass of milk:

- *Tangibility:* Unlike a cold glass of milk, data are generally abstract and intangible. If there was a problem in one or more of the steps described for dairy distribution, such as the content having exceeded its shelf life, we would have a chance of detecting the issue with our senses—certain cues would alert our nostrils or our eyes. The indications that a particular data set is out of date can be far less apparent. With some thoughtful design, however, visualizations can help compensate for this difference and provide immediate visual cues that there may be something problematic about the data before we consume too much of it (see Figure 1.33).

- *Familiarity:* We all understand the basic properties of milk and what can be done with it. We know how to use it in conjunction with other foods. But how do you mix different kinds of data and visual elements to make something that works well as a whole?

FIGURE 1.33
Obviously out of date!

- *Concentration:* Generally, the proportion of elements in milk is at a level that can be assimilated by people. Data is necessarily super-concentrated, and that makes assimilation all the more difficult—it's 100,000- or 1,000,000-times concentrated milk.

Milk run

Staying on the subject of milk, a data analytics company called Palantir Technologies has created a set of tools that helps users track food production issues from farm to store shelves. The ripples in supply chains can be difficult to see, but specialized software makes the process of detecting these ripples much more simple. The "trace back" study shown in Figure 1.34 is an example of that software. All data are real but anonymized.

The view in Figure 1.34 shows the entire trace back without any data filtering. Because there are too many data points to fit comfortably on one screen, the data view can be panned and zoomed.

It's often useful to filter data based on when the shipment or event occurred. The screen shot in Figure 1.35 shows an analyst highlighting and isolating blocks of time with the Timeline Helper (notice the shaded area near the bottom right of the screen). Elements not part of the chosen time block are grayed out to provide a quick reference that they occur outside the chosen time field.

In Figure 1.36, the Selection Helper (upper right) is highlighting milk. The red arrows indicate directionality of the shipment, and the size of the arrow indicates the absolute shipment count. This gives analysts a quick view of where and how much of a given item came through each distribution channel, which allows them to visually discount irrelevant channels.

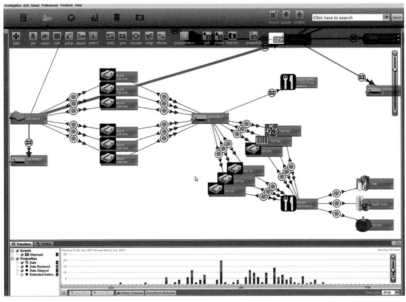

FIGURE 1.34

Example "trace back" study. *Source: Courtesy of Palantir Technologies*

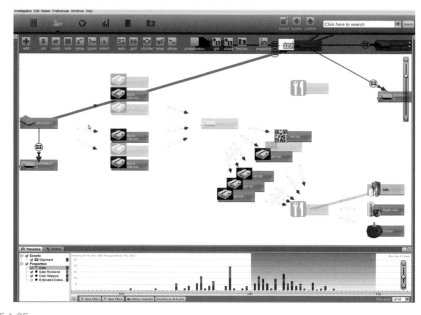

FIGURE 1.35

Timeline Helper can highlight and isolate blocks of time. *Source: Courtesy of Palantir Technologies*

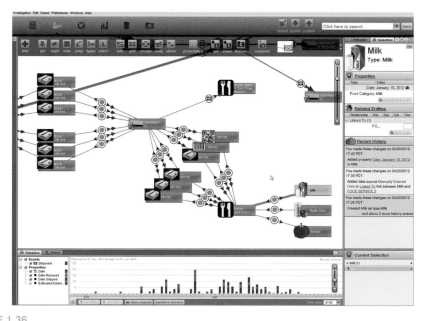

FIGURE 1.36

Milk being highlighted by Selection Helper. *Source: Courtesy of Palantir Technologies.*

www.palantir.com

Back in Thoreau's day, a trout in the pail may have been one of the best visual indicators that there had been some tampering with the milk. Now, the problems can be much less apparent, far more dangerous, and embedded in vastly more complex networks of supply. Companies, such as Palantir, are helping to reveal the sources and evidence of problems that would otherwise be beyond the unassisted abilities of people to detect (Figure 1.37).

FIGURE 1.37
More than meets the eye.

The tip of the iceberg

When you look at a chart, what do you see? I used to see just a chart, but now I view it as only the tip of the iceberg. As we navigate through oceans of data, we are starting to see more breaking through the surface, just as tips of icebergs are made visible at the surface only with the support of a lot below that we cannot see. Just because we can't see it, doesn't mean we shouldn't at least be aware of it. That awareness could mean the difference between a pleasant sightseeing cruise and the voyage of the *Titanic*. Over the years working as a user experience designer, and even more so while working on this book, I've come to see charts and visualizations as pointers to many other things. Now, when I look at a chart or visualization, I can't help but think about the data and decisions that went into it—I see it as much more than a chart.

One goal of this book is to get you to see some element of this topic from a different perspective or think about some aspect in a different way. That's a big part of what good data visualization does. It helps you to see something you otherwise might not have considered, prompts you to explore some interesting feature yourself, and lets you draw your own conclusions from it all.

Data visualizations of various kinds are an increasingly important part of how we inform—or misinform—our conversations. I'm seeing more and more charts describing data about everything from employment figures to diet and exercise patterns for some of my health-conscious, tech-minded friends. That's great. But if we are to have even more clear, honest, and inclusive conversations, most of us need a handle on the language of data visualization and infographics.

Data visualizations, infographics, and related data-driven designs have become increasingly mainstream over the past decade, thanks to the democratization of technological tools, their adoption by graphic designers, and the patronage of cutting-edge blogs and print publications. These sense-making tools could help many of us engage with the information and data we want and need. Those earnest *USA Today* infographics of the 1980s helped paved the way for open-source tech tools that allow everyone from web developers to Aunt Helen to import a data set, connect some statistical dots, shine it all up with design software, and post it online. An individual's graphic design chops, social media skills, or ability to stir up a little controversy—using sketchy statistics—can capture the attention of the collective online mind.

And therein lies the rub: the tools that give us the ability to visualize data with so much ease, beauty, and sophistication today also can cause complication and consternation because their key points and true meaning get lost in translation. This book celebrates style and creativity in visuals, but it is equally about communicating information effectively—and honestly. We should have tools that are easy to use, reliable, high quality, and able to evolve, but, along with highly complex visualizations, we also need "quick-draw" tools.

In many instances, it is simply not worth spending a lot of time or effort doing an infographic. The reason some of the current infographics are problematic is that they often do not illuminate the information at all. If you can read the story without looking at the graphic and know just as much then as after you've looked at the graphic, what's the point? On the other hand, if you can create a better infographic or a more elaborate, but still effective, data visualization, then why not try to do it? In concert pictures, words, and numbers can propel a story and illuminate the supporting data in a clearer, more informative, and more persuasive way, but their use needs to be appropriate to the purpose (Figure 1.38).

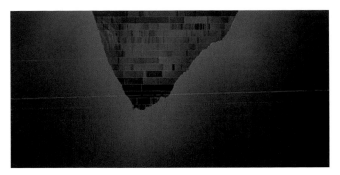

FIGURE 1.38
Getting to the bottom of things.

ATTRIBUTES OF DATA VISUALIZATION

Creating stories about data is only human: it's the ability to revise consistently that makes a story sound.

– COCO KRUMME

Here are some of the specific attributes and benefits of data visualizations that I'll highlight in this book. I believe the best examples of data visualization do the following:

- Help us understand and manage important data streams that are flowing around us. (We can do this in real time or otherwise.)

- Move easily from "the big picture" to the minute details at will. Again, Ben Shneiderman's mantra applies: "Overview first, zoom and filter, then details-on-demand."

- Allow us to quickly spot errors in the data. The problems visually "pop out" in front of us.

- Enable us to perceive things we were not considering or expecting and help us to better deal with the unexpected.

- Have deep simplicity: The interfaces are absolutely as simple as possible, but not any simpler, even if they are based on complex or deep data sets.

- Reduce what information visualization researcher and the author *of Information Visualization Perception for Design*, Colin Ware, and others describe as "the cost of information"—they should help us think about the important issues without wondering about things such as "What does that button do?" or "What am I looking at?"

- Have some level of interactivity and qualities of good collaborators.

- Help a spectrum of people make better real-life, day-to-day decisions.

- Help viewers gain new insights and enjoy exploring data.

- Have some flexibility and be able to adapt and adjust to the changing needs and contexts of the user.

- Don't tell "visual lies"—intentionally or otherwise.

I'm going to devote much of this book to looking at the ways in which visualizations and other tools can help us make more informed decisions and useful discoveries. That said, some problematic areas for infographics and data visualizations need to be addressed, as well. The following are a few of my pet peeves:

- Some polished presentations of charts and graphs are meaningless, contradictory, or outright deceiving. If "Past performance is no guarantee of future results,"—as it often says in these kinds of documents—then why use glossy graphics? Sure, it is a required bit of verbiage, but it always strikes me as basically dangling a bright shiny object in one hand and reaching for my wallet with the other. This is the downside to participating in the data. It is in that gap between the words and the pictures where you might be constructing your own narratives. Something like—"Well that's just 'legalese'…the pictures are telling the true story. It looks like I'll be able to retire when I planned."

- The charts you see are not the charts that really matter. Short of crystal balls and time travel devices, it's hard to find the proper kinds of visualizations to make the type of financial plans one might really want. That said, I can imagine, right off the bat, some that could make a difference. (Those would be good predictive models or tools to help the Time Bandits on Wall Street more effectively practice the dark art of "front running.")

- A complex problem is reflected with a complex visual response. Big deal! After college, I was a freelance science writer with two kinds of jobs—technical writing and writing about science for lay audiences. Which was harder? Yes, the popular content. Creators of infographics and data visualizations: why not put in a little more effort to help the viewer get through with less? As Einstein famously said, "Things should be as simple as they are, but not simpler." Part of the job, I believe, is to strive for finding that line.

- The charts and graphics look cool and get circulated a lot, but if you ask anyone what they mean or what insights they've gotten—crickets.

- Just because a complex problem is presented in a cartoon format, doesn't mean that it's any clearer or easier to understand. I'd rather have a theoretical physicist explain the expansion of the universe than, say, Captain Galactic, if the former understands it well enough to say it simply.

DIVING INTO THE WELL OF MACHINE DATA WITH SPLUNK
CIO DOUG HARR

Errors like straws upon the surface flow:
Who would search for pearls must dive below.

– JOHN DRYDEN

Whether it's calling a friend on your cell phone, booking travel tickets online, or countless other kinds of interactions, all of the resulting electronic exchanges generate "machine data" about these processes. Mostly, these data are the unnoticed ripples and wakes left by user and computer activities. At first glance, these digital traces may not seem particularly useful, but, in the right circumstances, they can offer important insights for many purposes. Let's start with a tangible illustration of this idea. Imagine that you're a castaway on a desert island and have been walking along the sandy shore searching for some sign of a ship. As you walk, you leave a set of footprints in the sand. You're not trying to make these tracks, they just get made while you're moving along, formulating a plan, and looking for help. However, rescuers see the seemingly inconsequential impressions and patterns you leave behind and follow them directly to you (Figure 1.39).

Machine data are like those footprints in the sand—a sometimes extremely useful consequence of the activities of people in particular kinds of environments. Also, like those footprints, machine data can be ephemeral. Without intervention, they simply

FIGURE 1.39
Making an impression.

disappear. The amount, variety, and complexity of this kind of unstructured data is on the rise, and this presents opportunities to see the tracks and traces of the people who made them.

Doug Harr is Chief Information Officer at Splunk, a company that specializes in mining and visualizing machine data. It is squarely in the "big data" business, and some of the company's larger deployments involve tens of terabytes of new data each day. Harr says the value in this kind of machine data is "not as much about what happens at a surface level of an interaction, such as booking a reservation or buying a product at a particular time," rather, "it's far more about how the process unfolded, what the experience was, and how long it took. Businesses want to see data that shows if the credit cards used were bad or if there were attempts to defraud the system," he says.

www.splunk.com

Because these businesses were getting vast pools of data in web logs, they found they could start doing a new form of web analytics and business intelligence (BI) by drawing from that source. Harr notes, "One difference between this and more traditional BI is that you don't have to do up-front schemas [a description of a database's organization and structure]; in fact, you don't want to do that." Instead, businesses can start to pull the data in and see what's useful. Harr adds that, as one of his colleagues puts it, "There are questions that you didn't even know you wanted to ask." In any case, he says, there's no way to schematize all the machine data anyway because there are too many formats for that kind of approach. He continues,

It is almost the opposite of the traditional BI world, where you carefully plan what tables you're going to pull, and transform them, load them, and clean them up. In this scenario, people pull up data, look at what might be interesting, organize it, and try to determine how long they are going to keep it. They hold onto the data and make discoveries as they go, even when they are not sure what they are going to do with it. They build on initial attempts to gain insight out of the data and keep going until they have something really compelling. This is a new area, so we have to allow for invention by early adopters in this green field, and there's inevitably a certain amount of trial and error involved in the work. We've often noticed with our customers that a systems administrator will download the software and start to work with it and see what's possible. Then they share their findings with colleagues. It might cross over silos in the organization and eventually trickle up to the CIO or somebody else at a high level who can see what might be done with the data.

That systems administrator, Harr believes, "can be a hero who discovers a new understanding of something or have key insight that changes the game for the business as a whole, not just for the IT department." These insights can save huge amounts of money from the bottom line. For example, a leading telephony company started to review call details records and looked at the rate tables in relation to where they routed calls. The client put the rate data together with the routing data and created a kind of real-time cost chart showing where they were spending more money than necessary. They were able to save many millions of dollars by making adjustments to their system.

Although the ability to capture, store, and retrieve data is improving rapidly, those capacities are still finite. Factors ranging from basic physics to budgetary constraints impose limitations, so there comes a point where practical decisions about what data to keep become necessary. Thoughtful analyses and discussions are essential to make determinations about what are the most useful kinds of machine data and what to do with it all. Harr says, "Despite the 'data nirvana' idea of just keeping everything and figuring out what to do with it later, thoughtful analysis and planning all the way through are still crucial."

He points to some kinds of machine data, such as web logs and application logs, as generally "safe bets" for being useful. The digital footprints left in these logs reveal people's paths through a website and are instrumental in many kinds of analyses. They can offer important insights into the *who*, *what*, *where*, *when*, *how*, and sometimes, perhaps, even the *why* of user behavior. Along with various elements of the machine data representing storage, server, and network utilization, the data can tell important stories about the interactions of consumers and systems. For businesses that want to better understand their customers within a particular technical infrastructure, that's data worth keeping.

In addition to identifying the kinds of data that are clearly useful, there's the hard work in the sometimes gray areas of figuring out what other data might also be good to keep and explore. "There's a lot of coaching to try to develop frameworks around what could be done with machine data," according to Harr. Part of this process involves working with customers to figure out what kinds of data could be valuable, and therefore worth saving, and then making it more rapidly accessible (Figure 1.40). Says Harr, "Sometimes, we'll have consultative meetings with clients who might not know what's possible, where we'll pull some data up on the screen and have an exchange, walking through the data saying, 'What can we learn from this, and what can we do with that?'"

Another approach to helping make the machine data influx manageable and useful according to Harr is creating a kind of "snapshot." He explains: "You choose a subset of the machine data, and you create a kind of summary index of that information, at a certain period of time, and snapshot it and keep what you believe might be the most useful, but not all of it."

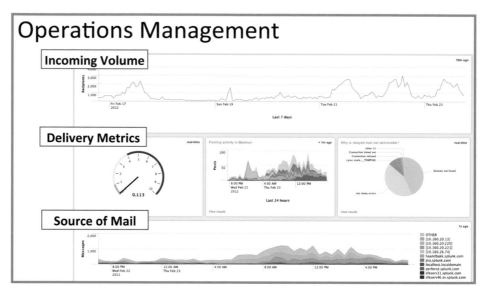

FIGURE 1.40

A framework for analysis. *Courtesy of Splunk.*

Keeping hot, warm, and cold buckets of data

In the course of discussions with colleagues and clients, different kinds of data might emerge as clearly valuable, and other elements may not be as essential to collect at that point, as Harr explains:

> We have regular discussions about how long we want to keep certain kinds of data and what is 'hot' versus 'warm' versus 'cold'. We can help people manage buckets of this machine data so that they can secure it, manage it, and retain it. We'll take a hot bucket and put it in better storage and do real-time analytics on it that might only last seven days. The next 30 to 45 days might be a warm bucket after that; when it goes cold, it might go to very inexpensive [and slow to access] storage.

Just because a bucket of data goes from hot to cold doesn't necessarily mean its value is gone for good. At times, the discovery of a particular trend of interest about consumer behavior in a hot bucket may suggest further investigation to see how far back the trend extends. "Developing a trend line over an appropriate period of time is very important," says Harr. "We might decide that a particular trend line is interesting over a three-month period, but then wonder what happened over the last year or two."

Because it can be hard to know up front how far back in time an interesting trend line may go, Splunk keeps some kinds of data for long periods to ensure it will be able to take those retrospective looks. For example, a company might save its web logs for a seven-year retention period. These web logs have a record of everyone who used the web services and what that process was like. That includes details such as the operating system the user wanted for the download and what version of the software they were accessing.

Harr has seen a shift in attitudes about the value of keeping and mining machine data. "People are starting to realize the benefit of grabbing and keeping data," he says, "because there is quite a bit that might come up in the future that we might not anticipate today." As that shift accelerates, Harr and his colleagues are working to develop new sets of best practices that include ways to handle the data and determining cost-benefit models for storage. Figuring out these new rules of the road will take a range of participants who bring different kinds of experience and expertise to the table. "Some people would say this effort should be done only by data scientists, but we are really trying to democratize this a little more than that," says Harr. "To IT practitioners who have a lot of experience in this area and have been through some of this before, we say let's work with that knowledge but also turn it on its head a little bit, because machine data is different."

Visualizing operational intelligence

As part of the ongoing discussions about managing and mining data at Splunk, there are also conversations about, and interest in, how to most effectively and meaningfully visualize machine data. Says Harr, "We are seeing a renaissance around how to visualize what we are calling *operational intelligence*—people are very excited about it and are turning to new and old sources about the art of the infographic. They ask, 'How can I get the most insight from the visual representation?' We talk a lot about how to present the data in the most useful and compelling way."

He notes that, sometimes, it doesn't have to be a graphic representation to get the point across in the most effective way. "At the end of the day, a table can be very effective in some circumstances." Even so, a good visualization can make a compact and compelling case based on data that is difficult to ignore (Figures 1.41 and 1.42).

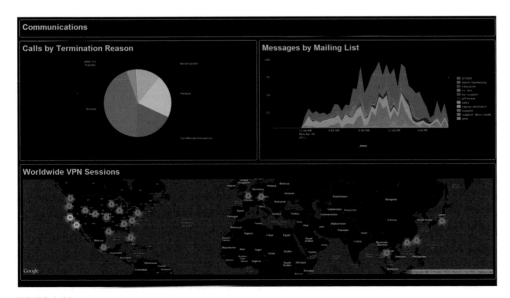

FIGURE 1.41

Dashboard for situational awareness. *Courtesy of Splunk.*

FIGURE 1.42

Close-up of dashboard. *Courtesy of Splunk.*

DEEP SIMPLICITY (COMPLEX DATA IN SIMPLE FORMS)

One sometimes finds what one is not looking for.

– ALEXANDER FLEMING

Perhaps one way to think about adapting to the opportunities and challenges presented by the move to democratize data is to create more interfaces that appear to be simple, but represent complex relationships and interactions. Just because a visualization isn't complicated, doesn't mean it can't produce powerful, even world-changing, insights if it is put in front of the right person. Consider the glass or plastic petri dish and the special kind of clear goo called "agar" that fills the bottom of the container. These are relatively simple things that allow people to see the presence and growth of simple kinds of organisms such as bacteria and molds (Figure 1.43).

One day in 1928, Alexander Fleming noticed that a cover had been left off one of the dishes in his lab that contained a staphylococcus bacteria culture. Some bluish-green mold found its way to the dish and took up residence. Fleming looked at the contaminated dish, and instead of simply disposing of it, he noticed there was a zone around the mold where the bacterial growth was inhibited. Although the visual was fairly simple, Fleming had the training, mindset, and insight to see something profound that would be meaningless to most people and simply a bit of sloppy lab work to others. This led to the introduction of penicillin, which has saved countless lives. Without the accidental visualization, Fleming might never have asked the question that led to the development of penicillin. Without the right user looking at it, that world-changing petri dish may have literally ended up in the ash heap of history. Hans Selye (Mintzberg, 2005) said:

> I doubt that Fleming could have obtained a grant for the discovery of penicillin on that basis [a requirement for highly detailed research plans] because he could not have said, "I propose to have an accident in a culture so that it will be spoiled by a mould falling on it, and I propose to recognize the possibility of extracting an antibiotic from this mould."

FIGURE 1.43

What's growing on? *Source: Andreas Feininger.*

To me, that petri dish is a particular form of what I'll call *deep simplicity*. What I mean by that is, in essence, using relatively simple elements (such as, in the penicillin example, glass, clear goo, and microscopic creatures) that help properly prepared minds make new insights. The meaning and significance is in the eye and mind of the beholder. Sure, that sounds very theoretical and hard to accomplish in practical terms, but it might be another way to approach the creation of some forms of visualization. After all, we are entering a period of many experiments. Not all will work, but, then again, one person's lab blunder could be another's Nobel Prize–winning moment.

If every aspect of a system is narrowly defined, highly constrained, tightly scripted, and over-engineered, then it can be difficult, if not impossible, to find what one is not looking for. One of my motivations for writing this book is that, although the promise and potential of data visualization is great for enabling more insights to more people, more can be done to increase the power of visualizations of data while making the fundamental as open and accessible as possible. To me, just because someone is very smart and has great expertise in an intellectually challenging area doesn't always mean he or she is also an expert in working with complex visualizations. Those skills are not necessarily linked by either inclination or by training in their subject.

Achieving deep simplicity with the use of visualizations and language is not "dumbing down." It is, in many ways, the exact opposite. In my own experience as a science writer for a range of audiences, the easiest work was often that which looked the most difficult—a piece for researchers or practitioners of technical information in a no-nonsense way. Some of the most difficult, and also rewarding, work was to take a challenging scientific topic and make it understandable and interesting to lay readers.

As someone who worked with some pretty difficult subject matter said, "If you can't explain it simply, you don't understand it well enough." That's true, Albert Einstein. Getting to the essence of deep simplicity requires a lot of work, and the goal is to make a great number of people more knowledgeable. I would suggest that even experts well versed in their fields might benefit from looking at their work in a deeply simple, more visceral way. When possible, I like to consider a problem at as fundamental a level as possible and, once I have a better understanding of that, step through additional layers. This may not work for everyone, but I imagine there are many out there who might agree.

Inspirations for simple visualizations can come from many sources. Could the data be imagined as a sphere with layers that can be peeled back like the skin of an onion…or sliced in a cross section…or diced into chunks that could be put into different piles? Could the data be imagined as a rubber band—something that is stretched in a particular direction, but only so far, before forces pull it in another direction?

WHAT'S NEW?!

It's what you learn after you know it all that counts.

– ATTRIBUTED TO HARRY S. TRUMAN

So much has been written about visualizing data—is there anything really left to add? Of course there is. In anything as quickly changing and broadly encompassing as this field, there are fresh ideas to consider and old themes to view through new lenses. That doesn't negate the value of all the important work that's been done. However, just as the most effective ways to present content on the radio didn't all translate to television, perhaps the same is true for presenting data in 2D versus fully immersive 3D environments.

Some considerations transcend the particulars of a specific medium, and some don't. In the case of television, it took at least a decade for the medium to start coming into its own. Some of the emerging technologies and forms of visualization will take time to mature and develop best practices; some will be taken from the past, and others will be drawn thoughtfully from current contexts (Figure 1.44). Along with the burst of interest and creativity, of course, waves of hype are almost guaranteed to come as part of the process as well. Figure 1.45 provides another way to visualize it.

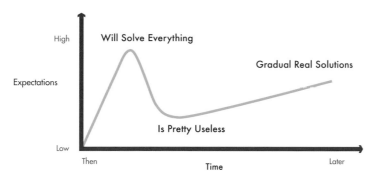

FIGURE 1.44

The hype curve.

FIGURE 1.45

From hype to progress.

Only with the passage of time can we say what has met—or exceeded—expectations; however, several of the themes and trends listed below will play an important role. At various points, this book will touch on many of these ideas and explore new ways to visualize and make sense of data, as in the list that follows.

Democratizing data

More kinds of people are able to access more sources of data. This opens the door for many new perspectives and ideas about what to put together and what to do with it. Along with all the fresh starts, there will be failed attempts, but that comes with the territory of innovation. With thoughtful approaches to data in general and visualizations in particular, the good that emerges from the ferment likely will far surpass the bad.

Abundance of data, scarcity of context

The availability of various kinds of data about people and subjects is expanding, while the amount of time, money, and effort required to obtain it continues to decrease. Within seconds, a simple search can return a vast amount of data points, but they are often a collection of largely unconnected dots. Without context, a cursory scan of search results and other presentations of data can lead to inaccurate assessments, misinterpretations, and other problems. Technology may be better at producing data than the context needed to form a clear and accurate picture. This imbalance can be problematic, but visualizations can help us come closer to equilibrium and validity of interpretation.

Connections, collaborations, and communities

As more people get involved in working with data, more groups and collaborations of various kinds will emerge. People with divergent skills and abilities—all connected and focused on the same problem—can collaborate in ways an individual or narrowly defined group cannot. This increasing connectivity means sharing and working with data, among not only members of teams, but also departments and affinity-based communities, as well as across countries and cultures.

Increased *sensoring*

From weather satellites orbiting in space to the phones we hold in our hands, more sensors of all kinds are collecting a variety of data about us and our environments. For example, detectors installed in some high-crime neighborhoods are able to pick up the point of origination and trajectory of a bullet being fired.

The delta of data

Sometimes, the most important aspect of data is how it changes over time. The technical barriers to capturing and keeping this dynamic data are getting lower. At the same time, the ability to present this influx in meaningful ways is becoming ever more practical and potentially useful.

Fluid interactivity

As interfaces such as touch screens make it easier for people to interact fluidly with data, more opportunities may emerge for trying out new kinds of visualizations that may have been impossible or simply too cumbersome with a keyboard and mouse. Motion and gesture capturing capabilities and evolutions in 3D technologies may help make working with abstract data a far more tangible experience. Some of our devices will detect inputs of which we are not consciously aware, such as facial expressions. Like it or not, while we're watching TV, our TV will be monitoring *us* and adjusting content, such as targeted commercials, accordingly. New breeds of highly responsive visualizations would not necessarily be replacements for older approaches, but they would add more arrows to the quiver.

Upwardly mobile

The growing range of options we have for receiving, sending, sharing, and saving data will allow us to work with it in the times and places we prefer. Of course, that assumes the challenge of designing interaction to make the data visualizations useful and meaningful in some way is attainable at various levels of screen size and resolution.

The need for speed

Timing matters. You can get all the right answers to the key questions, but if they arrive too late, what then? Because visualizations often can communicate at a more preconscious and immediate level, we can get feedback on multiple concerns quickly. In environments such as operating rooms and battlefields, rapid streams of interrelated data may be flooding in to the various participants. Much of this flow somehow needs to be considered and addressed to get their respective goals accomplished.

Many conversations about these topics would extend well beyond the scope of this book, but they are good to keep in mind as factors driving the evolution of data visualizations.

A More Beautiful Question

2

Always the beautiful answer who asks a more beautiful question.

– e.e. cummings

FIGURE 2.1

All Over Coffee #507, Visitacion Valley, San Francisco, by Paul Madonna.

THE ART OF INQUIRY

You can look at data visualizations from many different perspectives. For one, they can be seen as a means to arrive at answers to complex problems. But visualizations can play an even more essential role in sparking important *questions* that would not have arisen otherwise. When people begin problem solving, they may start off with a baseline set of assumptions and premises that are vague or misleading. To respond effectively in those cases, they may have to accept the idea that their initial set of ideas could be wrong or that the most important question to ask is one they never considered. The willingness to change one's mind and the ability to respond with new sets of questions can be more useful than the skill of crafting queries that can prove to be irrelevant.

In this chapter, we'll dive into the process of interactions between people, data, and displays that lead to better questions and more useful answers. If you'd like to first learn more about, or review, some of the basic building blocks of data visualization designs, please take a look at Chapter 3, and then come back.

We will explore two fundamental questions that visualizations can help answer: asking questions and weighing answers.

Asking questions

Sometimes, it can be challenging to know where to start with a question—make it too broad (e.g., "Where is the best place in the world for me to live?") and you might not get back a useful response. Make it too narrow (e.g., "What is the best block for me to live on?"), and you may cut off important aspects of the results.

Data visualization tools can take some of the pressure off these decisions by making the precise entry questions into a data set less important. The ability to visually dive in and out of various layers of data on a map or social network diagram means you can work with the right density of detail for your needs. These tools have filters and feedback loops that can help in refining a general inquiry and point to the next steps. The feedback loops can be considerably shorter than the ones involving the queries that go from, say business intelligence (BI) teams to IT departments.

In addition, visualizations can provide a common platform for collaboratively generating and revising questions in ways that a more traditional process involving SQL statements cannot. The original question can be very broad—even potentially disposable—but helps set a question-and-answer (Q&A) process in motion that is more easily understood by all participants.

Weighing answers

You've succeeded in getting some interesting results from your investigation, but do the numbers add up? Among other things, it's important to consider where the underlying data originated, how it was processed, and what it reveals. Data visualization tools can help you more easily identify, zoom in, and assess the underlying sources. The supporting facts should not be mere footnotes at the end of the article but, ideally, a clear and continually updated connection to the original material. For example, take the question of where to live mentioned before a step further.

Let's say I'm considering moving to a new town, but it appears to have a high crime rate. If I took that one statistic at face value, I might knock it out of consideration. However, if I dug a little deeper, I would find it was part of an MSA (Metropolitan Statistical Area) with an overall high crime rate, but this area in particular was quite safe, and then I'd have a different attitude. Visualization tools can prompt me to ask about what I'm seeing and let me address those questions. This is an entirely different experience from simply looking up where the source material is buried.

GOOD QUESTION

A good question is never answered. It is not a bolt to be tightened into place but a seed to be planted and to bear more seed toward the hope of greening the landscape of ideas.

– JOHN ANTHONY CIARDI

What makes a good question? Many times, the best questions are not necessarily the ones that lead to a single, direct answer. Instead, they invite conversations, counterpoints, and, ultimately, new insights. They enable a person's ideas about a subject to expand and evolve. This kind of iterative Q&A process does not have to be just person-to-person; something analogous to this can happen with a combination of user, computer interface, and database.

Ben Shneiderman coined the term *dynamic querying*. By putting questions into interactive visual forms, we can easily see, save, and compare various versions of a single basic question as "snapshots." Shneiderman says that the chart or graph is only a part of the whole visualization. The visible controls allow us to fluidly and effortlessly "fly through the databases." With these tools, we can begin with a "big picture" and then quickly filter out the elements that are not of interest. As mentioned in Chapter 1, Shneiderman's data visualization mantra is—"Overview first, zoom and filter, then details-on-demand."

Dynamic querying can offer a more fluid and direct kind of experience for asking questions about data, compared with the typical use of SQL statements. For readers who are interested in the topic of data visualizations but are not necessarily familiar with all the terms tossed around by an IT department, SQL stands for "Structured Query Language." It is a data manipulation programming language that works on relational databases and has been around since the 1970s. SQL is a way to ask questions of highly structured data and is an excellent way to retrieve things like airline flights or credit card transactions, but it's not good for anything that isn't contained in the neat rows and columns of a database or spreadsheet. Another shortcoming of SQL is that the relative complexity of the language means that even users who know the basics of SQL statements still generally need IT departments or database specialists to turn natural language questions into ones that are machine-readable statements.

Here's a simple example:

Mary wants to look in her customer database for the names and addresses of everyone who became a customer before the year 2000. The SQL for this question is as follows:

```
SELECT firstname, lastname, street, city, state, zip;
FROM customer_list;
WHERE join_date < 1/1/2000;
```

Large and complicated SQL statements can take up pages and pages of space when printed out of a standard office printer. This kind of approach, although often useful and necessary, can make the process of getting answers from data more stilted and difficult.

WASHINGTON, D.C.'S 1100 POINTS OF LIGHT

One example of a tool for dynamic queries is embodied in the "DC HomeFinder," which I think of as an archetypal and elegant data visualization tool. This type of interface is called a Starfield display, and this particular one was created in the early 1990s. It displayed regional housing data and presented, in a visual format, the homes on the market. It was an inspiration to me as I was starting out on my interactive design career path in the late '90s; it also shows that people have been working on interesting approaches to visualization longer than we might think.

The DC HomeFinder was created by Christopher Williamson, under the auspices of Ben Shneiderman, at the University of Maryland Human-Computer Interaction Lab (www.cs.umd. edu/hcil/spotfire). It showed a map of Washington, D.C. and, as one Shneiderman description of the tool puts it, "1100 points of light indicating homes for sale" (Figure 2.2). Slider controls allow the rapid selection of the number of bedrooms and cost, and buttons select air conditioning, garage, and other features. Within seconds, users could see how many homes matched their query and adjust accordingly. Shneiderman writes:

> One of the amusing stories about this project was the unwillingness of corporate or university sources for regional housing information to share their data. Undaunted,

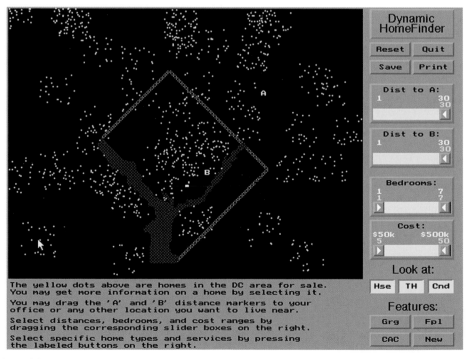

FIGURE 2.2
DC HomeFinder.

Chris Williamson and his friends took a Sunday *Washington Post* and typed in the data for the 1100 homes. One of the amazing stories is the resistance of these same institutions to learn about or apply our approach.

Let's take a brief trip back in time to the early '90s and say that a user named Alice wants to buy a home in D.C. She may not be exactly sure where to start, and that's okay, because alongside the map, she has an easily changeable set of choices. The interface reduces the level of effort to modify the question, so she can easily ask about various combinations of alternatives. The first step could be stripping out attributes of a home she's sure she doesn't want and then setting geographic and price ranges. Figures 2.3 and 2.4 show some aspects of the DC HomeFinder that show these ideas in action.

Seeing a set of range sliders that can help rapidly narrow the parameters of the search provides a visual reminder of all the main factors she should keep in mind, rather than having to track all the variables in her head. They can help her figure out what to ask without being bogged down by concerns about getting her search terms just right.

For this kind of exploration and discovery process, interface controls can allow intuitive and fluid interactions with the data and can be very effective and even absorbing and fun.

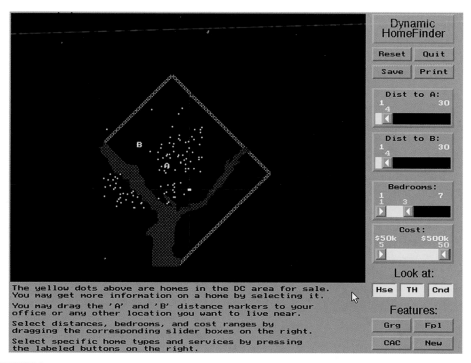

FIGURE 2.3

Alice wants to narrow down the field by distance from points A (e.g., office) and B (e.g., health club) of the homes that have one to three bedrooms.

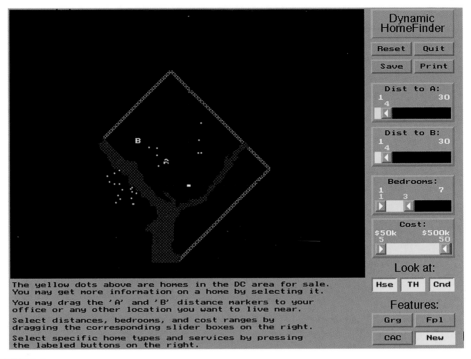

FIGURE 2.4

She may also want to further limit her selections to only new homes.

TWENTY QUESTIONS

If we would have new knowledge, we must get a whole world of new questions.

– SUSANNE LANGER

Whether it's checkmating in chess or scoring high in bridge, successful game play can demand sharp observation, fluid adaptation, and asking yourself a series of sometimes nonverbal questions in rapid succession such as, "Given this arrangement of options, what's the best move to make next?" These same key skills can be essential in finding meaningful and reliable insights in data. In many games, the starting point is far less crucial to winning than how we respond to changing variables and competing priorities as we play. Extracting meaning from data with visualizations can be a similar experience. Instead of focusing on how best to construct an initial query and going down that one path, we can put more emphasis on exploring differing lines of potential interest from the beginning. The visual feedback and level of interactivity that data visualizations provide can help us engage and figure out what to do next as we go.

When even slight changes in the syntax, emphasis, and details in the words of a question can lead to wildly divergent answers, it can be hard to start asking for what we need. Important nuances in formulating questions and understanding the results are not always clear. Not everyone asks questions or reaches conclusions in the same way—and our assumptions, beliefs, and views of the world dramatically affect how we interpret the answers we receive. The more flexible and rewarding it is to ask questions of data, the more likely people are to engage in it. This can encourage exploration of a wider range of alternatives and also potentially more complete answers to a particular question. It can be an art: a game of exploration in which the more beautiful questions arise through the process of inquiry.

That said, on their own, even the best formulated questions and queries ultimately can prove pointless without a way to readily judge the scope and quality of underlying data. Is the deck stacked? Let's say you've just discovered very interesting and important findings and are anxious to report the results, but you're feeling uncertain about the depth and reliability of the sources. What do you do? Without clear and easily accessible validation, your options may lead down a rabbit hole.

How about when you're confronting an overwhelming number of questions all at once? Another reason data visualizations can be so powerful is they can help to satisfy the increasing need for speed in reliably assessing and responding to large, real-time incoming data flows in various environments. They can help reduce the time it takes to get feedback on a burst of questions arising in critical situations and accelerate good decision making.

PATTERNS, CONTEXTS, AND QUESTIONS

Words differently arranged have different meanings, and meanings differently arranged have a different effect.

– BLAISE PASCAL

Question: How do you start to turn a jumble of data into something interesting and useful?

Consider a game such as Scrabble®. You begin with a general goal in mind—putting together more high-scoring word combinations than your competitors. The specific questions you need to ask are determined by the particular handful of tiles you have to work with. You go through the process of looking at the letters and rearranging them, physically or in your mind's eye, so that the most meaningful (highest scoring) pattern emerges (Figure 2.5). A number of questions arise in this process: What combinations are possible?

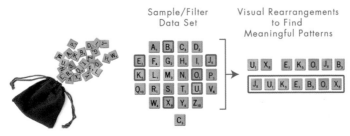

FIGURE 2.5
Arranging tiles in Scrabble.

Does this arrangement yield the highest score possible? Does that word really exist or is it just a product of wishful thinking? How long should I take to figure this out?

At least for me, there is often a lingering doubt if I have the strongest combination, but at some point you do the best you can.

Depending on the context, one pattern can produce many widely different things. For example, in the context of Scrabble, the arrangement of letters to spell J-U-K-E-B-O-X offers you a high score that could help you win the game. It doesn't matter what the word actually means as long as I can point to it in a dictionary. However, how was I able to come up with that arrangement of letters? I can't really tell you exactly. I just moved things around and saw what patterns matched. I noticed the "X", "O", "B" formed the word "box" and thought of what else could be added to that. Somewhere from the recesses of my mind, word meanings and images surfaced. To make the word, I relied on more than the abstract context of Scrabble. It came from memories, associations, images, and who knows what else?

I may start with one context to think about something, but I employ others as I go. I have one question in mind, but I may need to go to surprising places to get the best answer. I see B-O-X and also see J-K, and I think about a dive bar in Long Beach, California, and picture a jukebox. In many kinds of processes, our abilities to recognize patterns are remarkable and mysterious, and vary from person to person. A narrow set of particulars, such as people's level of attentiveness, and broad factors, such as cultural norms, can influence the interpretation of a pattern of data. The level of experience and expertise that someone has in a particular discipline is only one of many factors that can sway the perception of a pattern.

Different angles, perspectives, and resolutions

To raise new questions, new possibilities, to regard old problems from a new angle, requires creative imagination and marks real advance in science.

– ALBERT EINSTEIN

Sometimes, you need to view data from different angles and perspectives to find the most interesting facets. You may discover they're not the ones you expected. You have to be prepared to let go of a favorite question and replace it with one that yields an even more important and interesting answer. A recurring theme of this chapter is that there can be real value in the process of question generation and iteration. The ability to generate many questions and answer them easily in rapid succession, while not being overly attached to a single line of inquiry, can be a productive exercise. Sometimes, it's simply not realistic to think that crafting that perfect question will yield the best answer.

Let's try a thought experiment in this kind of process using the pattern of Scrabble tiles that we saw earlier. Here's a question we could ask about it: What are some of the different kinds of outputs that can arise from a specific combination of letters that are considered in different contexts? As I arrange the combinations of letters, there is a rapid sense of recognition that this combination forms a common word with a clear definition (at least in an English language dictionary). This conjures up a mind's-eye visualization of one of these beautiful machines (Figure 2.6).

Pattern:

Context 1 (Game): JUKEBOX—Seven-letter word worth 77 points

Context 2 (Dictionary): juke·box (jōōk bŏks) *n.* A money-operated machine that plays music, usually equipped with pushbuttons for the selection of particular recordings.

Context 3 (Image):

FIGURE 2.6
Scrabble leads to visualization.

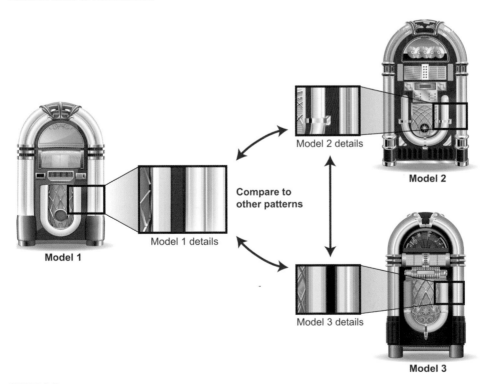

FIGURE 2.7
A jukebox comparison.

Moving away from the game, the linguistic pattern transforms into a visual one and invites all kinds of new questions, if one were inclined to explore them. Because this is a thought experiment, let's try it. I've never really looked too carefully at jukeboxes and wondered if there are any categories or styles by which they're grouped. Is there any kind of visual that connects them, and what are the similarities and differences that might make interesting design elements for other purposes? Are there color and texture patterns that might be good for future reference for a new user interface design? I selected a detail from one of them and then looked for how it is similar to and how it differs from other jukeboxes (see Figure 2.7 on previous page).

For the purposes of this book, I won't go into the details, but I did learn some interesting history about the evolution of jukebox design styles, and an engineer named Paul Fuller. Trying this experiment and gleaning this new information has changed the way I look at these devices. This may be a whimsical example, but the approach might be generalized to a visual exploration and summarized this way:

1. Start with a pattern in one context.
2. Put the pattern into different contexts and see if anything of interest emerges.
3. Look at the item of interest in overview and then pull out interesting details.
4. Compare those details to other related items.
5. Zoom out to see the larger context.

What can we learn from this thought experiment? A pattern, such as a sequence of letters, can be the springboard for explorations of entirely different kinds of patterns. It can spur ideas and lines of investigation that may not have occurred to you initially but still may be interesting. It is a matter of being open to different perspectives and perhaps having some willingness to occasionally engage in a little creative exploration.

Unasked questions about the 999-year-old patient

Be careful about reading health books. You may die of a misprint.

– MARK TWAIN

Large organizations can have such overwhelmingly vast and continuously accumulating data that important questions about elements of it never get asked as it flows in. Carried along with the onrushing tide are many otherwise obvious questions that are moving by too quickly and are obscured by too much other material to be noticed. The result of these unasked questions can be the introduction of errors into the data pool that can contaminate everything around it. Visualizations can help people to look at these large pools of data to see if anything interesting bobs to the surface and suggests a useful question to ask.

For example, when Ben Shneiderman was asked to review some hospital data, and he loaded it up in the data visualization application TIBCO Spotfire, he noticed that three patients were listed as 999 years old. Undetected, this kind of error could have skewed any information from the data. When properly visualized, problems with a data set "just pop out at you," Shneiderman says. "Data visualization is worthwhile if for the data cleaning capabilities alone." According to Shneiderman, "Organizations haven't realized until recently, the majority of their data sets have something wrong with them. Using visualization sometimes allows us to see potentially dangerous errors and omissions."

DESIGNING SOFTWARE FOR WHEN YOU DON'T KNOW WHAT YOU DON'T KNOW

I am wiser to this small extent, that I do not think that I know what I do not know.

– PLATO

Jason Marsh is Chief Information Architect at Acesis, Inc., an enterprise software company that works with healthcare organizations to help improve the quality of patient care. He says that in his area, "Not knowing what to look for in the data, or even knowing what data to capture, is a huge issue." He adds, "There's a whole class of problems in which there are many actors that are not easy to relate to each other and whose interactions are extremely complex."

Marsh says there can be many unintended consequences driven by a set of decisions and actions in one part of the system that emerge in sometimes unexpected areas and unanticipated ways. In healthcare, Marsh says, solving problems can be analogous to "pushing on a balloon," in which squeezing one area simply causes a bulge someplace else. "Narrowly addressing a problem in one part of the system, such as focusing on a single metric, merely pushes the concern into another part," he explains.

A more encompassing, systemwide view, and appreciation for the potential unexpected impacts, can be helpful. This kind of approach requires not only a certain level of open-mindedness on the part of the people working in these systems, but also a flexibility and agility in the software that supports them in their efforts.

Don't go chasing waterfalls

When designing software to manage highly complex systems, it can be a good idea to avoid jumping to conclusions about that system too soon in the process.

It's all too easy to build an application based on a set of known assumptions that leave out key unknown considerations. In these instances, the developed application misses the mark even if all the subsequent development steps are perfectly executed. Software processes traditionally set workflow into stone, so new knowledge and assumptions can't be applied quickly. You can get drawn down a bad path, and the further you go, the harder it becomes to change course. Marsh likens it to a typical occurrence in the traditional "waterfall" software development cycle: "Once you have the program done, you realize you have the wrong model in mind, but it is too late to change." The currents generated by this waterfall get stronger as it gets closer to the end, and a variety of pressures, from institutional to logistical, increase dramatically.

The key, says Marsh, is to have extremely nimble systems. "That nimbleness changes the whole equation." He believes that speed and flexibility in data capture and analysis fundamentally change the way people think about problems, and the process becomes an entirely different experience. "Once you see new relationships between data and causality, you need to be able to re-ask your questions in the first five minutes rather than five days later. This often leads to new data capture requirements," he explains. "We designed the Acesis platform to allow the process redesign to be nearly immediate, and that gives problem solving a whole different quality." Although he sees this kind of dynamic in healthcare, Marsh notes that it is a broadly applicable phenomenon in many different fields.

Rather than trying to come up with the "right" question and then undergo a long and often sluggish process to get the answer, "just start with something, and then try to discover what you don't know, and see if there are questions you should have been asking but didn't realize yet," suggests Marsh. When you don't know what you don't know, there are ways to try to address that uncertainty. One approach he particularly likes is to start asking questions that you believe, or guess, might be relevant, and then rapidly test them. "With those starting points in mind, you can begin to analyze data and iterate. Good visualizations raise as many questions as they answer."

The right track

Visualization tools that make it easier for people to see if they're asking relevant questions, making effective decisions, and accurately evaluating outcomes are a critical component of healthcare performance improvement software. Marsh says one illustration of this is the hospital admissions system, in which it is important to rapidly assess the causes of subsequent readmissions. When problems and their potential relationships are revealed, that can open the way to rethinking some of the steps that may have contributed to the concerns. Flexibility and adaptability let the users ask the right questions at the right time. "How quickly can you change the form of the question?" says Marsh. He adds that, in the tools he creates, "Cases are analyzed and sub-categorized in any dimension defined in real time by the user."

In the dynamic dashboard of the app shown in Figure 2.8, "Human Error Type" is subcategorized by the seriousness of the patient outcome. To the right is a popup edit pane,

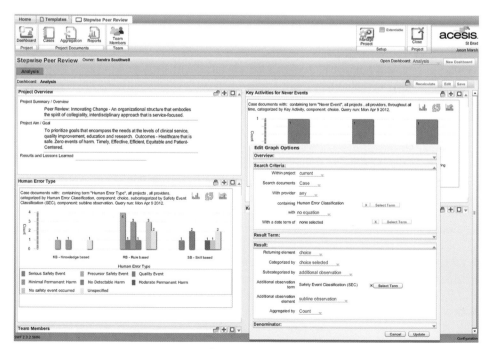

FIGURE 2.8
Acesis Software screen shot.

where the user can choose any two document elements (uniquely identified by an underlying "terminology") to look at in relationship to one another. A relatively simple interface enables certain users to explore the data in real time and iteratively zero in on what questions to ask.

Trust but verify

Another key element of a visualization, Marsh says, is that "you need to trust the data and the process. When you are working with so many unknowns so much of the time, trust is a central concern. It needs to be a part of the culture in which there is transparency of the data, including the process, and sources." For Marsh, any visualizations should allow you to drill down through a graph and immediately see the source of a data point. "When using navigable graphs in an important performance improvement committee, we can look at an outlying data point in a graph and within 30 seconds dive in to the source document and verify if it is valid," he says. "Since it is easy for physicians with poor results to claim that 'My patients are sicker,' clarity is vital. True problem solving can only be accomplished when everyone can trust the data."

Personal questions and public answers

Certain kinds of personal data clearly can have a big impact on decision making at the individual level. But when these same data are pooled in meaningful ways with those of others at the population level, they can serve important purposes at much greater scales. For example, my phone's GPS system can help me find the best way to drive from Point A to Point B, but that same data, when combined with fellow motorists' data, also can add to a useful, real-time picture of regional traffic patterns.

Similarly, Marsh says, in healthcare, an electronic patient record can be helpful in treating a single patient, but when it is anonymized and aggregated with others, medical researchers can mine an entire set of hospital records to better understand the causes of disease and effective therapeutic options. Although the data's primary application may be to help the individual, whole new classes of problems can be addressed as a consequence of that data's existence. Data visualizations are increasingly helping to answer the bigger public health questions along with the ones from individual patients and healthcare providers.

THE QUESTIONS WITHIN A QUESTION

There is nothing like looking, if you want to find something... You certainly usually find something, if you look, but it is not always quite the something you were after.
— J.R.R. TOLKIEN, THE HOBBIT

Arriving at the answer to one question often depends on stepping through a succession of other questions along the way. The solutions to these intervening riddles are the keys necessary to unlock the larger puzzle. To demonstrate how visualizations can help people step through this kind of process, Huey Kwik, Engineering Lead at Palantir Technologies, describes a scenario in which an anti-fraud investigator at a bank uses his company's software to find the answer to an initial question by asking a series of other kinds of questions involving relationships, locations, and activities over time.

Kwik says that for the most part in daily life "people don't think relationally—we don't have mental models like rigidly structured tables." Instead, he says, "we start off with a question in our heads, but don't know how elements that are part of the question might connect together." If an investigator tries to narrowly define too much too soon, she may never arrive at the right answers. Sometimes, it is only by allowing the facts to constellate in the patterns and relationships of forms that were not imposed, that the most important question can be answered.

- *Initial question:* Does new information indicate fraudulent activity is being perpetrated against the bank?
  - An investigator receives an alert about three IP addresses that are suspected of engaging in fraudulent activity (Figure 2.9). As a result, she begins to search for any inbound traffic from the various IP addresses in the web server logs of the

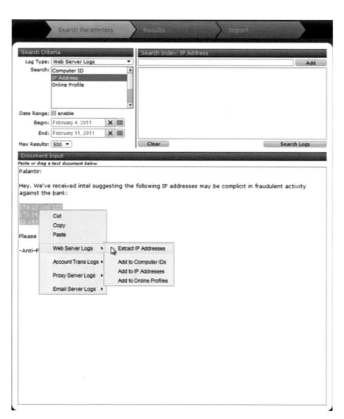

FIGURE 2.9
Finding IP addresses.

bank (Figure 2.10). When this initial task is completed, the investigator needs to proceed to the next questions.

- *Question:* What does the data related to the alert look like?
  - Assigning affordances, such as icons, instead of IP addresses to designate people allows the investigator to more easily identify and delineate individual data points

FIGURE 2.10
Searching for inbound traffic.

that potentially are related to the investigation. These visual cues can offer her a more immediate sense of key elements in the data and also act as important building blocks for doing additional visual analysis (Figure 2.11).

- *Relationship question:* Are there any interesting patterns in the networks of relationships that warrant a closer look?
  - A few different network patterns are visible in the overview (Figure 2.12). Some are small groups of connections, and others form larger clusters. To a trained eye, each type of pattern may suggest a few key qualitative attributes along with the quantitative ones. It's time to take a closer look (Figure 2.13).

- *Narrow the question:* Zoom in on one set of relationships (Figure 2.14).
  - In the context of a web server log, this is the data model we would expect to represent regular activity—a computer with a unique identifier uses a browser (Firefox) to connect to a single Online Profile using one IP address.

- *Narrow the question:* Zoom in on another set of relationships.
  - The relatively large cluster in the middle shows a single computer that is connecting to many online profiles using just one IP address. In the context of this data model, this is not a standard access pattern and can be classified as suspicious activity that warrants further investigation.

FIGURE 2.11

The people behind the IP addresses.

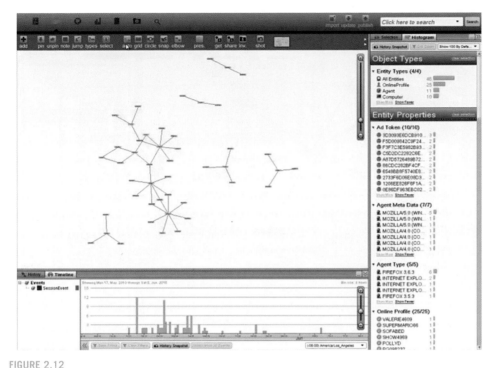

FIGURE 2.12
Network overview.

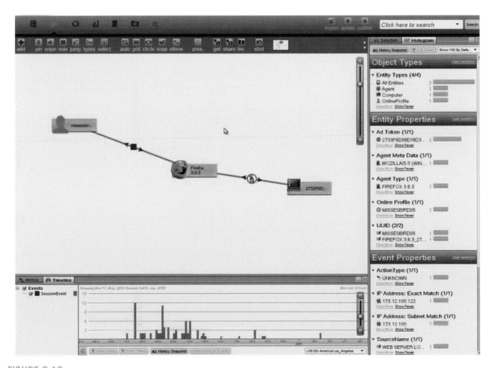

FIGURE 2.13
A more focused view.

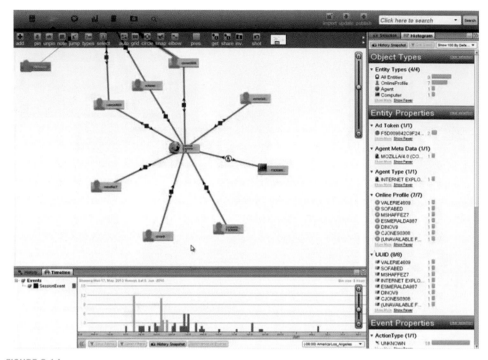

FIGURE 2.14

A different zoom.

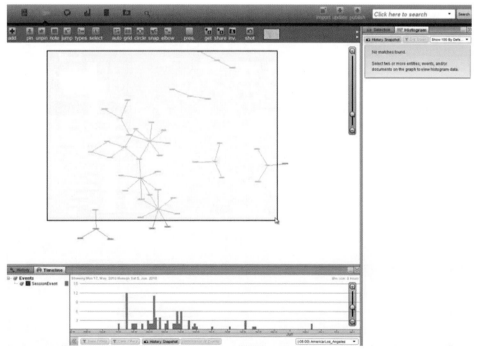

FIGURE 2.15

Digging deeper with the histogram.

- *Questions about particular people and patterns:* Which profiles in this data set are associated with similar unusual patterns of activity?

  - We can investigate further by using the histogram, where we quickly identify the online profiles showing the most unusual activity patterns—the profiles with the most session events (Figure 2.15). The investigation started with 3 suspicious IP addresses but has uncovered related traffic from about 20 others.

  - Overlaying visual representations such as network diagrams with compact user interface tools (such as the "search around" widget pictured in Figure 2.16) can provide a way to dive into certain questions while maintaining a sense of the broader context. This method of inquiry can be more effortless and natural than trying to keep in mind many disparate facts all at the same time.

- *Questions about place:* Is there anything interesting about the locations of the individuals of interest?

  - Each IP address is geocoded so that the origin of all the incoming network traffic can be displayed on a map. There is inbound activity from expected locations, but there's also an isolated cluster coming from Nigeria that appears suspicious (Figure 2.17).

- *Timely questions…*

  - After narrowing down the field to a single online profile, the investigator looks for suspicious activity in bank accounts. She will need to quickly search through a new data source showing all account transactions, which requires integration of two massive, disparate data sets: the web server logs and the account transaction logs. She examines all activity on the same graph—online activity as well as transaction activity. The timeline pictured in Figure 2.18 on the next page shows two clear periods of activity: late May and early June. In late May, there were nine microtransfers of $0.50 or less, which is a classic pattern of setting up access to external accounts. In early June, the transactions went up abruptly—massive money extractions on the order of $10k, $30k, and $350k.

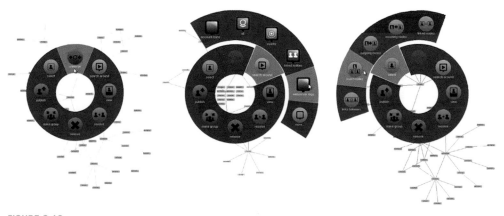

FIGURE 2.16
The tool augments the data.

FIGURE 2.17
Unexpected activity in Nigeria.

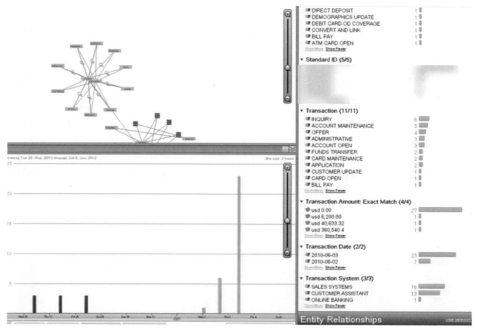

FIGURE 2.18
An abrupt change.

At this stage of the process, it becomes evident to the investigator that the original concerns prompting the analysis were justified, and she now has the answers to take clear and actionable steps to address the threat.

Making it a snap to put in the missing pieces

Sometimes, no matter how many good questions an investigator poses, there simply isn't enough data to get the answers. As discussed in Chapter 1, the idea of *what to leave in and what to leave out* can be a profound challenge, so you may find yourself with a set of data that is missing certain key pieces needed to solve the puzzle.

One way to address that problem is to make it as quick and easy as possible for users to fill in gaps in the data with the help of the same visualization tools they are using to pursue a line of investigation. For example, Kwik asks us to imagine a scenario in which an analyst has determined that the current question cannot be answered with the data sets that have previously been integrated. The analyst finds an open-source structured data set and imports it into the Palantir Front-End Structured Data Importer (shown in Figure 2.19), which has a graphical interface that allows users to visually "draw" what they are integrating, mapping source data fields directly to the Palantir Dynamic Ontology.

Once the new data is integrated with other disparate data, the analyst is able to answer the current question in the full context of all relevant information. Of course, when adding a new data set to the mix, considering the origins of and vetting the fresh material can help ensure that it's helping to clarify and not muddy the waters.

Figure 2.20 on the next page shows a network diagram of integrated data, including data brought into Palantir through the visual front-end data importer.

The process of investigation is one of back and forth between the data and the investigator, and it can shift between questions of time, place, and relationships. Visualizations help make that interaction possible in ways that would be hard to imagine taking place strictly in the world of rows and columns.

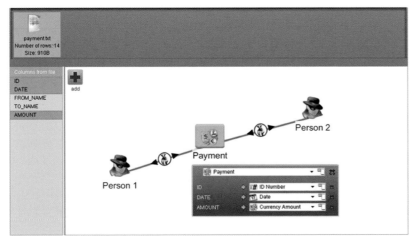

FIGURE 2.19

Adding in some missing pieces: a payment transaction.

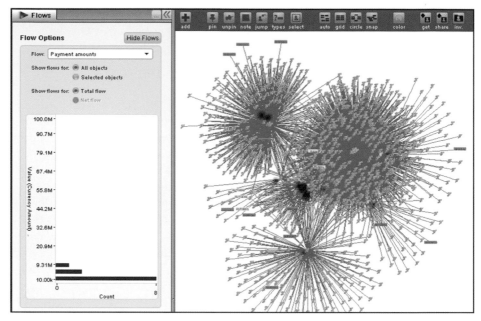

FIGURE 2.20
Integrated original and imported data.

KNOWING WHAT YOU'VE GOT

Is something important because you measure it, or is it measured because it's important?

– SETH GODIN

Imagine you're climbing a sheer rock wall, and about halfway up, the stone starts to take on a different appearance. You find yourself reaching for the next ledge but are no longer so sure that it's as strong as the material that got you this far. It might be fine, but without some clear indication, you'd be wise to pause and reflect on whether you feel confident about putting all your weight on the outcropping. Ropes and other equipment may be there to protect you, but that doesn't mean that you want to chance it. You don't have to be a geologist to be a rock climber, but it helps to know at least some basic qualities about the supporting substrate. Is it solid granite or sandstone? The distinctions can have a big impact.

Getting a good grasp of a visualization begins with a sense of where the underlying data came from, how it has been handled in the process, and how solid it is. You don't have to be a data scientist, but every step of the lifecycle can raise questions about how we should interpret what we see (Figure 2.21). As a reminder from the discussion in Chapter 1, the remainder of this section presents the types of questions various kinds of people who work with data, and those who design visualization displays, might consider for each stage of the basic data lifecycle.

Overview...

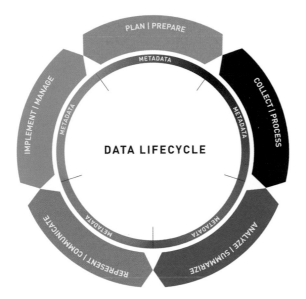

FIGURE 2.21
Data lifecycle infographic.

Zooming in...

Planning and preparing

Why might you want to collect data about something, and are you sure you know what you really need? How wide a net should you—and can you—cast? For this net, how fine or coarse should you make the filtering mesh? How much will it cost, and who cares enough to pay for the work to be done?

FIGURE 2.22
Plan and prepare.

Collecting and processing

How is all the data stored? As boxes of papers? Computer files? What are the file formats? Is the data "cleaned" or "preprocessed" before storage? How is it organized, indexed, and arranged? How easy is it to retrieve the metadata?

FIGURE 2.23
Collect and process.

Analyzing and summarizing

How much processing does the data undergo? How is it summarized (statistically) and modified? Has there been extensive processing with many different outputs or just a high-level view with a few simple pie charts or bar graphs showing, for example, seasonal sales changes?

FIGURE 2.24
Analyze and summarize.

Representing and communicating

How are the charts displayed, formatted, and presented in the context of the overall user interface? Are the content and format a good match? Who disseminates data outputs such as graphs and charts, and where do they go? Do the producers share them, or do third parties? Do the third parties perform additional data analyses or massaging, and, if so, do they make it clear that they're going further? Does all the necessary metadata get packaged along with the summarized data?

FIGURE 2.25
Represent and communicate.

Implementing and managing

Now that the time, effort, and money have been spent on collecting and transforming the data, how are you going to put all of that into practical use? What data do you want to keep at your fingertips? What do you want to store farther away for another day so you have more room for more new data? Have any questions been raised in the process that make you want to collect other kinds of data or change some of the measures and methods you use?

Thinking about these kinds of questions, even at the most basic levels, is essential for designing the right tools for the job and making good judgments about the quality of the supporting data.

FIGURE 2.26
Implement and manage.

QUESTIONS AND METADATA

If a man will begin with certainties, he shall end in doubts; but if he will be content to begin with doubts, he shall end in certainties.

— FRANCIS BACON

Even for seemingly clear-cut questions, there can be hidden twists and turns in the roots of source material used for the answers. Here's an example: How did the rates of childhood obesity compare in different counties in California in 2010? On the surface, that might seem straightforward, but some of the basic premises required for an answer may be more complicated than meets the eye.

In this case, one important underlying question is, exactly what is meant by the term *obesity*? Regan Foust, Data Manager at the Lucile Packard Foundation for Children's Health, has to confront these kinds of questions on a daily basis in her work maintaining *kidsdata.org*. In her mind one of the best available indicators for local (school district level) California data on child weight is provided by the California Department of Education (CDE). On its site, CDE provides the percentage of public-school students in grades 5, 7, and 9 with body composition falling within or below the Healthy Fitness Zone (HFZ) of the Fitnessgram assessment (Figure 2.27).

Although you might assume that the percentage of students not falling in the HFZ are overweight or obese, you actually can't say that using the data as reported. With additional calculation, what you *can* come away with is the percentage of children neither at a healthy weight nor underweight, which is a more difficult concept for the average person to understand than "obesity." Foust believes, "Finding ways to clearly explain exactly what's being

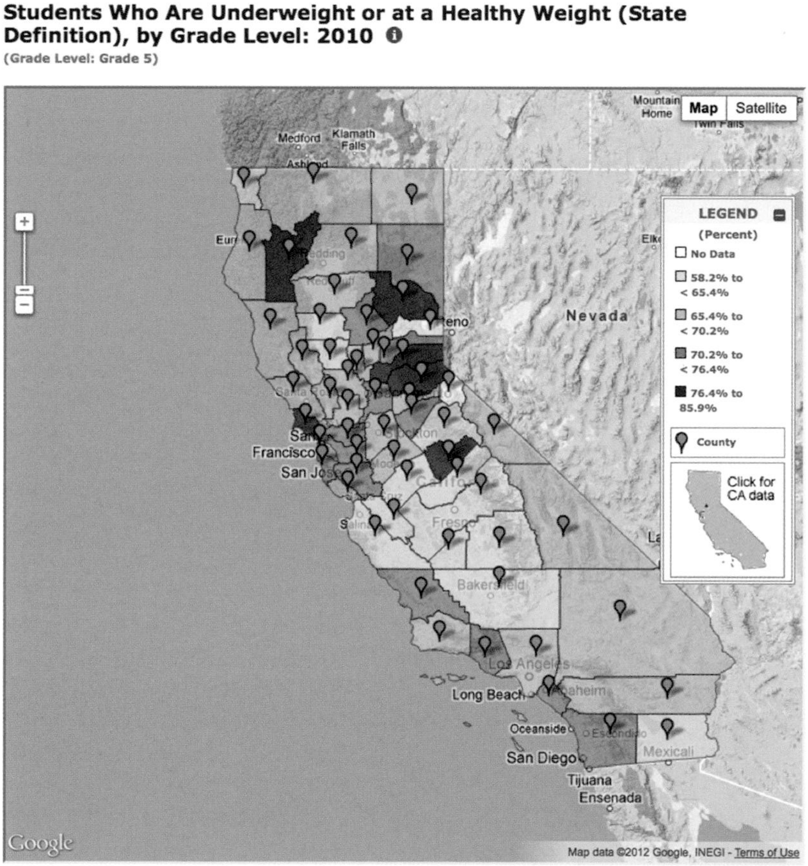

Students Who Are Underweight or at a Healthy Weight (State Definition), by Grade Level: 2010 ❶
(Grade Level: Grade 5)

FIGURE 2.27

Underweight or healthy weight students by county in California (see the Lucile Packard Foundation for Children's Health *kidsdata.org* website or the first QR code on the next page for more information on the organization or these figures).

measured to people is a key challenge and one that is a common issue in describing data from any public source."

http://goo.gl/qgopK

Determining how many students are overweight/obese requires deeper analysis, such as the work done by the UCLA Center for Health Policy Research and the California Center for Public Health Advocacy (Babey, 2011). These researchers examined the original CDE data to determine height and weight from the body composition component of the California Physical Fitness Test and used this information to calculate BMI, allowing them to create a measure of children who are overweight or obese. Figures 2.28 and 2.29 on the next pages illustrate the findings.

Telling the full story

Multiple measures can be useful in telling a full story. In this case, the related measure of "fitness" can help round out an understanding of how students are faring regarding obesity, weight, and physical activity. Foust says, "We hope that providing multiple measures on kidsdata.org will help users get a deeper understanding of an issue." She adds that "we are very selective about what we provide. It's a balancing act. Ultimately, our goal is to identify key data and information, and present it in engaging, strategic, and effective ways."

Foust notes that, as with any measure from public sources, the data can be constrained by factors such as how it's collected and analyzed. The "healthy weight" data mentioned earlier, for example, offers data by race/ethnicity, but the breakdowns that the state uses aggregate a number of racial/ethnic groups together in a category called "Asian American," making it hard to determine weight scores for, say, Vietnamese children in San Jose, or kids of Hmong descent in Fresno. Put simply, data often are not collected in a way that allows for breakdowns that may be desired at a local level.

Similarly, these measures come from fitness tests that evaluate students in 5th, 7th, and 9th grades. "Useful data at a very local level for kids in lower grades—or in preschool—are not as readily accessible," Foust says. "While there may be local communities or organizations individually collecting data for younger students—or in a

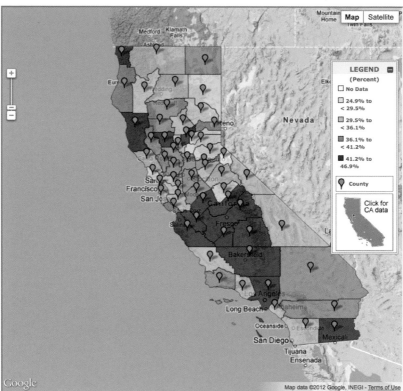

Overweight/Obese Students (Federal Definition): 2010 ⓘ

FIGURE 2.28

Overweight/obese students by county in California (map view).

http://goo.gl/1pkVB

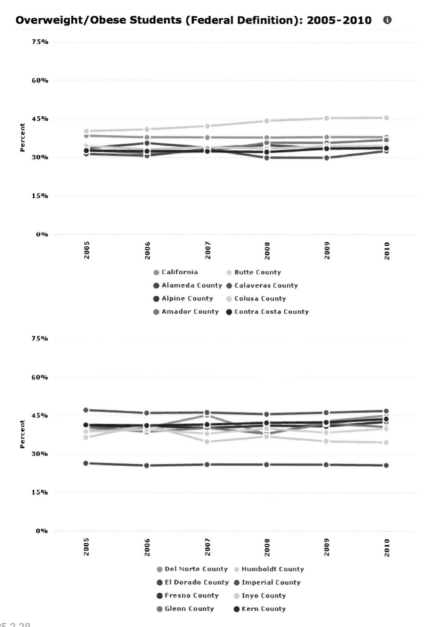

FIGURE 2.29

Overweight/obese students by county in California (trend lines).

more detailed way for racial/ethnic groups—we limit ourselves to publishing data on kidsdata.org that have been uniformly collected across communities, for reasons of data credibility, expediency, and to ensure people can compare one region to another or compare data over time." The organization is careful to publish data that is from sources that are credible, relevant to public policy, and "understandable to a broad audience."

Locally produced

Foust and her colleagues have also discovered that the more *local* the data, the more relevant it is for most people. "School district-level data is quite useful, and we have that for the fitness and healthy weight data," she says. "The data about overweight/obese children are available only at the county and city level, given the time it takes to conduct this analysis." Other data, such as about children with special healthcare needs, is only available at a statewide level. And for some users, school-district data is not local *enough*; many need data at the zip code or school level.

Foust says, "As with any data from a public source, you have to be careful that you have a large enough 'N'—number—to report reliable rates and percentages." On the website, she explains, "we use the term LNE (low number event) to inform our users that we can't report weight/fitness data for a particular region/demographic group in cases where fewer than 20 students were represented within that group." She maintains that larger numbers are needed to provide reliable percentages/rates. "The integrity of the data on kidsdata.org is critical."

Thinking it through

This book has several recurring themes, including the idea that visualizations are only the tip of the iceberg in the data story and that human factors play a much more profound role in the process than is always appreciated. The work done by Foust and her colleagues exemplifies some of the challenges that go with these themes. Although you may or may not be interested in childhood health issues in particular, the issues raised by the work at kidsdata.org are applicable to many different areas involving data analysis, presentation, and communication. "Before you can even think about how to visualize the data as a trend/bar graph, a simple rank-order list, or a map, you first need to think through these kinds of issues," says Foust. "We need to do that for every measure on kidsdata, and there are roughly 400 on the site!"

QUICK QUESTIONS

Observe due measure, for right timing is in all things the most important factor.

– HESIOD

Although many people have to work with increasingly large amounts of data, the amount of time they have to make sense of it all does not grow accordingly. It's often quite the reverse. In environments such as operating rooms and battlefields, a rapid-fire series of interrelated sub-questions may be flooding in that all need to be considered and addressed to manage the overall situation. Visualizations can help users process information more rapidly by putting it into more compact and easily digestible forms. However, software alone will not always complete the picture. Training and practice with fast-paced scenarios in highly fluid situations involving real-time data can ensure that dense displays are a help and not a hindrance.

Designer Ron Gregory, Owner of G2 Media, has designed a "serious game." In the visualization of it shown in Figure 2.30, the clock plays an important role in keeping the player focused on the problems as they occur.

Gregory explains that the dashboard represents a series of challenges for a hospital administrator, including allocation of resources at hand, not the least of which is cash reserves. This state of play has the player in the ninth day of an epidemic's outbreak. Occupancy, emergency room capacity, and other data are reported as an alarming national death toll continues to tick upwards. Notice the spike in "infected" cases compared to noninfected cases. Staffing and HR resources also are given their due, as well as the cash reserves to pay for the operation of the hospital. A news media outlet allows reporting on a national and global level to keep the player/administrator abreast of current events and outbreaks, both local and international. Behind the video pop-up is a "heat-map" showing the areas with the most reported cases of influenza.

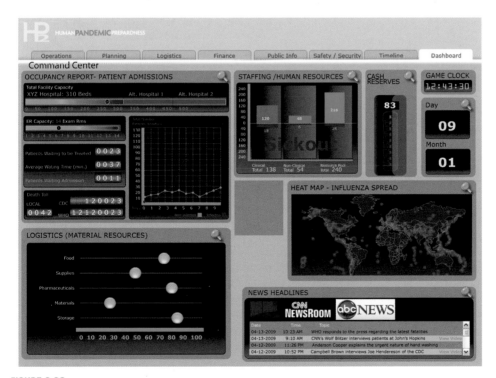

FIGURE 2.30
It's a serious game. *UI design: Ronald J. Gregory.*

In this game, the user can set the size of the hospital they want to manage; usually it corresponds with the size they ordinarily manage on a day-to-day basis, but they're not limited to that one choice should they want to test their abilities in either a smaller or larger facility. The people that play this game are typically hospital administrators—not just the executive in charge, but also the next tier down the chain, such as HR or logistics staff members. The scenario and data visualization can help train users to work with data when the need for speed is essential.

FINDING "PERSONAL BESTS" (BASED ON WORK BY INFORMATION SCIENTIST, DAN GILLMAN)

Every fact that is learned becomes a key to other facts.

– EDWARD LIVINGSTON YOUMANS

It's not a one-size-fits-all world, and the cost of customization can be steep. This applies to data as much as anything else. Even if there's a fire sale of facts and figures, you still have to sort through it all. It takes time, effort, and money to find the things that most meet your needs. The more places you cut corners doing that, the more likely it is that you're going to get stuff that doesn't fit, is made from shoddy materials, or both. How can you be a value shopper of information and data?

Let's look at a scenario based on a topic explored in many books, articles, and infographics: What is the "most livable" city? Good question, but far too generic to be personally meaningful to many of us without serious refinement. This is a situation in which interactive visualization tools can offer a better approach than static lists created by people we don't know using criteria we don't really understand. How would you find the "most livable" place for you? One way of starting could involve rendering a lot of data on a map and then filtering out various kinds of details. You also probably would want to have the visual output tailored according to your own unique set of criteria. For example, the weighting of crime rates versus cultural amenities or quality of education.

The following scenario describes our friend Alice, who is wondering, "What is the most livable city for me?" The reason she's considering a move is for a potential job change. She wants to get a sense of how "safe" and "livable" the candidate destinations are. She's not sure of the best way to find out, but she starts with researching "safe cities" and finds several recent articles. Although the term *livable* is widely used and understood in a general way, it can be hard to pin down the specific criteria that would apply for any particular person. In addition, no standardized definitions are used to determine "most livable" across articles and data sets. These varying descriptions provide mixed results.

Alice has her own unique set of interests and priorities. She finds articles that aggregate data of all kinds about city attributes and then puts them together for herself. Collecting the data and packaging it up is convenient, but she is relying on their criteria and sources, which may not necessarily be the best fit for her.

LOWERING THE "CURIOSITY TAX" FOR BUSINESSES

All life is an experiment. The more experiments you make the better.

– RALPH WALDO EMERSON

When the financial future of a company can depend on asking precisely the right questions, the pressure sometimes can limit adaptability and innovation. Mark Lorion, Vice President of Marketing at the Spotfire Analytics Division of TIBCO Software, a business intelligence (BI) and analytics software provider, says, "It can be daunting and hard to feel confident about figuring out key questions in advance, something many 'traditional' BI tools require." He adds, "Many businesspeople and researchers have long had to formulate a precise question up-front for their IT teams, who then configure the reporting systems structured query language [SQL] statements." This process can shut out more natural and exploratory approaches—asking something, getting a result, and immediately asking logical follow-up questions.

"Why give businesspeople only static, centralized, highly regimented systems?" asks Lorion. Visualization tools can lower what he calls the "curiosity tax" by making it easer for users to generate and test questions. He says they turn the tedious and effortful devising of query variations into a more tactile and visual experience. It's about tightly coupling the immediacy of a visual interface with an interactive control system that allows people to ask questions without a lot of extra effort. "People can work with their data like a Rubik's Cube," he says. Lorion believes that in these ways people learn things they didn't know and develop a greater degree of confidence. "They are able to look around the corner and see what might be hiding there because they are not only looking at one data aggregation."

Many times the most important commodities are the *outliers* (values that appear to lie outside the range of others in a random sample) or clusters that get lost in typical reports that focus more on aggregating values. If the outliers arise from clean, well-organized data, they can act as red flags, signaling problems lurking in a data set or pointing out important and interesting dynamics that may have been overlooked. As Lorion puts it, the real "gold in the hills" can be found in both great nuggets of insight or in identifying the places where there are pockets of "fools gold" (bad data) that can be cleared away.

As an example, the following is a brief scenario of a fictitious online store, "Bob's Model Toy Store" (Figure 2.31). Starting with Figure 2.32a on page 91, the images show some sales data that Bob has collected.

When data is imported (from a database file or from dragging and dropping files), Spotfire automatically builds a filter panel, which allows users to dynamically control every column in the data set and how much information is shown on the screen. Spotfire assigns each data type an appropriate filter for the kind of information it includes (e.g., check boxes or item sliders for categorical values, etc.; Figure 2.32b).

1. Because these filters are "grayed out," we can also immediately see there were no orders of "Ships" or "Trains" in quantities greater than 56.

2. Also note other visual "clues" that depict where "empty" data resides in the filtered data set; e.g., there are no records in these lighter portions—meaning that further

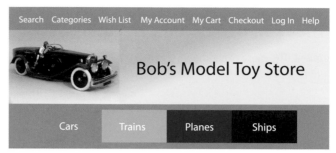

FIGURE 2.31

Planes, trains, and automobiles.

filtering of this "Order Date" would not change the resulting data set. We've learned something we were not even asking: there were no sales ordered with a quantity greater than 56 outside of this very narrow data range.

3. Dragging or selecting/deselecting these filters in any combination automatically reduces/expands the data set. (Note how the data table is now smaller.)

Adding a basic bar chart visualization depicts the distribution of orders >56 units across toy types (Figure 2.32c). Most big orders were for Classic Cars, followed by Vintage Cars.

The user now drags and drops the "Ship Method" filter right onto the bar chart color palette to automatically color by the categories in that filter (Figure 2.32d).

Adding a basic bar chart visualization depicts the distribution of orders >56 units across toy types. In Figure 2.32e we see most big orders are being shipped via "Regular Air," with very few big orders being rushed via Express Air. The fewest orders are being shipped via Delivery Truck because this is an international distributor, and only a few customers are local.

By adding a different visualization type, we can simultaneously uncover more insights. The scatter plot is good at showing outliers and clusters. The colors are being driven by Product Category, the size by overall revenue of each product, and the shape by sales territory (Figure 2.32f). By selecting these outliers, we see in the bar graph where those orders reside. The three individual highest orders were for planes and classic cars (Figure 2.32g).

By highlighting any of these markers, we can see detailed information about the order, too. This appears to be the highest revenue-generating order. It's for classic cars and was shipped to APAC via Regular Air. (We can tell it was Regular Air because the bar chart below the scatter plot is showing the "Regular Air" portion of the classic car bar as highlighted; Figure 2.32h.)

By replacing the scatter plot with a box plot and bar chart combination, we easily can spot the distribution of quantity ordered by product category. These plots help to bring users the most statistically relevant records. In Figure 2.32i we see generally tight

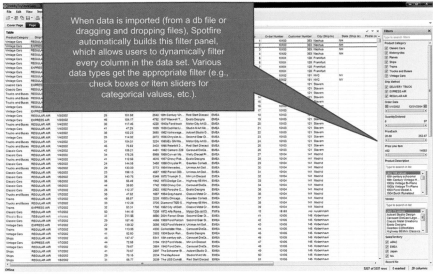

(a)

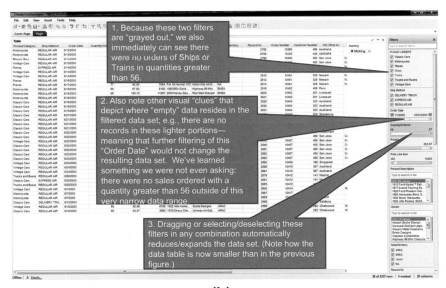

(b)

FIGURE 2.32a-i

TIBCO Spotfire toy sales data.

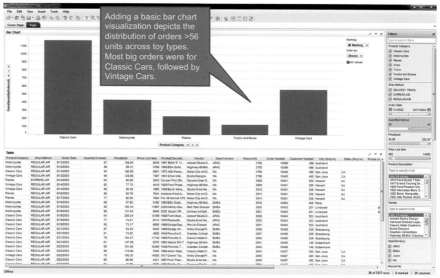

(c)

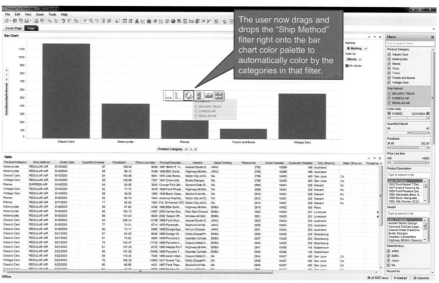

(d)

FIGURE 2.32a-i—(Continued)

(e)

(f)

FIGURE 2.32a-i—(Continued)

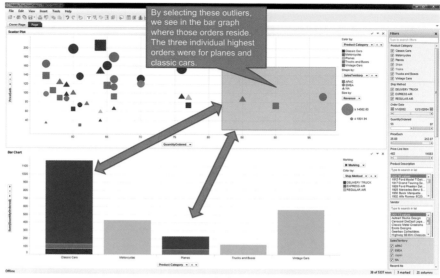

(g)

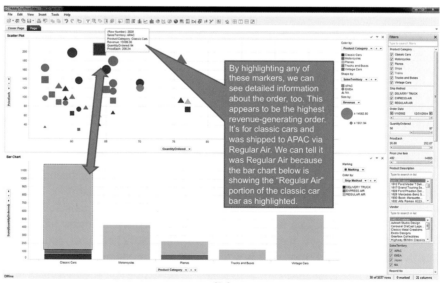

(h)

FIGURE 2.32a-i—(Continued)

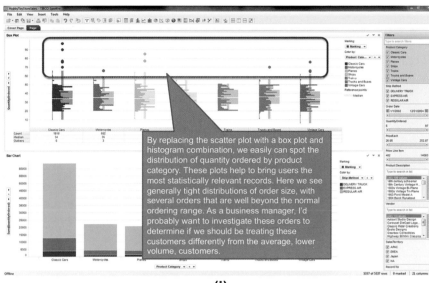

By replacing the scatter plot with a box plot and histogram combination, we easily can spot the distribution of quantity ordered by product category. These plots help to bring users the most statistically relevant records. Here we see generally tight distributions of order size, with several orders that are well beyond the normal ordering range. As a business manager, I'd probably want to investigate these orders to determine if we should be treating these customers differently from the average, lower volume, customers.

(i)

FIGURE 2.32a-i—(Continued)

distributions of order size, with several orders that are well beyond the normal ordering range. As a business manager, I'd probably want to investigate these orders to determine if we should be treating these customers differently from the average, lower volume, customers.

The examples in the series of images in Figure 2.32 show how using visualizations can highlight different facets of your business and provide you with practical and actionable insights to affect, and potentially improve, the bottom line.

ASKING GOOD QUESTIONS

Although visualization tools offer new approaches for asking and refining questions, if the contexts and quality of the source materials are not easy to evaluate, the whole process can be compromised. The next section will look at how the transformations of data can affect the results and show why that matters. Before we move on, here are a few last thoughts for generating productive and useful lines of questions. Current data visualization tools support some of these, and more might be considered for future designs:

- *Ask the same questions in different ways.* Can you ask questions from significantly different angles? For example: What if the exact opposite were true? Could the same results come from alternative conditions?

- *Uncover the questions you* really *should be asking but haven't thought of yet.* When I'm interviewing someone in my role as either a journalist or a user experience (UX) designer, at the end of the conversation I will generally ask if there's a question that they might have expected but I didn't ask. Sometimes the answer is "no," but in other cases the interviewee raises a question that had not occurred to me, and ends up enlightening the conversation in important ways.

- *Make your assumptions compete.* In *The Psychology of Intelligence Analysis*, Richard J. Heuer, Jr., calls this idea the "analysis of competing hypotheses." Make the question that you favor the most the one subject to the greatest challenges. In visualizations, this could equate to setting up alternate paths of inquiry and observing how they progress.

- *Consider the possibility that you are engaging in confirmation bias.* Is it possible you are selectively, but unconsciously, seeing data that confirms and supports your hypotheses and conclusion while discounting contrary indicators? Hey, it's part of human nature to do that, so we have to keep ourselves honest, and perhaps good visualizations can help us with that.

- *Ask "compared to what?"* This is one of my favorite questions because it can be easy to lose sight of the meaning of something we're analyzing when there's no context.

- *Are you detecting zebras or horses?* In medical slang, a "zebra" represents an atypical diagnosis such as the cause of a patient's symptoms being a rare disease. The term comes from the saying, "When you hear hoofbeats behind you, don't expect to see a zebra." (The idea here is that if you're in North America and hear the sound of hoofs, it's probably horses, not zebras.) For various reasons, novice physicians may tend to be overly biased in terms of finding zebras, whereas experts may have a tendency to overlook zebras when they do appear because they're focusing on the more common causes of the patient's symptoms. Although you'll usually detect horses, keep your eye out for any zebras that may appear from time to time (Figure 2.33).

FIGURE 2.33
Not all questions have black-and-white answers.

APPROACHING DATA WITH A BEGINNER'S MIND

In the beginner's mind there are many possibilities, in the expert's mind there are few.

– SHUNRYU SUZUKI

I was asked for my opinion on a project in which a UX team was trying to represent complex relationships using a specific type of data visualization. I asked why it was done that way. The answer: a designer "liked it." Perhaps not enough foundational thinking had gone into what they were really trying to accomplish.

UX practitioners, and the growing variety of users working with these kinds of visualizations, need to consider and ask fundamental questions about the full process that determines what data gets collected, stored, processed, and ultimately displayed. Otherwise, they become part of the problem of misinterpreting data rather than helping to make it clearer and more meaningful. Sometimes, the simplest questions are the most important to ask, especially when designing visualizations for complex data sets.

The Japanese term shoshin, or "beginner's mind," describes the mindset of a novice—full of openness, enthusiasm, and fresh perspectives in learning something new. This approach and attitude can help someone who might have a lot of knowledge about a subject but might be stuck in a cognitive rut. Experts and novices alike can make important contributions to problem solving and innovation. Beginners' minds can help make breakthroughs with the help of collaborative data sharing and visualizations.

If we approach with rigidity and unwarranted certainty when we work with data, we may miss key patterns hiding in plain sight. On the other hand, rigor and expertise are necessary to help guide and validate our understanding of what we're looking at. Ideally, we can find an optimal combination of these perspectives. The visualization tools will need to be able to enhance this balance rather than feeding into and reinforcing preconceptions and biases.

TMD (TOO MUCH DATA)?

You never know what is enough unless you know what is more than enough.

– WILLIAM BLAKE

Just about anytime, anywhere, I can get nearly instant feedback to an infinite set of possible searches or look at an increasing stream of data packaged up in the form of infographics or articles. Sometimes, they are thought provoking and enlightening, but often they are diversions, distractions, or simply noise. Whether it's ad banners or charts showing an economic trajectory, we can quickly become acclimated to them and no longer perceive them as visual aids—we develop "ad blindness."

The ability to screen out much of the cacophony of life is a good and necessary trait to function in just about any environment—from prehistoric times to the present. As our lives become more and more filled with data and information, the ability to filter for relevance and significance becomes increasingly important. Working with data, from collection to analysis and visualization, demands imagination, creativity, and discernment. It also may benefit from the idea of "beginner's mind."

Filtering is essential at every stage of the life cycle to deal with this data. That said, it's also important to keep in mind that the filtering process itself can lead to, and reinforce, false conclusions and bad decisions, as well as good ones. There's an infinite supply of data out there but a finite capacity to work with it. The ability to collect, store, and analyze data is on the rise in a big way, which can help address the problem of what to keep and what to toss. If more is captured and saved in retrievable forms, then we have the possibility of going back to data that once might have looked like trash but is, in retrospect, a treasure trove of vital metadata. From this perspective, arguably, "all data is good data."

Finding the right level of information is a balancing act. Perhaps the best way to determine that balance is, as Blake suggests, by being more aware of the full range. We should take a closer look at the process in which data visualization is only one aspect of a long, complex path that can be repeated every nanosecond or in decade-long intervals. Every phase presents its own costs and challenges and sometimes continues indefinitely… or at least until someone tells somebody else to stop, or the sensors die, or the batteries run out, or the satellite de-orbits….

Some of our best insights might not come from simply increasing the volume of data but from working more effectively with what we already have—"asking" the data we already have new and better questions.

A MORE BEAUTIFUL QUESTION

Do not seek to follow in the footsteps of the wise. Seek what they sought.

– MATSUO BASHO

Sometimes the most important and interesting part of asking a question is the process of arriving at that answer. Life would be far less interesting if every answer was available the minute a question was raised. Imagine this: you've just had a nice dinner with friends on a rainy night and are settling in for a board game. Just as you roll the dice, someone blurts out, "Colonel Mustard did it with a croquet mallet in the gazebo." That may be correct, but it totally misses the point. The process of discovering *why* may be more important than the final answer…not to mention more fun.

We make interesting connections and associations on the path to discovery. Although this kind of search process obviously can be done with key words and queries, that approach doesn't always make it the most inviting for all of the people all of the time. The form of text searches does not always allow us to easily and pleasurably wander through data. The ease and enjoyment factor should not be underestimated. If we're able to seek information in a more primal and engaging way, we may be more inclined to do these tasks, or at least not avoid them. Furthermore, with relaxed and effortless interactions, our minds might be more receptive to new ideas and insights than if we feel the pressure of coming up with a "perfect" narrowly focused question.

So, what is a "more beautiful question"? To me, it has several qualities:

- It encourages exploration and leads to other interesting questions.
- It leads to useful results but also reveals additional questions.
- It can be asked in different ways.
- Its answers are relevant, reliable, and meaningful.

The more beautiful question is one you are willing to ask because, whatever the answers, the process itself is helpful and rewarding.

Winning Combinations

Working with the Ingredients of Data Visualization

3

JUST THE RIGHT MIX

Great things are done by a series of small things brought together.

— VINCENT VAN GOGH

Helping people find meaning in large, complex data sets is becoming an increasingly important consideration for many kinds of organizations and the people who work for them. Although the need may be clear, the steps for transforming unprocessed data into effective visualizations are not always so apparent. As discussed toward the end of Chapter 2, when you're looking for a solution to such problems, a different perspective can help, and one of the most useful perspectives is that of "beginner's mind."

Sometimes, being a beginner, or taking on the mindset of one who is, can yield unexpected insights. Getting back to fundamentals and being reminded of the origins and the purposes of the basic building blocks we use in data visualization can pay off. This chapter explores those fundamentals in detail for those readers who are new or who see the benefit of a review.

Data comes in a variety of "flavors," and each kind can be paired with certain types of visual representations. Some combinations mix well, and others just don't mix at all. For example, certain visualization designs are more effective than others in summarizing and highlighting various characteristics of data (I show examples of this a little later in the chapter). How do you assess and assemble all of the disparate elements in the most informative way? At least for me, the more familiar I become with different data types and their related depictions, the more confident I am in applying and exploring visualization design ideas.

COUNTER INTELLIGENCE: FIGURING OUT WHAT TO DO WITH MANY INGREDIENTS

Imagine that the Food Network has randomly selected you as a contestant in a challenge. They'll provide a state-of-the-art kitchen and a wide assortment of ingredients. You have an hour and a half to prepare a winning meal. There are no rules, other than the ones dictated by the physics of cooking (temperature, time, etc.) and basic food safety. There are no instructions, other than that the final results should be as tasty and nourishing as possible. You do get points for using as many ingredients as possible, provided the end results are satisfying. Containers are scattered everywhere—some well-labeled and others not—brimming with more items than anyone could possibly use in one meal, and the clock is ticking. How would you start? How would you assess what you had and how to put it together?

Although having so much at your fingertips might seem to make the situation easier, in many ways it makes it harder. With all the jumbled abundance, the decisions you'll need to make will expand as the choices expand. If I were the contestant, I'd try to organize it all in some way, and might know how to prepare something passable; however, without a lot of guidance, it's unlikely I'd be named the next Iron Chef.

Whether it's cooking or data visualizations, combining a variety of elements is both an art and a science, and the less practice and experience you have, the more you may need to rely on existing guidelines and "recipes" to start off. These recipes represent the distilled trials, errors, calculations, and experiences of predecessors—the collective wisdom of how to form raw elements into a well-done final preparation. Yes, there is often much room for improvisation and experimentation, but there's also a basic order and process for many of the steps along the way. You don't fold in the eggs after you've baked the cake. The more familiar you are with the fundamentals, the more free you can be in experimentation and innovation or, simply stated, the more comfortable you'll be with using visualizations, creating them, or both.

In the preparation and consumption of raw ingredients—be it data or otherwise—the levels of experience and expectations of all the participants play an important role in the process. An experienced sushi chef, for example, might be happy to serve up a plate of fugu fish for patrons who—one hopes—understand the limits, consequences, and rewards of eating the neurotoxin-laden flesh. The chef, in turn, needs to be aware of how much fugu is too much.

People who are charged with transforming the contents of extensive tables filled with raw data into visualizations should keep in mind their own familiarity with the underlying materials, as well as the knowledge and understanding of the people who will be the ultimate consumers. If it is well done and served in thoughtful proportions with end users in mind, a visualization can provide satisfying insights. If prepared poorly or with no appreciation of users' expectations, it could easily turn into a stew of confusion and lead to false conclusions. In this chapter, in three parts, we'll explore some fundamentals of bringing together raw elements into digestible visualizations. The intent is not to show all the ingredients and combinations. That would be nearly limitless. Instead, the ideas are to highlight some key elements in the context of data visualization, to whet your appetite about exploring the different aspects, and then see how they can come together.

Part One—Selecting, Storing, and Combining the Ingredients of Data: There's strength in numbers. All things being equal, a larger set of data can be the wellspring of more reliable, robust, and comprehensive insights than a comparable, smaller one. But that's only if an accurate, valid, and truly representative set of numbers has been collected. The more we expand the quantities and types of data that we include in analyses and visualizations, the more depth and dimension we have...and the more ways that we might mix data inappropriately—producing misleading results. The task of managing data, and the key metadata accompanying it, can be truly monumental. Even so, the choices made in this process will determine the value of everything that follows.

Part Two—Fitting Data Types with Visual Forms: Different kinds of data lend themselves to different forms of visual representation. A line chart, for example, works well for a series of continuously varying data values. There's a reason they call them time*lines* and not time *squares* or *circles*.

Part Three—Putting Together Different Visualizations: To get the best understanding of a problem or an issue, it's important to view it from different perspectives. Someone may get usefully different insights by looking at the same data set depicted as both a bar chart and a pie chart. In a sense, it is a combination of combinations—merged multiple data sets, transformed into a few different visualizations, which are then collected in an interface for easy comparisons.

SETTING THE TABLE

You can have all the best ingredients at your disposal, but there's always the question: what are you going to do with them? How do you start? Will the end result be what you wanted? Let's say you have some potentially interesting but unprocessed data and are not sure how to put it into digestible form. How do you put the elements together to best represent the data? If we were talking about food, it might involve thinking about whether it is breakfast, lunch, dinner, or a snack. In at least a general way, you might put some thought into the proportion of protein and starch.

In the realm of data and design, the basic ingredients and the way they are served up are much more abstract, so the difference between good and bad combinations is much less apparent. One way to get a handle on this issue is to carve out some general distinctions between types of data and how they are served up. In giving visual form to data, a few considerations are fundamental to what kind of representations to use. However, the things we do with visual representations of data don't always fall neatly into distinct packages. It's far more complex, intertwined, and nuanced than that. The following breakdown is simply meant to offer a general approach to selecting the best visual for the data at hand.

- Visualizations of various forms, such as bar charts and pie charts, can **summarize and showcase** what would otherwise be hard-to-digest sets of numbers. An easily digestible visual representation can reveal useful characteristics of a data set, such as the typical value or approximate center (the *central tendency*) in the data, as well as the spread (or *range*) of the data. What did the sales of apples, oranges, and pears total last month? Bar charts can provide a specific answer for this kind of question.

- Let's say you're interested in knowing how a couple of different data points relate to each other...or not. For example, are there any interesting connections between the sales of milk and cookies during a typical week? Is there a potential link between the two (perhaps a promotion in the dairy section offering 30% off of a box of chocolate chip cookies when you purchase a gallon of milk), or are they unrelated and, if so, can this in turn help stimulate decision making? These kinds of **interrelationship questions** can be addressed with visual representations like scatter plots and their associated "trend lines."

- Another kind of insight we might want to glean from certain data is if there are any **trends** suggested by the numbers. Orange sales have steadily increased over the past three years, but apple sales seem constant over the same time period. These kinds of data can be conveyed by line charts.

PART ONE: SELECTING, STORING, AND COMBINING THE INGREDIENTS OF DATA

Whether it's preparing a meal or creating visualizations with a large data set, at a fundamental level, some of the same considerations and processes need to occur in putting everything together, as described in the following subsections.

Selection

Although we know of many staples we'll want to buy, it's not always easy to anticipate everything in advance. The same is true for data—we might need many "staple" data sets but might also have a lingering concern that we're leaving some key ingredients out of the mix. And by the time we figure that out, the data may no longer be easily obtainable. The store may be closed.

Specificity versus serendipity

When I go to the store, I have a list of the specific things I'll need for the week, but I also typically make many more purchases as I'm walking through the aisles. I see things that I had not thought of and get a direct visual reminder to buy them (Figure 3.1). If I'm looking for groceries or books online, there's a continuum between specificity and serendipity. Sometimes, I may know exactly what I want for dinner and will get exactly those things. Other times, I may know I want some proteins and starch, but whether that means steak and potatoes or scallops and linguini depends on what I happen to see at the store. Same consumer, different day.

Specific Search   Scanning and Serendipity

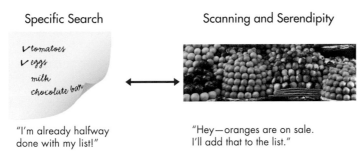

"I'm already halfway
done with my list!"

"Hey—oranges are on sale.
I'll add that to the list."

FIGURE 3.1

Specificity vs. serendipity: shopping.

Specific Search   Scanning and Serendipity

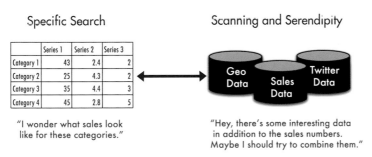

"I wonder what sales look
like for these categories."

"Hey, there's some interesting data
in addition to the sales numbers.
Maybe I should try to combine them."

FIGURE 3.2

Specificity vs. serendipity: data.

The same basic idea can apply to acquiring the ingredients of data. Sometimes, users may have a highly defined data point to examine, and at other times, they may be interested in a whole class of data and want to see what is and is not there (Figure 3.2).

Storage

During busy times, many of us might want to purchase as many groceries as we can at once to save trips to the store. But we have only so much room in the refrigerator and cabinets (Figure 3.3). Of course, the foods we buy can have a range of shelf lives. The boxes of mac and cheese may have long expiration dates, whereas the avocados have only a few days to exist in an edible form. Properly storing the food in your pantry can be a challenge, but managing what to select and store from the torrents of data is a monumental task. The capacity for storing data is vast and increasing, but the amount being generated is greater still. In their own ways, data also can have different shelf lives (Figure 3.4).

Sorting

The way we select and store what we need can be influenced by the network of producers and vendors that are available to us. Let's say a new produce stand has opened nearby. While the proprietor, Dale, works out the logistical details of his store, several local

Bulk Package

My Capacity to Organize,
Store, and Retrieve

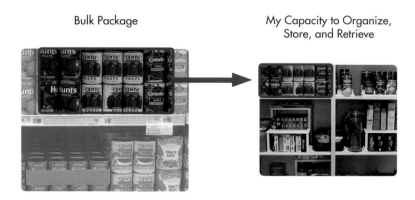

"This value pack is a great deal, but I won't
be able to manage all of it now. I can only
fit part of it in my pantry."

FIGURE 3.3

Food storage.

Data

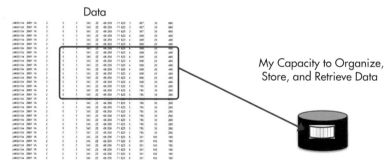

My Capacity to Organize,
Store, and Retrieve Data

FIGURE 3.4

Data storage.

suppliers are aggressively vying for his business. Three trucks, full of freshly harvested fruit, rush over. One truck is brimming with apples, another is full of oranges, and the third is packed with tomatoes (which are technically a fruit, although not commonly described that way). The trucks pull up at the same time, and the drivers are all in a hurry. They want to offload their cargoes and go on their way.

It's great to have all the fresh supplies, but Dale's stock clerk has to sort through them all and place them in the right bins. Imagine that the stocking person dumps the new items nearly randomly into various bins. At one level, these items are all available, but customers would not visit Dale's stand if they had to go through the laborious process of picking out the same item from three separate bins. Separating, labeling, and organizing these items would make life easier all around. That said, the way to do that is not completely clear-cut (Figure 3.5).

Who is making decisions in sorting this...

...to this?

Who (or what) is making decisions in sorting this...

...to this?

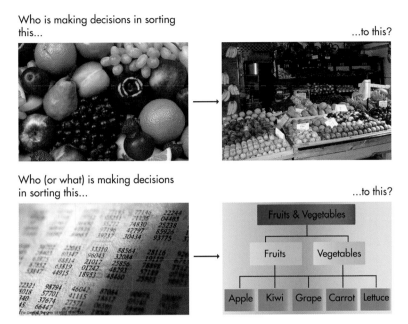

FIGURE 3.5
Who sorts?

Now a new stocking clerk gets hired who is the complete opposite of the first one—conscientious to the point of being compulsive, and this clerk is also a literalist. Perhaps he knows that a tomato is a fruit and not a vegetable, but although we would never put it in a bin called fruit, because that's not how it's generally thought of, the stocker is a purist.

Let's say another stocking clerk is very detailed in his approach, but is not much of a big-picture thinker. He properly places the apples into "Red Delicious" and "Granny Smith" bins, but their placement on the shelves makes one variety difficult to see. A customer who comes in shopping for apples may see the bin of Red Delicious and completely overlook the obscured Granny Smiths. The customer might end up with something, but not the full range of what he or she might have wanted, and may never realize their preferred apple is actually there. Dale loses out on a sales opportunity, and the customer loses out on choices.

The issues with sorting are important in the discussion of merging and managing big data. Because the automation and machine learning that are needed to work on these scales don't always get the nuances and distinctions that might make a big difference in the final analysis, this is something to consider when organizing and combining data. The automation and machine learning are like robot assistants; they can do certain tasks very effectively and efficiently, but they also can work in ways reminiscent of the two bad stocking clerks described before—they can't sort carefully enough, or they do it so narrowly that they create almost as many problems as they solve. With tangible items such as produce, the fact that they may be jumbled up in the wrong bin can be relatively easy to recognize and remedy. However, when working with intangible data, once the elements in the columns and rows have been improperly joined together, it can be extremely difficult to detect the error and separate them back into their correct categories. This, in turn, can distort the true picture that the data is capturing.

To help stocking clerks, data wranglers, and machines do their tasks most effectively, we have to be thoughtful about considerations such as labeling and categorization. For example, consider various other attributes and derivatives based on our three produce items. We can buy "apple juice," "orange juice," and "tomato juice," but typically you can only buy "tomato soup," not "apple soup" or "orange soup." A computer working with data about fruits, vegetables, and products derived from them won't "see" the problem of "orange soup" that a human would, unless the vocabulary and rules that accommodated the distinction were programmed into the software. As the volume and complexity of data drives an increasing need for algorithms and automation to handle it, the need for well thought-out labeling systems is going to be ever more crucial.

As Dale and his employees try to organize their store's shelves and bins, the trucks continue to arrive with new inventory. Dale is so fixated on categories and placement, that he forgets the temporal dimension of sorting the goods. Before long, the older produce starts to get mixed up with the newer shipments. As a shopper at this store, it could be difficult for you to get a good sense of the inventory or how long some of the items have been sitting on the shelves. In this case, one bad apple truly could spoil the whole barrel.

The metadata about the length of time the item has been in the store can be an important determinant in how it is arranged in the bins (near the front and top). This, in turn, can help ensure the produce is used in a timely manner, which serves both Dale and his customers. Whether it's a produce stand or an organization working with large complex data sets, defining a good system for identifying, storing, organizing, and retrieving the things you want is essential.

Using the right measures

Let's say Dale wanted to compare the change in prices of some of the exotic fruit drinks he has bought in the last couple of years. He sees the price of "Mango Madness" has gone up 50 cents a bottle, as has the price of "Pineapple-Palooza." They seem the same if he charts out the change with the x-axis showing time and the y-axis displaying the absolute price (Figure 3.6).

It looks pretty unremarkable, but Dale remembers that "Pineapple-Palooza" used to be a lot less expensive than "Mango Madness." If he looks at the percentage change between the two data sets, where the y-axis now shows percentage change over the same time period as in Figure 3.6, he gets an entirely different perspective (Figure 3.7).

He makes a note to find out from the distributor what accounts for this differential change. By calibrating the scales (making the y-axis show percentage change over a certain time period, rather than reflecting the absolute price change), he has been able to gain useful insights that, in turn, have prompted him to ask questions about the fruit drink portion of his supply chain.

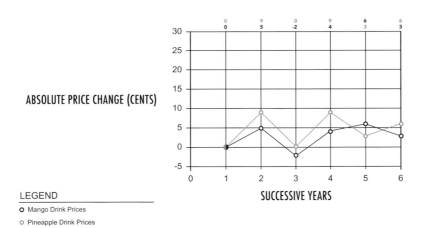

Absolute price changes for "Mango Madness" and "Pineapple-Palooza."

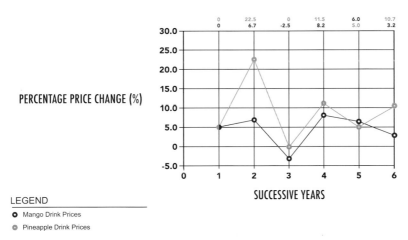

Percentage/proportional price changes for "Mango Madness" and "Pineapple-Palooza."

Combining data

Data sets are joined together for many reasons—adding brand new categories, for instance, or updating existing databases. This might sound straightforward in principle, but it is often anything but that in practice. Merging data can introduce many errors and, once joined, the problems can be hard to untangle, if they are ever even detected at all.

As an admittedly crude example, say a couple of spreadsheets about produce inventory have been created by two different people at Dale's store. Although both individuals are very hard working, they don't always find the time to meet and compare notes about apple nomenclature. In one of their spreadsheets, there's a column containing data about "Granny Smith Apples." In the other person's spreadsheet, there's a column with data about "Green Apples." In fact, they are the very same apples on the store shelves, but different stockers think about them in different terms and have given them different names in their respective spreadsheets.

If these two tables are merged into one master table, and the disconnect on the wording goes unnoticed, then the number of "Green/Granny Smith Apples" appears to be double what it actually is, rather than the two types being identified as one and the same. Let's say that, unknowingly, Dale then creates a report based on this table with the unnoticed duplicate numbers. If, at some point, he adds a third green apple variety, such as Pippin, to his stock, the potential for error increases. The more data are pooled and consolidated, the more potential errors can multiply and the source of the initial problem can become increasingly difficult to detect.

As another example, say a doctor has patient records for "Joe Smith" and "J. Smith"; are they the same person or two different people? If they're different people, but the records are merged, that can have serious consequences, such as a medical misdiagnosis. If they're kept separate, but are in fact the same person, then data might be left out and unavailable to the healthcare provider when it's most needed. Even when updating existing records, there can be mismatches in the new data—say, for example, a customer has changed phone numbers, but the records show that both numbers are still valid. Good data visualizations can be helpful in quickly and clearly revealing problems of this kind in data sets.

Basic ingredients: Varieties of data

I've seen several variations, not to mention had a few philosophical discussions, on how to break out and describe data types, and it can sometimes get confusing, but here's a basic way to look at it. At a broad level, data can be broken into two major classes: *discrete* and *continuous*. Discrete data specify distinct, separate items that fall into qualitative categories (Figure 3.8). An apple and an orange, for example, are "discrete" or "nominal" items that have no intrinsic order in relation to each other. Conversely, continuous data are things that are in a particular *ordered* way—for example, days of the week, temperature, the shelf life of snack cakes (Figure 3.9).

Along with discrete and continuous data, other kinds of broad classifications also are used; we'll focus on just a few.

Measuring the ingredients

There are many ways to slice and dice things we're interested in, different kinds of questions we can ask about them, and different ways to measure them. Certain kinds of measurements apply to certain kinds of things, and others don't. Take a box of mixed fruit, for example. You can measure the total mass of the box, list the individual items, order them by weight of each piece, categorize them by color, determine what percentage of them are citrus, rank them in order of popularity, and so on. However, certain questions you can't readily ask about this box of fruit, such as how many fluid ounces it is or what tax

Discrete (unordered) items   ...**not** continuous

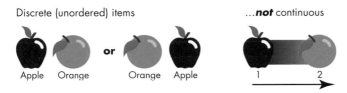

Apple   Orange   Orange   Apple   1   2

FIGURE 3.8

Discrete, not continuous.

Continuous...

Can be safely consumed until?

Date of manufacture   Heat death of the Universe

FIGURE 3.9

Long-lastingly continuous.

Apple   Orange   Tomato

FIGURE 3.10

They are what they seem.

bracket it's in. Think of this box as a representation of a data set. These considerations about data types and measurements play a critical role in determining what kind of visual representations you can use.

- *Nominal scale:* This is simply putting items together without ordering or ranking them (e.g., an apple, an orange, and a tomato). These items can be arranged in various ways that all still convey the same basic information (Figure 3.10).

- *Ordinal scale:* Elements of the data describe properties of objects or events that are ordered by some characteristic (e.g., how would you rank oranges as a snack food compared to tomatoes?). The order of the objects does not, however, provide any information about the distance along the continuum between any two adjacent items (Figure 3.11).

- *Interval scale:* These are data that are measured on some kind of scale, often temporal (e.g., the days of the week, hours of the day), where the differences between adjacent scale numbers are equal. A degree of temperature is the same size in the 95 to 100° Celsius range as it is in the 0 to 10° Celsius range. Another example is—how many apples and oranges were sold each day last week? (See Figure 3.12.)

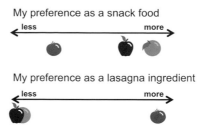

FIGURE 3.11

Legitimately ordinal.

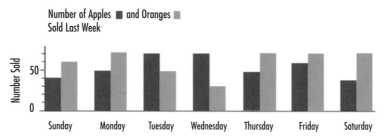

FIGURE 3.12

The intervals of fruit.

FIGURE 3.13

A citrus ratio.

- *Ratio scale:* An ordered series of numbers assigned to items (objects, events, etc.) that allow for estimating and comparing different measures in terms of multiples, such as "half as many" or "four times as heavy." What makes this scale possible? *Zero.* That is, it has to start with a value of zero (as in the current orange inventory = 0), and things can scale up from there (Figure 3.13).

Setting the table: Data types and representative forms

Question: What's wrong with this chart displaying data about the number of these items sold last August? (Figure 3.14)

Answer: Among other things, the line, in this context, is not an appropriate visual representation of this kind of discrete, categorical data because a line represents a continuum with no delineation of the discrete items of fruit (Figure 3.15).

Number of items sold last August

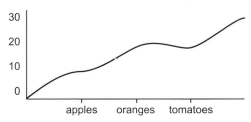

FIGURE 3.14

A continuum of fruit?

...***not*** continuous

FIGURE 3.15

The appleorange.

Finding the right fit between data and visualizations can be a subtle and complex process. As a consumer of infographics and other visual representations, it can be well worth it for you to ask if the image does justice to the meaning or if it's even legitimate and sensible to use, or it even makes any sense. For designers, it's important to consider how the visual may clarify or confuse the point. This process is called "visually encoding" the data. Here are two generalizations from information visualization researcher Colin Ware about relating different kinds of data type displays:

1. Using graphic size (as in a bar chart) to display category information is likely to be misleading because we tend to interpret size as representing quantity.

2. If we map measurements to color, we can perceive nominal or, at best, ordinal values, with a few discrete steps. Perceiving metric intervals using color is not very effective. Many visualization techniques are capable of conveying only nominal or ordinal qualities.

These kinds of considerations are only just scratching the surface of chart selection. Even so, keeping in mind the basic ideas discussed here in this section can be helpful for making quick assessments about chart usage and also for anticipating potential usability issues for the people who will be using the charts.

Figure 3.16 shows some common examples of basic charts that work well with discrete data. The histogram is an example of a chart that shows continuous data—as compared to bar charts, which generally display categorical data—whose x-axis has the intervals of

Percentage of each of these three items in the basket...

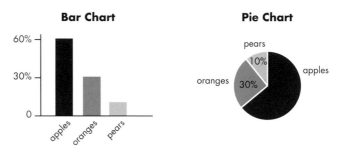

FIGURE 3.16
Fruit bars and fruit pies.

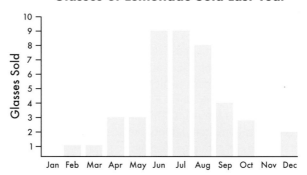

FIGURE 3.17
Citrus juice histogram.

months, as in Figure 3.17, which, unlike categorical oranges and pears, have a particular order.

Bit by bit: A brief look at data, units, scale, and storage
Units of measure

Imagine you're driving down a lonely stretch of highway late at night, and a yellow light on your gas gauge is glowing ominously, indicating that you're getting close to E. It's getting a little scary, but then you notice a road sign just up ahead (Figure 3.18).

FIGURE 3.18
Meep-meep.

Okay, what's a *KiloMeep*? (In this case, I just made up the unit of measure "KiloMeep," and, fortunately, in the scenario, you won't run out of gas.) At that moment on that desolate highway, the unit of measure suddenly becomes of great interest for any number of reasons. Even a general sense of what a Meep is and how it compares to units of measure you recognize can suggest what kinds of plans you will need to consider.

Without that kind of information, you really are left stranded in the dark. Having even a very general sense of some units of measure can be helpful for planning how to work with data. To be honest, it's easy to talk about getting a "general sense" of the scale of data, and it's quite another thing to have it really be comprehensible. Most of us have a difficult time wrapping our heads around big numbers—I certainly do. With that acknowledged, let's take a quick crack at it anyway.

Just how big is a terabyte?

You've seen the various measures of data storage and their respective sizes in bytes. The following examples should help you get a general sense of how much can be stored in any given quantity of data.

- One byte can store a single standard keyboard character or a number from 0 to 255.

- One kilobyte can store 1000 characters, or about the length of the KiloMeep discussion.

- The King James Bible, with no formatting, can be stored in 4.44 megabytes (MB).

- A standard college-style dictionary is about 25 MB worth of data, including some formatting.

- Assuming such a dictionary is exactly two inches thick and contains 25 MB worth of data, a stack of these books 6' 8" high represents a gigabyte.

- A terabyte-high stack of these dictionaries would be more than five times the height of the Empire State Building.

- As another example, 4 days and 19 hours of over-the-air terrestrial broadcast television transmits just over a terabyte of data.

Data and units in the worlds of atoms and bits

I can discover facts, Watson, but I cannot change them.

   – SIR ARTHUR CONAN DOYLE'S CHARACTER SHERLOCK HOLMES, The Problem of Thor Bridge

Many of us spend a lot of our time inhabiting two worlds—the world of atoms and the world of electronic bits, or, in another sense, the physical world we inhabit and the realms we experience with computers. There are many interesting similarities and important differences between them, but we can easily forget or overlook some of the key distinctions. Those differences have important implications for how we work with data.

The distinction that I want to emphasize here is that the world of atoms is governed by rules that don't come from people but, rather, from the laws of nature. The realms generated by computers, on the other hand, ultimately originate and are defined by humans and are constrained by the intrinsic properties of machines. That can have important implications for working with data.

Consider an example. Let's say we have a large set of flasks containing different kinds of chemicals. We systematically mix one with the other and see what happens. Maybe a mix of chemical A and chemical B instantly turns glowing green, begins to bubble, and produces voluminous vapors. The reaction we observe is due to the individual properties of the two chemicals and the way they interact with each other. The thing we observe is a result of the laws of physics and chemistry and human intervention in setting up the particular experiment. That is the world of atoms.

Now, let's do the experiment in the realm of bits. We have a computer program that has a simulated chemical A and chemical B, and we mix them. In this instance, nothing happens. Why? Because everything in the simulation, such as the properties of A and B, was ultimately defined and decided by people who may not have had all the key data, made assumptions that don't match what is going on in the physical world, or may have simply gotten something wrong.

Models, materials, and measures

Consider two new bridges spanning a deep river gorge. The first bridge has a structurally sound and elegant design but is made of balsa wood and bamboo; the second bridge is based on untested and possibly unsound assumptions by the engineers but is constructed from high-quality concrete and steel. To celebrate the grand opening of the bridges, someone holds up a set of keys to a fancy sports car and says the first person to drive over one of the bridges can keep the vehicle. Which bridge would you take? Neither is an especially appealing option, and, personally, I'd pass on the attempt.

Both the engineering models and the materials matter. In the world of atoms, the results of a significant problem or deficiency in either can lead to catastrophic results that can be immediately apparent, such as the splintering of wood that occurs if the sports car

FIGURE 3.19
Ill-fated space venture.

starts to make its way across the balsa bridge. In the world of bits and computer simulations, where basic materials are numbers and data, the problems with models and materials may or may not be as apparent, unless and until they are put to the test in the real world.

This all may seem theoretical, but it has real-world implications. In the world of computers and simulations, everything can be completely, internally consistent, but if human assumptions are not well connected with physical realities, things can go really wrong. Take the untimely demise of the Mars Climate Orbiter that disintegrated in the Martian atmosphere in 1999 (Figure 3.19).

The cause of the problem was determined to come from the fact that one team on the project was using metric units of measure and one used Imperial units of measure. They're two perfectly reasonable units of measure for data, in themselves, but this was not a mix-and-match kind of scenario. The flight control software was doing what it was supposed to do, maneuvering the orbiter in its fast, precise, and literal way, but the discrepancies in human assumptions and data input led to a catastrophic conclusion. In the contest between the world of atoms and bits, nature won, and a potentially very interesting $300 million-plus mission vaporized over the red planet.

PART TWO: FITTING DATA TYPES WITH VISUAL FORMS

Every kind of chart, graph, or other visual form has its own unique set of strengths, weaknesses, and limitations in displaying and bringing out important features in the data. Although a few different kinds of representations may be appropriate for a given type of data set, one form may be particularly suitable and effective for a specific purpose.

Part of the beauty and power of data visualization is that key elements don't have to be complicated to stimulate complex ideas and insights. But, as with so many things, our strengths can also be a weakness. We can easily read meaning into patterns of data that is just not there. On the other hand, as great as our cognitive-perceptual equipment is, it still has limits, and it can be overloaded to the point where we overlook the key patterns. The way to achieve optimal visualization design is to be aware of the full assortment of ingredients and how they reinforce, detract from, or otherwise interact with one another.

When you look at the graph in Figure 3.20, you probably notice some basic patterns immediately. Even as you consciously consider what those patterns might mean, you don't really have to think about the fact that there is a distinct pattern. The clustering of dots simply seems to emerge from the chart. This is based on the idea of *pre-attentive attributes* of visual perception. Essentially, we are wired for noticing differences in such visual elements as shape, color, and pattern without conscious thought or effort. These basic visual elements that enable pattern detection can be associated with data to create visualizations that allow us to process at least part of what we are seeing in a nearly automatic way.

Exploring any one of these visual elements of data visualizations easily could fill a chapter on its own. I'm going to mention a few aspects of each here, simply to stimulate your own thinking about them.

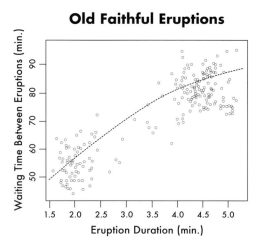

FIGURE 3.20
Dual-cluster plot.

Raising the bar

Shapes are the building blocks of visualization. Simple forms, such as the rectangle, for example, can pack a tremendous amount of meaning into a few straight lines. The arrangements of a few rectangles in bar charts and histograms can tell the tale of the distribution of a data set, the central tendency (the tendency of data points to cluster around the "middle" of a distribution of a data set, e.g., median and mean), and the range (Figure 3.21).

A rectangle, and its quadrilateral cousins, in conjunction with other shapes (Figure 3.22), can be used to describe different categories of data and their relationships in network diagrams (Figure 3.23). Different shapes can be used simply to help differentiate several lines in a chart without the need for color (Figure 3.24).

There's another kind of simple, rectangular form of data representation that I want to briefly mention. That is the *box-and-whisker plot* or *box plot*. Although at first it may look like a peculiar kind of bar chart, the boxes and lines pack a lot of statistical punch.

FIGURE 3.21

The bars are raised.

FIGURE 3.22

Easy differentiation.

US TECHNICAL SALES TEAM

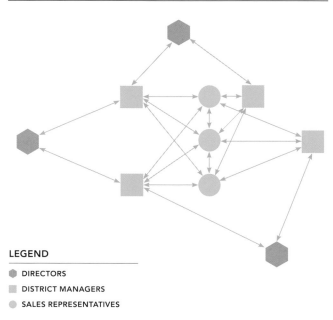

LEGEND

- DIRECTORS
- DISTRICT MANAGERS
- SALES REPRESENTATIVES

FIGURE 3.23

Shaping up the network.

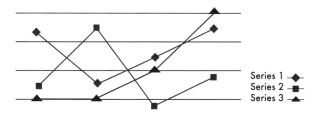

Series 1 ◆
Series 2 ■
Series 3 ▲

FIGURE 3.24

Clarified lines.

The top and bottom of the vertical lines projecting from either end of the box (the "whiskers") represent the maximum and minimum values, thereby showing the spread of the collected values. The top and bottom of the box itself indicate the 25th and 75th percentile, and the line that occurs inside the box is the median. Box plots (Figure 3.25) do a lot of work with a few lines, but they do require more knowledge from the person looking at them.

Well-arranged, stacked bar charts can provide effective support for helping time-strapped experts make better decisions about vital issues, such as the medication side effects when multiple drugs are prescribed to a patient (Figure 3.26).

BOX PLOT

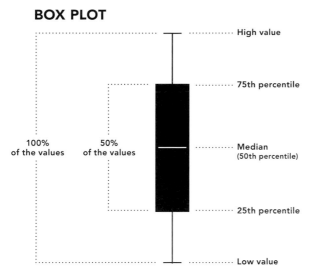

FIGURE 3.25
Boxes full of information.

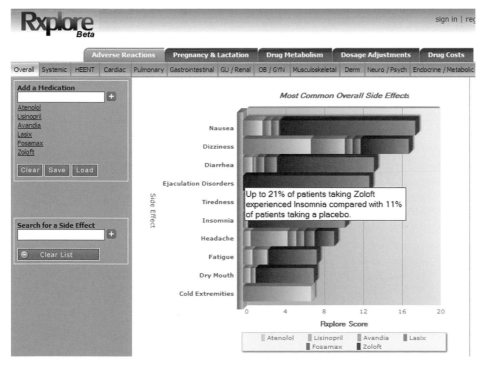

FIGURE 3.26

Multidrug comparison. *Credit: Jon Duke.*

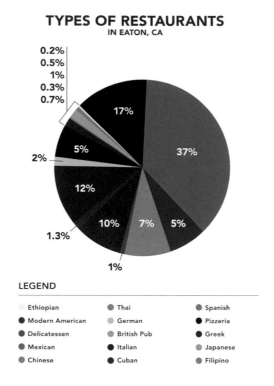

TYPES OF RESTAURANTS
IN EATON, CA

LEGEND

Ethiopian	Thai	Spanish
Modern American	German	Pizzeria
Delicatessen	British Pub	Greek
Mexican	Italian	Japanese
Chinese	Cuban	Filipino

FIGURE 3.27
Too many slices.

Virtuous circle?

Over the years, I've seen the pie chart vilified. I suppose that for many uses, the pie chart format doesn't provide a very precise visual reference—it can readily be used to create some pretty bad charts (Figure 3.27).

The supply of bad pie charts out there is limitless fodder for the ranks of purists, yet the pie chart still seems to be a staple of basic data representation. Perhaps it's because there's something about the qualities of a circle that, when used properly, convey an immediate sense of comparing parts to a whole. Circles, like other shapes, can help us differentiate multiple lines in a line chart or different *nodes* in a network diagram, but their role as a main ingredient in pie charts makes them interesting and unique.

Right on the dot...

Consider the lowly dot in Figure 3.28. It may not look like much, but the humble dot and lines can have the potential to describe some of the most complex problems and issues imaginable (Figure 3.29).

FIGURE 3.28
Microscopic.

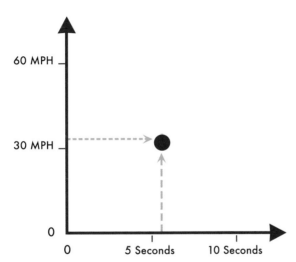

FIGURE 3.29
Complexity with simplicity.

Put two lines together, with some regular intervals on them, and you have *x*- and *y*-axes that define a space in which the location of a dot now can potentially have meaning and significance. Dots become embodiments of individual data points in a defined space to reveal otherwise invisible patterns.

Beyond single-variable (univariate) data, there's a vast realm of paired-variable (bivariate) and multiple-variable (multivariate) data that can be explored with visualizations. For example, if you become interested in investigating the relationships between pairs of data points, such as the harvest date and sugar content of grapes, then a scatter plot, not a bar or pie chart, is the best way to present the data (Figure 3.30).

The points on a scatter plot can represent two or three dimensions of continuous data. Scatter plots are commonly displayed as 2D, but some scatter plots come in 3D and have small spheres floating in space rather than dots on the page (see Figure 3.31).

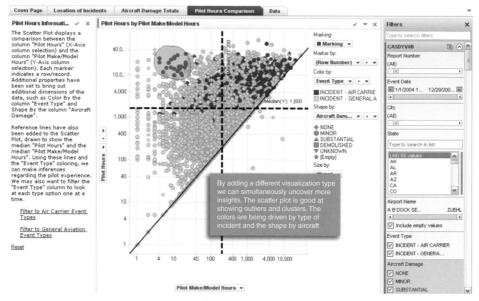

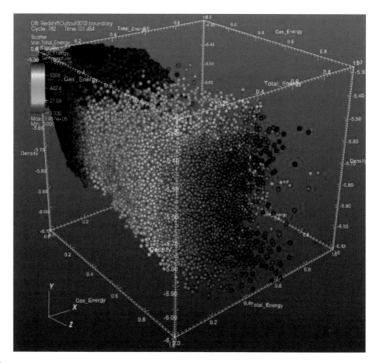

Certain kinds of 3D representations of data can be problematic. For example, "3D" projections on 2D can create instances when dots in the foreground area block dots in the background and there's no way to move around the dot that's in the way. However, with the addition of interactivity to 3D visualizations, users can view the data points from different perspectives so the dots, or other data shapes, won't necessarily block the view. Immersive and interactive visualization can help make exploring high-dimension data with 3D more practical, intuitive, and useful.

This idea is nothing new. Human-computer pioneer Douglas Engelbart's lab was working on this issue back in the early 1960s. The increasing availability of ever more rich and complex data sets, coupled with the advances in computer interfaces, may accelerate this trend.

Drawing the Lines

Although shapes are building blocks of data visualizations, the way they're visually related to each other is what turns it all into a meaningful structure (Figure 3.32). The relationships can be constructed in a range of very different ways—including lines that, depending on the context, can take on many roles. In a network graph, such as that shown in Figure 3.33 for example, the lines reveal who is communicating with whom, the nature of the communication (e.g., one- or two-way), and, if desired, the strength of the relationship (with line thickness and color).

As simple as a line may be, when a number of lines are used to display connections of large, complex networks, they quickly can become badly tangled. Collections can turn into dreaded "hairballs" or "spaghetti bowls" that make these kinds of diagrams completely unintelligible. However, with the inclusion of interactivity and well-designed controls, that kind of messy view can be cleaned up to a great extent (Figure 3.34).

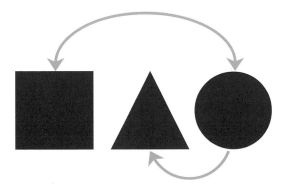

FIGURE 3.32
Connect the blocks.

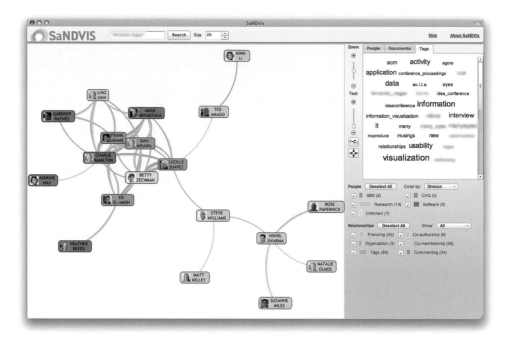

FIGURE 3.33

A network graph. *Courtesy Adam Perer (2011).*

In addition to showing relationships, lines help us to see the trends in data. They are very effective at showing changes over time and hinting at the future.

That strength is also a weakness, because lines can be manipulated in ways that might mislead the viewer. With a few changes to the scale of the *x*- and/or *y*-axis of a graph, a gently rising or declining line can suddenly become very dramatic (Figures 3.35 and 3.36). Because the line is simple and compelling, it's important to look carefully at who is tracking the data and what scales they're using.

Lines can also be very suggestive. The slope and direction can point in ways that seem like they will continue in that direction. There's a saying on Wall Street that "the trend is your friend." Perhaps that may be true in some cases, but seeming trends and trajectories can sometimes lie. The lines presented in glossy financial brochures, for example, can suggest returns and outcomes that will not materialize. When it comes down to the line, caveat emptor.

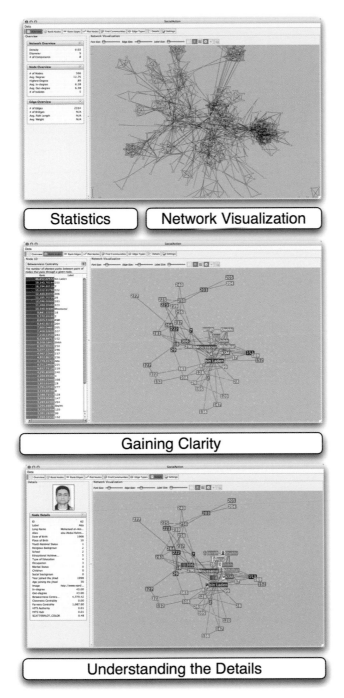

FIGURE 3.34
From hairy to clarity. *Courtesy Adam Perer (2010).*

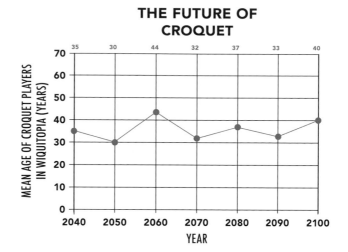

FIGURE 3.35

Calm seas.

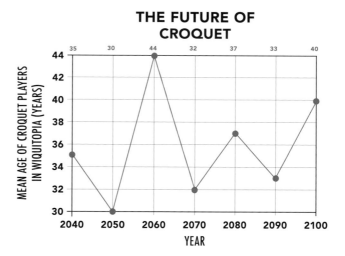

FIGURE 3.36

Tsunamis!

COLOR!

As I'm writing this, a hummingbird is surveying my balcony, checking out several plants there. It quickly focuses on two richly colored flowers on my Chinese Lantern plant and zooms in for some long sips. The plant is not in full view, but the ability of these birds to very quickly detect when these vibrant nectar sources are in bloom is amazing. Color can

FIGURE 3.37
Pick a color, any color

be important for survival, and people are good at locating it, although perhaps not as good as hummingbirds.

It makes sense, literally, to use color (Figure 3.37) as a way to enhance our ability to find meaning in data. However, it's possible to have too much of a good thing. Because it is so powerful, it can be tempting to use a lot of it, but as a great art teacher I know, Walt Bartman, often says, "The less you use of a color in a painting, the more you see it." A less judicious use of color can become overwhelming and drown out the main message.

It's important to be consistent, systematic, and thoughtful in associating colors to represent data (Figure 3.38). It's also good to be mindful that a substantial number of people are colorblind, and so are unable to distinguish between red/green or blue/yellow color combinations (Figure 3.39). That's one good reason to think about designs that don't make color the sole basis of discriminating among data elements. Shape, size, and other elements can help colorblind people get the gist of the visualization while also providing reinforcement for everyone else.

Order, position, and hierarchies

For certain aspects of our daily lives, a specific arrangement and ordering are essential. We shower first and then get dressed, versus the other way around. Some variation may occur, but the sequence of putting on socks and shoes is very specific. Simple enough. But like so much else in life, even the simplest things get unwieldy when they scale up. Trying to

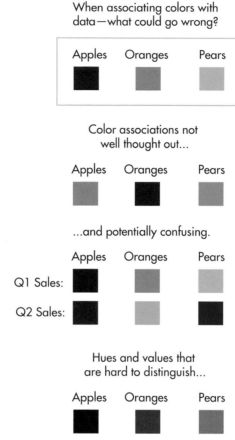

FIGURE 3.38
Don't pick just any color.

capture the relationships and hierarchies of data can be no small feat. Shapes and lines can show relationships, but their arrangements display hierarchies (Figure 3.40).

There are many ways to display hierarchical relationships. We're all familiar with the tree-like representations of various kinds, with a trunk or root that then spreads out to successively smaller branches, and even leaves. As abstract as it may be, it still has a pattern that is fairly similar to its real-world model—the tree. But the kinds of data that people have to deal with nowadays are so massive and varied that our conventional solid trunk and branch lines can't support the weight.

Enter the treemap. Treemaps have been around for a good long time, arising from work done by visualization maestro Ben Shneiderman. When I heard about treemaps and then saw one, I had a momentary need to shift my thinking to a more abstract level. The colorful patchwork of nested boxes did not immediately seem all that maplike or treelike. It's an

FIGURE 3.39
Colorblind conundrum.

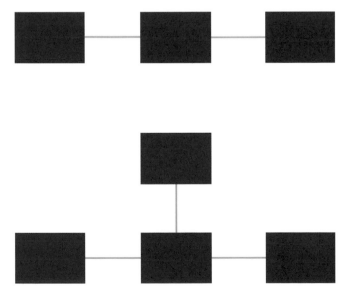

FIGURE 3.40
Connect the boxes.

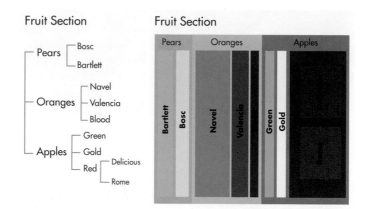

FIGURE 3.41

The fruit treemap.

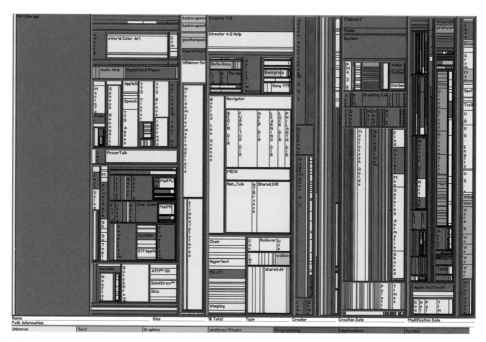

FIGURE 3.42

The Shneiderman treemap.

interesting fusion of the two concepts that can contain, in a compact space, an immense amount of information about a lot of relationships of categorical data. This combination can visually encode many dimensions by relying on such ingredients as the size and color of the rectangles.

Treemaps also offer many great advantages over more commonly used forms of hierarchical diagrams. Even so, they may not always convey the key attributes of a relationship the way good old boxes and arrows can. I've made a comparison in Figure 3.41 of two ways to display the hierarchical ordering of fruit. The treemap is simplified and doctored a bit to make the point. It not only displays the hierarchy of the diagram on the left, but conveys quantitative information, as well. The areas of the rectangles reveal the amount of each kind of thing; there are four times more navel oranges than there are blood oranges. Figure 3.42 shows a picture of a treemap from Dr. Shneiderman's Lab.

A selected menu of chart types

I've discussed bar charts, histograms, line charts, and pie charts a good deal so far in this chapter to help make some points about data types and visual forms to make them as clear and direct as possible. Of course, there are many different kinds of charts and many variations on a theme within each chart type. There are compound versions of forms we've seen—stacked bars, pie charts, and line charts. There are chart forms, such as the box plot, that, although reminiscent of a bar chart, display a combination of statistical measures in a compact form.

I'll call out a few kinds of visualizations for special note, and you'll find more in the figures below. We'll see how some of the factors brought up earlier in the chapter come into play with these different chart types.

The things we do with visual representations of data don't always fall neatly into distinct packages. It's far more complex, intertwined, and nuanced than that. Early in this chapter, I mentioned a few broad categories of descriptions—**summarizing and showcasing** distributions of what might otherwise be hard-to-digest sets of numbers (e.g., histograms, bar charts, box plots, pie charts, pictograms); **showing relationships** among different data points (e.g., link diagrams, scatter plots); and **revealing trends** suggested by numbers (e.g., line charts).

Playing well together: Data, visualizations, and people

It is as deadly for a mind to have a system as to have none. Therefore it will have to decide to combine both.

– KARL WILHELM FRIEDRICH SCHLEGEL

The big opportunities for problem solving and gleaning insights from large, complex, and diverse data sets often require that people with very different skills and mindsets all share in the effort. When tech entrepreneur Raffael Marty started looking into computer security and visualization, he found that "the visualization people didn't know about security concepts, and security people didn't know about visualization." Many of the different groups that need to collaborate on visualization efforts come from very different backgrounds and have very different ways of thinking about, representing, and communicating related ideas.

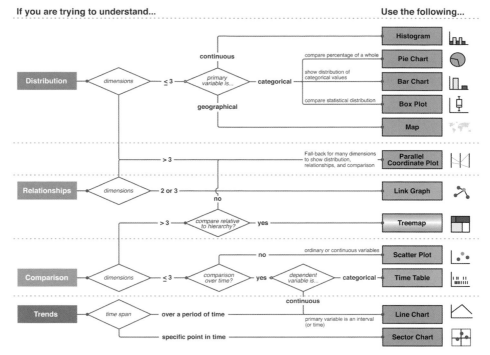

FIGURE 3.43

Data, design, and decisions. *Marty, R.,* Applied Security Visualization, *1st edition, © 2009. Printed and electronically reproduced by permission of Pearson Education, Inc., Upper Saddle River, New Jersey.*

The essential skill of effectively combining visual principles and theory to make meaningful representations of data requires an element of creativity. "In the end, I think visualization is not a hard science but an art," Marty says. For example, he says, "if you had a simple bar chart to convey information, and added a little color to it in an interesting way, it might make it more decipherable; understandable. How do you show the most information with the least amount of complexity?"

Marty created the diagram shown in Figure 3.43 for his book, *Applied Security Visualization*, to help users decide how they might take certain forms of data and present them in the most effective way. He says he has felt the pain himself of wrestling with how to represent the data that he needs to communicate. "I've had frustration that comes out of my own challenges about not being able to visualize data the way I want it." As a result, Marty has been inspired to start his own company, Pixl-Cloud, to work on these issues.

Note: In this chapter, I have looked at only single-variable (univariate) data as a starting point. However, paired-variable (bivariate) and multiple-variable (multivariate) data play a role in many visualizations. Figure 3.43 includes charts that can display more than one-dimensional data.

PART THREE: PUTTING TOGETHER DIFFERENT KINDS OF VISUALIZATIONS

Ideas rose in clouds; I felt them collide until pairs interlocked, so to speak, making a stable combination.

– HENRI POINCARÉ

The combo plate and multiple courses: combining different visualizations and views of the data

To get the best understanding of a data set, it helps to view it with a mixture of visual forms and different perspectives. Mixes and matches of different kinds of visualizations can be connected to tell a more complete and detailed story than any one kind of visualization could do by itself (Figure 3.44).

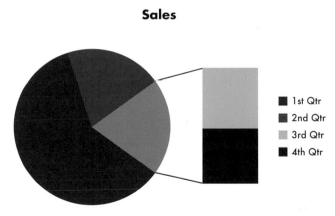

FIGURE 3.44

Quarterly breakdown.

Deciding what to combine is one of the interesting challenges of creating visualization interfaces. What are the elements that you add to the plate that the users will want to consume?

To take a simple example, using a bar chart in tandem with a pie chart to show aspects of a data set can be more effective than either one individually. Sometimes using multiple views of the same kind of chart, highlighting different parts of the same data, can better convey meaningful patterns than simply having a single version that shows all the data at once. For example, by breaking out and arranging in a matrix various elements of data in a set of scatter plots, rather than just using a single graph, meaningful patterns in the data become more recognizable…at least to a trained eye.

The process of gaining insight from visual representations can mean looking through a range of design filters. Like a gem that catches the light and glints brilliantly when held in a certain way, that key connection, pattern, and meaning may only make itself known when you've turned and viewed the facets of the data from many different angles.

How much is *too much*?

Combine the extremes, and you will have the true center.

— KARL WILHELM FRIEDRICH SCHLEGEL

In any good cooking, adding a little fat can enhance the flavor and substance of a meal, but overdoing it can spoil the presentation and harm the people consuming it. In data visualization, you want to add richness to the data to create the most effective display possible, but you don't want to overdo it and end up with something muddled or confusing. On the other hand, if the data aren't rich enough, you may end up producing something that is clear, crisp, and respectable but that really doesn't capture the depth of the situation.

Sometimes, too much is just too much. Showing too many data points may overwhelm the meaningful patterns. With artful visual combinations of data, you can differentiate the important aspects of the data from the statistical noise. A great combination of elements doesn't always mean that they become indistinguishable from each other. Sometimes it's quite the opposite. From music to food to visualizations, certain combinations make each individual element's unique properties and characteristics stand out all the more.

Let's consider this for a moment with a bottle of MetaReserva wine. It's been aging in the cellar for two years and, during that time, various chemical interactions have taken place with the different elements, including the varieties of grapes selected, their relative proportions, and the barrel in which the wine is aging. The result is something with a range of "notes." At first sip, you get a strong sense of berries and a hint of vanilla. It then offers up a bite of tannin at the end. The reason that our vintage commands a high price is that it offers a range of qualities all contained in one glass. With visualizations, we may look at the same display but see a larger variety of richness and subtleties the more time we spend looking at it.

Often, we put contrasting elements together to intensify their differences. Sweet and sour in the right proportions can work well in Chinese food or certain candies. Placing the complementary colors orange and blue next to each other can make each color seem more vivid and make the combination of contrasts pleasing. In data visualizations, by putting colors and shapes together in artful ways, meaningful differences and important outliers in data can be made to stand out rather than blend in and disappear within vast columns and rows of collected material (Figure 3.45). So the question is—what combinations can bring out the most interesting differences?

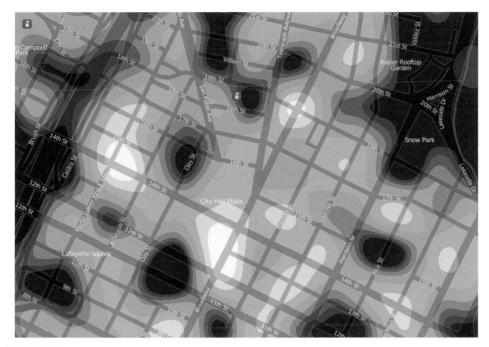

FIGURE 3.45
A heatmap.

A WINNING COLLABORATION ON A SMALL SCALE

There are very few human beings who receive the truth, complete and staggering, by instant illumination. Most of them acquire it fragment by fragment, on a small scale, by successive developments, cellularly, like a laborious mosaic.

— ANAIS NIN

Hack-a-thons are hotbeds of collaboration. They draw together people with a range of backgrounds and varied skills to create software focused on a specific area of interest. The intensity of these gatherings is heightened by their brevity—typically lasting just a few days at most. In 2010, I dropped in on one called "Hacking 4 Health," sponsored by the Palo Alto–based startup HealthTap. "H4H" focused on creating prototypes of applications that can help make health data that was recently released by the government more accessible and useful to the public.

I ended up leading a team that coalesced around the idea of creating a simple data visualization application that drew from various sources of health data and put it into a form that was simple, interesting, useful, and highly interactive. We called our team "First Steps" to reflect our basic goal for the application, which was to encourage people to take realistic first steps in the direction of making a positive change to enhance their own health.

During this collaborative process, we considered many ideas and approaches. One of the key recurring questions was: How do you present data in a way that feels immediate and meaningful to the individual? It's not just about numbers or lines on a chart. It's also very much about human nature, the power of habits, and how the combinations of visuals and interactions can most effectively and directly connect the data to someone at a personal level. And we wanted this visual to be easily used by "Aunt Helen or her 10-year-old niece."

We began with the idea of showing trend lines of long-term health consequences of different "first steps" but eventually moved away from that approach. Although trend lines can tell important and valid stories about daily health behaviors and their potential long-term consequences, for many people the long view is too abstract and simply not compelling. So we had to think about how to make the visualization elicit a more immediate and direct response in people.

Visualizing relationships of actions and outcomes based on solid data can help us see our health choices in new ways and make more informed decisions. It's all about getting insight into how one's own behavior relates to one's own health. If people could have a quick and easy way to see how behavioral choices might have an impact, relative to one another, on their risk of developing a particular disease, and if there was an easy way to mix and match those choices, they would be more likely to change their behavior.

Furthermore, health decisions often are not a question of "Yes" or "No." In reality, they're a series of negotiations, relative priorities, and tradeoffs. For example, one behavioral change may not be as positively effective as another, but it might be far more likely to be started and maintained over time. On the other hand, a big shift in one habit can have such an outsized impact that it outweighs the effects of many other smaller changes. Many of these kinds of decisions ultimately can be made only by that person alone.

http://goo.gl/bQfyo

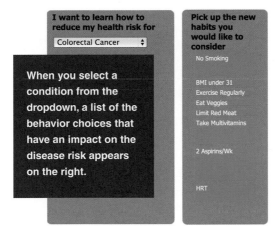

FIGURE 3.46
Weighing my options: select a condition.

Not all hackathons have a competition component, but this one did. Long story short, the judges liked our lines of thought, and we were given the opportunity to compete in an event at the Health 2.0 Conference called the "Developer Challenge" a few weeks later.

For our prototype, we decided to work with a set of data that focused on the relative risk of various factors associated with development of colorectal cancer (Figure 3.46). We used aggregated data from the CDC (Centers for Disease Control), the NCI (National Cancer Institute), NHS (Nurses' Health Study), and HPFS (Health Professionals Follow-Up Study). Our application showed the data using the idea of a common kitchen scale to represent the relative impact that diet, exercise, smoking, and medication use, among others, could have on colorectal cancer risk (Figure 3.47). Using this simple visual could help users make better decisions about specific behavior modifications, by seeing how each factor, either alone or in combination, would affect their own scale, and to identify which ones could have the larger impact (Figure 3.48).

The final idea and implementation occurred over approximately four days; the design was crude, and the details not all ironed out. Nevertheless, the prototype demonstrated how a simple interactive visualization that drew on real data could convey the idea of the relative impacts in a simple and immediate way. All the user had to do was provide a minimal set of basic information. After that, it was a matter of exploring different options.

We were honored by ultimately winning this Developer Challenge, and although our little design may not have been the most sophisticated, or the best looking, the point we were making was that simplicity of interactivity should be the goal. The more you can make a visualization fun, easy, and meaningful, the greater chance it can benefit a wide range of people.

Team Members: Hunter Whitney, Jeremy Johnson, Laurie Reynolds, Kathleen Sidenblad, Peter Vieth, Alex Kawas, Ash Damle, Maria DiLisio, John Bosley, Veena Kumar, and Gary Cieradkowski.

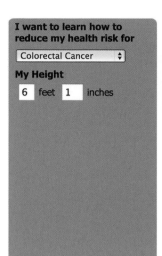
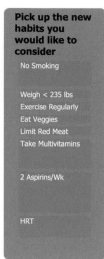

FIGURE 3.47

Weighing my options: choices to help reduce risk.

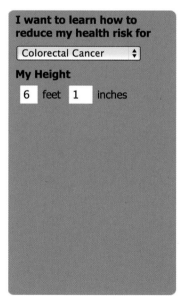

FIGURE 3.48

Weighing my options: notice how different choice combinations shift the white indicator toward lower risk.

CONCLUSION

Kitchen implements can help you make a great meal, but they can't do it without you. The same idea applies to preparing data visualizations. In many ways, the human mind is the essential ingredient. But with this power of decision making also comes the responsibility for the choices you'll make and the need for a basic grounding in fundamentals. Sometimes, this process can be as easy as pie, and other times not, but the final results should always aim to be satisfying.

Pathways, Purposes, and Points of View

4

ALONG THESE LINES . . .

The trail is the thing, not the end of the trail. Travel too fast and you miss all you are traveling for.

— LOUIS L'AMOUR

Often, the most interesting aspects of data are not individual data points but the pathways connecting them. Whether it's showing patterns of people moving from one place to another or revealing links between individuals in various kinds of networks, one of the most powerful capabilities of visualizations is using graphical elements to make relationships within the data plainly visible. When these paths are made visible with color, lines, and shapes, many interesting stories and questions can emerge. For example, in the visualization shown in Figures 4.1 and 4.2, Jon Bruner used anonymized and aggregated IRS records to let people select counties and see within them the patterns of inbound and outbound migration over the course of five years.

FIGURE 4.1A

Pick a county, any county.

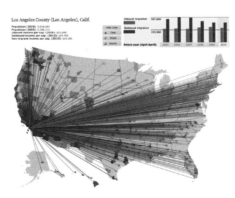

FIGURE 4.1B

L.A. stories.

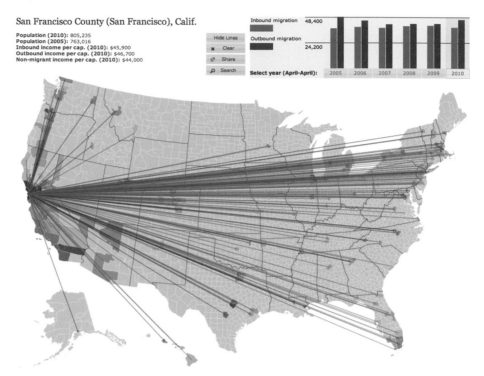

San Francisco County (San Francisco), Calif.

Population (2010): 805,235
Population (2005): 763,016
Inbound income per cap. (2010): $45,900
Outbound income per cap. (2010): $46,700
Non-migrant income per cap. (2010): $44,000

FIGURE 4.2
If you're going to San Francisco...

The quantity, direction, and color of the lines we see in Figures 4.1B and 4.2 tell a tale of two counties, in this case Los Angeles and San Francisco from the years 2005 to 2010. This chart doesn't explain the reason for the patterns, but it may raise questions about them or prompt an interested viewer to explore further.

http://goo.gl/KXHst

Even when drawing from the same data, different kinds of visualizations can serve different purposes, each with their own strengths and weaknesses. The IRS migration data could have been shown only with different color fills for each county, which would have been a valid approach and could be useful for certain kinds of explorations. However, this perspective of converging lines creates a particularly compelling sense of the patterns of movement that wouldn't come across in other forms. Depending on the purposes of the person looking at a visualization, there may be various, or many, points of view that go into making a complete picture.

Another example of Bruner's work shows an entirely different way to trace connections. In this case, the lines don't involve flows of people across geographic areas but flows of funds across political boundaries (Figure 4.3). To me, some of the most interesting lines are the ones that go more to the side, rather than the ones that go more directly down. Perhaps even billionaires have to hedge their bets to get some things done.

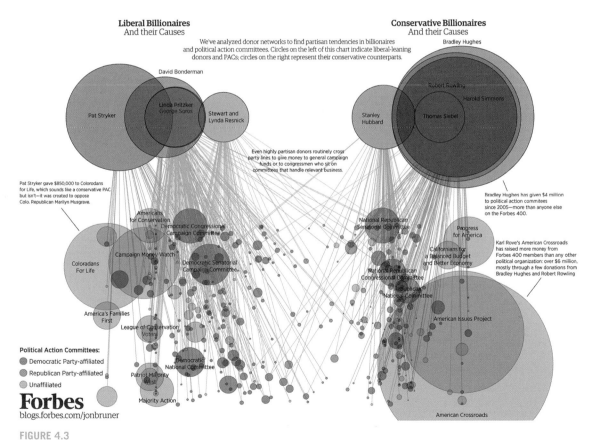

FIGURE 4.3

Spheres of influence.

http://goo.gl/MgKpo

FOLLOWING STRANDS OF DATA

At first glance, some visualizations can seem labyrinthine, but a few main threads of context and description can help us make our way through them and find interesting insights. In the case of the visualization in Figure 4.4, what ties the picture together is knowing the colored lines are representing transit data for the city of San Francisco. The data includes measures of average speed for different modes of travel during a particular period of time. Eric Fischer describes it as, "A day of Muni, according to NextBus."

San Francisco's transit agency, Muni, has been in the forefront of making all of its real-time information public. Working with a company called NextBus, and using satellite technology and computer modeling, the system can track mass transit vehicles on their routes. Real-time data is fed to displays on smart phones, bus shelters, and the NextBus website. Although NextBus is a great resource for commuters, Fischer came up with an interesting alternate avenue to make use of this traffic data. It may not have all the day-to-day practicality of informing a rider about the ETA of the next bus, but Fischer's map provides an interesting and memorable snapshot of the system as a whole. Visualizations don't need to be all things to all people; just enabling us to see otherwise invisible aspects of the world around us sometimes can be reward enough. They can show alternate ways to think about alternate routes.

Fischer's image in Figure 4.5 maps patterns of taxi accessibility in San Francisco, based on data from Cabspotting. Data collection of taxi GPS information and real-time bus information is provided by public transportation agencies such as the San Francisco Municipal Transportation Agency. The colors and densities give a feel for the congestion levels in different parts of the city.

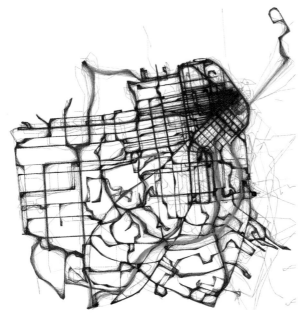

FIGURE 4.4

An a-mazing visualization.

FIGURE 4.5

Taxi! Taxi! *Image by Eric Fischer. Taxi location data from Cabspotting.*

http://cabspotting.org

ON THE ROAD AGAIN

Consider a purple line and blue dot...

They may not look like much in themselves, but visual forms similar to this have helped transform how many of us get around and experience our environment. Tracing their paths on digital map displays based on geolocation data, these lines and dots help ensure we arrive at our intended destinations. This visual form is so common and seemingly simple that it's easy to forget its power, but for me, the way it's implemented in the navigation app on my mobile phone makes it indispensable (Figure 4.6).

FIGURE 4.6

The most basic form.

The navigation app presents a suggested route from Point A to C based on a range of considerations and calculations, some apparent and others not. I can view the navigational line in several ways—for example, an overview of the whole trip or a step-by-step guide. It's a kind of conversation between the line and me. I feel satisfied when I manage to negotiate a particularly complex knot of highway interchanges and remain connected to the continually unspooling thread. Having this tool gives me a sense of comfort in unfamiliar surroundings when an unexpected detour suddenly appears. In those moments especially, I appreciate the dynamic, real-time data feed. I may decide to take an alternate route for a while and so endure a mild scolding (anthropomorphically speaking) from the app as it detects my straying and recalculates, but it quickly adapts to my changes and presents a new approach.

Pathways don't have to be only visual; they also can be auditory—or explained. Navigation using a phone app provides an important reminder about visualization as a cognitive tool—it's only one of a few avenues through which we interact with and understand the world. Along with the purple line leading the way forward, I also hear verbal instructions: "Exit highway in .3 miles and then make a left on 3rd Street." Sometimes, I want to see where I'm heading, and other times, I just want to hear where to go, when taking my eyes off the road even momentarily wouldn't be a good idea. This book focuses largely on visualizations, but hearing is important, too, and auditory cues and feedback can be important tools.

Some people prefer to get their information in different ways, have their particular manner of doing things, or have diverse needs based on their abilities. Beyond that, getting multiple inputs via different modalities can have a powerful synergistic effect. Even senses such as touch and balance may come to play an increasingly significant role as we navigate data in virtual spaces. Kinesthetic interactions are cropping up more every day, as we see games, virtual reality, and touch pad technology become mainstream.

TANGIBLE AND INTANGIBLE PATHWAYS

Beyond mapping geographic routes, lines and dots can also give visible form to many of the more abstract ways we navigate through our lives. For example, they reveal the tracks that we leave as we wander through a series of website pages and can show the lines of our communications and connections with others online. We've all heard about the six degrees of separation. You can trace different pathways or routes of connection from yourself to, say, the actor Kevin Bacon. The relational concept of "the shortest path between two points" has an important role in both getting from one physical location to another and finding a business contact. However, the definitions of distance and path length are very different. In a Point A traveling to Point C scenario, distance is measured geographically (miles, kilometers, etc.). In a Person A reaching out to Person E scenario, distance is measured by the number of intermediary people that Person A needs to go through to connect with Person E. In a social network graph, the intermediaries are "nodes" and the connecting lines "edges." (See Figure 4.7.)

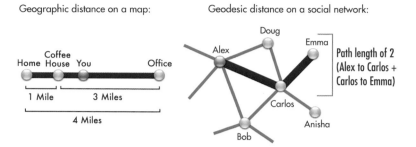

FIGURE 4.7

Geographic versus geodesic.

There is a "distance" and "quality" of connection, and they can be either tangible or intangible. Looking at the length and width of roads—for instance a four-lane highway, or a small dirt path with pot holes—it's quite easy to compare and contrast the amount of traffic typically expected, and in turn "rank" them by size and quality and determine what purpose they were made for. In a social network, connections between people can be shown by dots representing individuals and the number of connection lines. The strength of the connection can be measured by answering questions such as the following:

- How many times do you talk to someone per day, or per week?

- How often do you see them?

- How long are the conversations?

- What type of information do you share with one another?

This is often represented in social network graphs by lines; the thicker the line, the "stronger" the connection, and arrows, which can indicate the directionality of the interaction or give visual cues to show whether the interactions are a two-way street, and so forth. The qualities of the connections also are determined by the type and purpose of the relationship; is it professional or personal?

Lines are used to reveal geographic and network routes and distances. Many of our common activities and tasks can be shown in the form of pathways, which are another version of "lines." When considering potential uses and designs of various forms of visualization models, it can be helpful to picture some of the main pathways people take. Figure 4.8 shows some of the different forms used to represent process pathways.

Defined linear processes

For *defined linear processes*, such as filling out a form or completing a transaction, typically we won't want any surprises or deviations, and the views would confirm that (Figure 4.9).

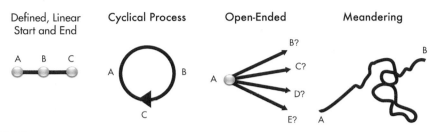

FIGURE 4.8

Pathways of the people.

FIGURE 4.9

Straightforward.

	Sales
1st Qtr	8.2
2nd Qtr	3.2
3rd Qtr	1.4
4th Qtr	1.2

Collect Data   Process Data   Present!

FIGURE 4.10

The process of presentation.

Rote process

Typically, for a *rote process*, we want to speed through it with as few steps as possible—for example, "one click" purchasing is quite popular. This is possible and will be successful only after the full path has been traversed and recorded by data professionals, with action-outcomes or "what if" scenarios taken into account for intermediate steps.

Less defined linear start and end sequence

An example of a *less defined linear start and end sequence* might involve creating a presentation that communicates findings to decision makers (Figure 4.10). This kind of process may become cyclical if the output results in feedback that, in turn, leads to further stages of collection and processing (Figure 4.11).

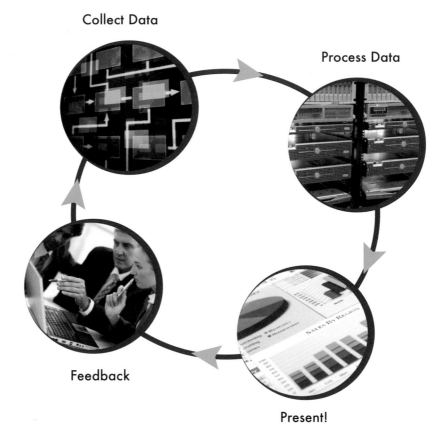

Collect Data

Process Data

Feedback

Present!

FIGURE 4.11
Linear becomes cyclical.

Open-ended processes

In *open-ended processes*, the results may come in multiple and sometimes unexpected forms. For example, a biomedical researcher may have a clear goal of finding a new treatment for a specific disease. However, she may not know what molecules and mechanisms are at work. Unlike an experience with a predetermined output, the key here is trying different things and discovering anomalies and seeing surprises that may lead to insights (Figure 4.12).

The tools and views that would be most useful for exploring the paths and steps involved in an open-ended process may be very different from the ones needed to create a visualization for a decision maker's clear and concise communication. In this case, looking for emergent patterns in a mass of data may be best shown as a heatmap (Figure 4.13). The researcher in this context can spend some time looking at and reflecting on the shapes and colors. Her mind, steeped in this open-ended process, can generate insights at its own pace.

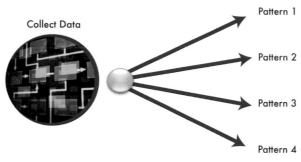

Goal and Question

Collect Data

Pattern 1

Pattern 2

Pattern 3

Pattern 4

FIGURE 4.12
Different paths to insight.

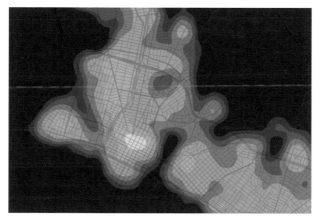

FIGURE 4.13
Emerging patterns of crime, "Oakland Crimespotting." *Courtesy of Stamen Design.*

Meandering

Sometimes, *meandering* is the best way to help us figure what we want or need. In both physical and virtual environments, we may peruse an area with a specific goal in mind but allow ourselves to see what other objects of interest enter our field of view (Figure 4.14). I might go to the hardware store, for example, to purchase a hammer, but wander the aisles and pick up other related materials that helped me to recall what I needed as I saw them, but not before.

Doodling

There's a lot to be said for doodling. Some scientific research suggests that people can retain more information if they're doodling while in a meeting. Researchers believe that doodling gives the brain just enough activity for an attendee to stay "present" in the discussion but not be drained or distracted. It seems safe to say that many people

Meandering

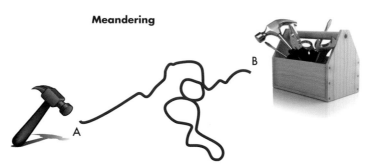

FIGURE 4.14
Just looking.

	Sales
1st Qtr	8.2
2nd Qtr	3.2
3rd Qtr	1.4
4th Qtr	1.2

FIGURE 4.15
The doodling habit of highly effective people.

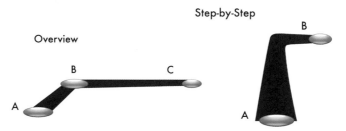

FIGURE 4.16
Overview versus straight ahead.

working for hours with a large data set may find they lose their focus and attention. Provide tools that let users doodle with data. Let them play in the sense that they easily and pleasurably can change how it looks or how it's arranged without altering the underlying data (Figure 4.15). In that way, they might be inclined to stay engaged with it longer and be in a state of mind that might be more open to possibilities in the patterns they're exposing.

Multiple perspectives or points of view

Sometimes the best way to present a pathway is from *multiple perspectives or points of view*. When we're trying to get from Point A to Point C, whether it's a location or a data point, we might want to toggle between an overview for context and a "street-level" step-by-step presentation (Figure 4.16). We might find a larger map view helpful if deciding between freeways, or a list of directions better for unfamiliar locations, for instance. As much as I have come to depend on the step-by-step view on my smart phone's navigation system, it can have its drawbacks. I tend to look less closely at the actual geographic details of the surroundings, instead letting my consciousness live in the abstract world of the purple line.

PATHWAY AND PROCESS

Whether your intention is to explore animal life in the Amazon or shop for books on Amazon.com, there's a pathway associated with that process. It could be a meandering path in the hopes of stumbling upon something interesting or a very linear and directed path for obtaining a particular item. The following are two examples of ways to connect purpose, pathway, and point of view:

- If you wanted to go on a quick day hike, you'd probably want to go on a pathway that had already been measured and marked out and was well maintained.

- If you wanted to embark on a journey of discovery to places where few had set foot before, then your goals would require entirely different kinds of equipment, planning, and level of effort.

Then, if you wanted to make a documentary of your grand expedition, that would introduce a whole new set of considerations and things to pack along for the trip. That's straightforward enough, but what about navigating through vast expanses of data? You may not have to get out of your chair, but you still are going on a journey, either by exploring data yourself or learning from someone else's discoveries.

FINDING RARE BIRDS IN DENSE JUNGLES: A PACKING LIST

As soon as anything new is discovered, the successful scientist immediately looks at it from all possible points of view and by connecting it with other knowledge seeks new avenues for investigation. The real and lasting pleasure in a discovery comes not so much from the accomplishment itself as from the possibility of using it as a stepping stone for fresh advances.
                    — W. I. B. BEVERIDGE, FROM THE ART OF SCIENTIFIC INVESTIGATION

Although a visualization showing the complex interrelationships of data can look very impressive, what strikes me even more is a visualization that captures a single interesting feature of the data and gets me to think about it. The distillation process involved is challenging and requires considerable creativity. Data visualization can sometimes seem exotic and abstract, but some of the same fundamental goals, skills, and challenges that apply today applied just as much when the first humans traced out lines in the ground with a stick showing the direction to a watering hole, or an ancient mapmaker drew a sea monster on an uncharted ocean. For the explorers and communicators, either in the physical world or the data landscape, what are the tools necessary to accomplish their goals? This table breaks it down and considers which kinds of equipment would be helpful along the way.

TABLE 4.1 Equipment List

Equipment for:	Exploration	Communication	Collaboration	Imagination
Context	(P) Maps (DV) Overview screens	(P) Maps (DV) Overview screens	(P and DV) List of participants	(M) A fresh clean surface to create and a box of crayons (or similar)
Way Finding	(P) GPS and/or Compass (DV) Displays that show how to navigate through the data	(P) Trail Markers, signs, etc.	(P) Communication devices (DV) Social media and other online collaboration tools	
Path Clearing	(P) Machetes, for example (DV) Dynamic filter controls (e.g., sliders)	Path has already *been* cleared		(M) Breaking out of biases, preconceptions and mental blocks (e.g., by showing multiple scenarios)
Recording and Representation	(P) Cameras, sound recorders, editing equipment, script or narrative (DV) "Bread crumbs," saving histories, screen captures, animation and editing tools, narrative flow representations	(P) Cameras, sound recorders, editing equipment (DV) "Bread crumbs," saving histories, screen captures, animation and editing tools	(P) Cameras, sound recorders, editing equipment (DV) "Bread crumbs," saving histories, screen captures, animation and editing tools	

P = the physical world
DV = data visualization
M = the mind

Exploration

Think about a visualization tool optimized for an expert analyst whose job it is to immerse himself in a data set to discover interesting anomalies and features. Exactly what kinds of tools would be most effective in helping him make his way through this jungle? Imagine an expert ornithologist in a lush tropical rainforest hoping to discover and record a new species of bird of paradise (Figure 4.17).

You have to go through this...   ...to find this.

FIGURE 4.17
In the jungle.

In this terrain, the primary tools for simply getting around would probably include a map, a machete to cut through the blocking underbrush, and a compass to indicate orientation in the landscape. For the data analyst, the equivalent of the map would be a high-level overview; the machete would be filtering controls (e.g., sliders) to weed out the extraneous material. The analogue of the compass would be an area of the display that allowed him to retain his orientation and a sense of context.

Selection

Now contrast that kind of expedition with another one in which the same analyst has to lead a group of impatient company executives through some data to an interesting feature he has spotted. Going back to the story of the adventurous ornithologist for a moment, let's say he has caught a fleeting glimpse of what may be a new species of bird. It's not absolutely certain, so he has to marshal the evidence he has, perhaps some visuals and audio captured on a brief video recording, and make a case to his colleagues.

He's not going to retrace his journey with them all back to the same spot. The goal now has shifted from exploration to a choreographed tour in which each element is selected, edited, and combined to make the best case for the significance and validity of his findings. The primary tools for this new purpose are not all going to be the same as for exploration. The interaction needs shift to include the ability to show a particular path in a concise, interesting way that provides context for the ultimate point of interest. There's no time for exploration or waiting for the magic to happen. It's much the same situation for the data analyst—none of the execs want to see all the footage of every moment of the investigation; that would be too much information and would lose the audience's attention. The more crisp and concise the representation of the progression is, the better.

The question is, are the people adept at wielding the metaphorical machetes equally adept at working the camera, and if so, do they have all the tools they need to master both pathways at their disposal?

A wildlife filmmaker would want an array of camera and sound equipment to capture the rare birds for his audience. A data analyst, or whoever will present his work, might similarly want tools that can capture and animate key segments or sequences that led to an interesting discovery or insight. They should convey the right amount of information so as to capture his audience, and not so much that he loses their attention.

For a presentation, key segments of the journey can be chosen and then edited together. Choosing "what to leave in and what to leave out" can be no easy task—just ask any movie director or film editor. When making a case about an interesting finding in the data, it can be important to show some of the steps for getting there, so you don't want to leave out too much (Figure 4.18).

A well-crafted animation of how data changes over time also can help viewers get a better feel for the context. Imagine a wildlife documentary that only showed still shots of animals against a white background and nothing about their environment or how they move through it. Not only is it interesting to see the animals in context, it's interesting to see the process that was followed to capture them in their natural element. It can be fascinating to see how the filmmakers made the trek to reach the creatures.

Animation tools that capture and present only key parts
of the discovery process that led to an interesting finding

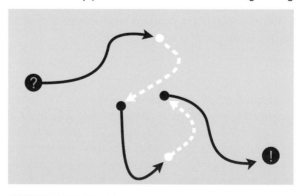

Full Data Exploration Process

FIGURE 4.18
What to leave out.

When creating a walkthrough or presentation, it can be a challenge to decide how much contextual material to provide (Figure 4.19). Too much, and you may lose the interest and attention of the audience as well as the thread of what's most important. Too little, and the audience simply may not have enough context, and the transitions may be too abrupt to maintain a meaningful narrative flow (Figure 4.20).

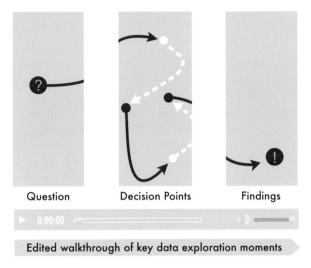

FIGURE 4.19

An optimized view—presenting the data.

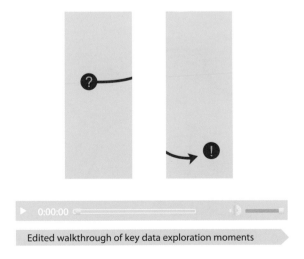

FIGURE 4.20

One cut too many.

Managers and data analysts have very different kinds of goals, so their paths through the data, the amount of time they spend going through them, and the tools they use are very different. The managers just want to see the birds; the analysts have to go out and look for them and then present them. Does the audience for the presentation want to see the "bird" in the data forest—or in a cage back at their base camp?

Analysts might try to increase their chances of finding the birds by collaborating with other analysts—by fanning out among the dense thicket of data.

Collaboration

The advent of online collaboration and visual pattern recognition tools adds another kind of process and new pathways through data. The concept of *open source computing* is based on sharing data and collaboration. *Crowdsourcing* is similar in that it is also based on pooling efforts and making data more widely available. It's a process that involves inviting people to participate and contribute their skills, time, and effort to complete a task or solve a problem.

An analyst could "crowdsource" the way the wildlife researcher could release all the raw audio and video he took instead of leaving most of it on the cutting room floor to create his documentary, and ask other researchers to view the recordings and see if they can find more within them. A highly motivated rare bird enthusiast might then pore through out-takes in the hopes of seeing something everyone else missed. She might even make her own discovery or documentary from that content based on someone else's footwork.

In Figure 4.21, each green square represents a person looking at only a section of the journey. Dividing up data about the journey into small chunks allows the participants to pay

Collaboration tools that allow greater participation
and closer inspections of paths through data

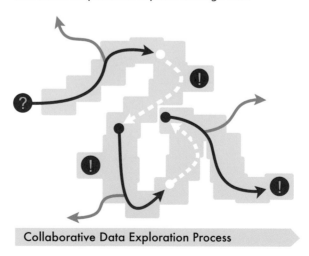

Collaborative Data Exploration Process

FIGURE 4.21
A tighter focus.

closer attention to their specific part of the whole. In doing so, there is a greater possibility of turning something up that might have been overlooked if only one person was reviewing all of it. Of course, tracing out new pathways doesn't always have to be strictly practical in nature. Lines also can lead down paths of the imagination.

Imagination

The most practical end points sometimes can only be reached by flights of the imagination. An architect or theoretical physicist can't do their job just through measurement. In their own ways, they create conceptual frameworks that can describe physical materials and forces. In those disciplines and many others, creatively analogizing and visualizing a problem can be very useful. In developing his theories of relativity, Einstein envisioned trolley cars hurtling near the speed of light, putting the unimaginable into something graspable at a human scale while still retaining key ideas. As another example, at least for me, it's easier to think of the nature of gravity and the warping of space if I first picture objects on a flexible sheet. Will data visualization tools help to stimulate people's imaginations by representing concepts in novel ways? That could prove to be one of their most important functions.

TIME TRAVEL, TRACKS, AND WAKES: VISUALIZING FLUX AND DATA

A lot of my works deal with a passage, which is about time. I don't see anything that I do as a static object in space. It has to exist as a journey in time.

– MAYA LIN

Pathways can help us find our way forward, but they also can show us where we've been (Figure 4.22). In the physical world, the tracks we make are often invisible or ephemeral. The footprints we leave in the sand at the shoreline or wakes behind a boat reveal the way we arrived at our immediate location, but they are temporary. Things are changing,

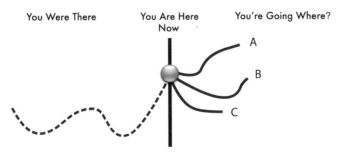

FIGURE 4.22
What's your move?

FIGURE 4.23
Fire in the hills. *Photo credit:* Bill Clayton.

however, as sensors, smart phones, high-powered computing, and visualizations make it possible, for better or worse, to track and display our movements.

Who knows what the ripple effects will be? Often, the lines displayed on a map are "hardwired" into the geography. These include state borders, roads, and personal property in a region. But sometimes very ephemeral lines can emerge on a landscape. Although they may be short-lived, they can instantly become the most important element in the terrain. Firelines are a prime example of this. They appear suddenly and don't play by the same set of rules as the other lines on the visualization. The lines of personal or state lands are formed in relation to each other and fixed, but a fireline will cross them or a road with impunity. The ability to effectively visualize these lines can be the difference between life and death (Figure 4.23).

Eric Frost, Director of the Visualization Center at San Diego State University, asks, "How do you display a dynamic and unfolding process, such as a natural disaster, in such a way that you can help the people dealing with it make better decisions?" One traditional form of visualization is drawing firelines on a map and tracking whether you're able to keep the fire contained within the lines. Frost says that in a major fire, traditionally the firelines would be generated only twice a day, and the quality of the lines would not provide much information about the nature of the wildfire. All the lines had a uniform thickness, but the conflagration was not so uniform—having a simple difference in line width in a visualization as an indicator could mean a big difference for the fire fighters. That picture now is starting to change.

Real-time data about a fire can provide simple but critical details about the contours of the blaze. Additionally, Frost says, the pattern of lines delineating that expansion and evolution can help firefighters formulate plans of attack. These patterns, like the rings of a tree, can tell a story about what is happening over time and from an overview perspective. For example, Frost says, in the case of the fireline's progress, a yellow ring is where the fire was yesterday, and a red ring is where the fire is burning today.

The information about the fireline from the people with their boots on the ground is vital, but so is the bird's-eye view. Each perspective adds more depth of understanding and forms a more complete picture of exactly where things are happening, what might happen next, and possible reasons why.

The lines and different perspectives of what is visible are not the only important elements in seeing and understanding the full picture. A pattern of arrows showing wind speed and direction provides an important layer of data in a simple form. Lines that show the overall pattern of wind direction can show the path that the fire is going to take in the future (Figure 4.24).

The shape of the smoke ascending to the sky also can provide important information. If the smoke rises directly up from the fire in a relatively straight line, that's an indication that there is no wind. However, if it flattens out, that suggests that winds are bending it, and the shape of the plume presents even more useful information. The wealth of data that comes from getting multiple views of patterns from all different perspectives can be a core feature of many kinds of visualization.

FIGURE 4.24

Which way the wind blows. The image shows the strong Santa Ana wind event in October 2007 that triggered multiple wildfires that destroyed 1500 homes. *Sources: The wind vectors were generated by a mesoscale atmosphere circulation model (MM5) for Southern California run by Professor Robert Fovell at UCLA. The Google Earth image was created by Peggy Li at JPL, Caltech.*

Infused with some design finesse and fed by real-time data, a simple line or icon can communicate key insights about the properties of a fire. For example, says Frost, in a 3D representation, an icon of a certain height near a fireline could indicate the temperature. An icon of one height may signify a 300° fire while another represents a 500° scorcher. The 300° fire is one that a firefighter can take on, a 500° one is not. The basic icon defines the line between the two conditions.

Data and the flow of commerce

In cyberspace, no one can hear you shop.

– PACO UNDERHILL

Just as people's pathways through physical space can be captured in a variety of ways, so, too, can less tangible routes through cyberspace be mapped. Visual representation of actions can tell us stories about patterns of human behaviors and actions. When combined with analytical tools and the insights of a practiced eye, visualizations can help fine-tune decisions about everything from online marketing campaigns to optimizing a website's landing pages. Web analytics help identify which landing pages are effective.

In the physical world, retail analysts can make direct observations about where and how people move around a store (Figure 4.25). These experts can predict and explain what people are going to gravitate toward and why. What are people looking at? Where are they hesitating and stopping? Jesse Nichols of Google Analytics says, "You would be able to get a good sense of this by watching the flow of traffic through a store's aisles."

FIGURE 4.25
Shopping circuits. *Source: Joyfull/Shutterstock.com.*

For online shopping, observations of people's passages through the retail experience have become easier to track. However, the process of observation is different and in some ways harder. If you're watching shoppers in a store, looking with delight and interest at a display or looking with uneasy puzzlement, you have a clear idea of the characteristics of their reaction to a specific thing. The representations that show people's movements and reactions in the cybermall are not tangible and have to be created by conscious effort and design (Figure 4.26). The shoppers' reactions must be interpreted from things such as "click-throughs," time spent on a page, transactions, and other traces left on the server logs.

Much more insight is needed as to why they're clicking on certain things and buying this or that. Being able to create visualizations that convey online shoppers' reactions would help marketers, supply chain professionals, business intelligence analysts, and others to make more informed, strategic decisions based on this information.

"Another barrier you can run into is a correlation threshold," says Nichols. "For example, what are the connections and the motivations behind customers purchasing various combinations of items? No machine can provide you with that kind of information." You need to understand the social context of a shopping list that, for example, would look like this:

- bag of rice
- newspaper
- water pistol
- toilet paper

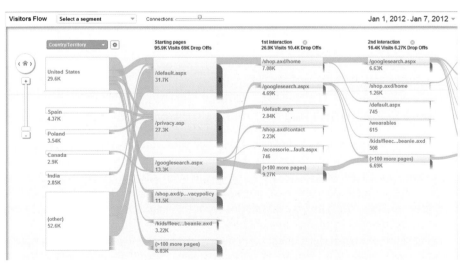

FIGURE 4.26
Click analysis, Google Analytics™.

Those may seem like a random assortment of items, but if you've ever been in the audience of a midnight screening of *The Rocky Horror Picture Show*, the picture is very clear.

Marketers and suppliers want to know the patterns of things you are purchasing, and understand the reasons behind them, so they can offer items you'll likely purchase in the future. For example, if you start buying a number of household tools online, you may notice many banner ads on your browser from home improvement stores.

Let's say a business invests $100,000 on a new interactive analytic tool intended to increase their sales volume or save money. How can you tell if this tool is really working as effectively as possible?

Nichols says there's a balance between taking approaches that are either overly broad or too narrow. You don't want to get too granular. "It often can be better to aggregate what you need," Nichols believes. That means pulling together the data you think might be useful. Too few data points can be tough to interpret in a meaningful way. On the other hand, sometimes you don't want to work with, or amass, too much as it will be hard to know what to do with it. You may then need to segment out by various demographic measures, for example, to get any useful information.

"Although most people do reporting with Google Analytics, they use it as a reporting tool rather than a tool for discovery," says Nichols. "The highest ideal is discovery." Many analysts do the investigation but stop short in the process, and the decision makers may not have the complete picture. Visualization tools can help accelerate basic analysis and foster exploration.

DATA AND THE NARRATIVE PATH

What is it that makes a film, a game, or a book great for you? For me, it starts with how well it draws me in. It's when I become an instant and involved participant. It's when I'm able to briefly go beyond my own field of vision and, when I return, see things in a different light. The best works of fiction and nonfiction also reflect the world as it actually is—full of complexity, ambiguity, and contradiction. They do all this within a framework that allows for a sense of coherency and meaning.

Whether it is for two hours or two minutes, they tell you an interesting story that has many dimensions. They make you think, but they don't tell you how. They can point you in a direction, but they don't force you there. Even better, at least for me, they can make you question your own biases and assumptions, make you more attuned to the unexpected and inspired to look for more. Perhaps most importantly of all, they can help you think about the world on multiple levels and recalibrate your own thinking. They take you on a journey, and the more you invest in them, the more they can give back.

Making sense of massively abundant and diverse data with interactive visualizations is a relatively new frontier, but there are already many great inroads; there are also many beautiful colorful mirages shimmering over the vast expanses of data. From a distance, they look like they will help us, but look a little closer, and they vanish before us, and our thirst for information remains unquenched. Then too, our deeply rooted tendency to construct stories from apparent patterns in unrelated bits of data can sometimes lead to what is called the "narrative fallacy." The ability of stories to capture our hearts and minds is double-edged—there's always the danger of creating, reinforcing, and proliferating misguided ideas. There's more work to be done in merging art and science together, using visuals, words, and numbers, to meaningfully and simply think about data.

Finding stories in the paths

The hard part of professional journalism going forward is writing about what hasn't been written about, directing attention where it hasn't been, and saying something new.

– SETH GODIN

"Follow the money," an iconic Watergate-era adage from the film "All the President's Men," have become words to live by for a good investigative journalist. The same could also be said for certain types of visualizations. Many new ways to follow the flows of money can be visually arresting and tell interesting stories. One of my personal favorite visualizations tells a story about movie genres and the film industry itself in a way that is memorable and engaging. Designed by *The New York Times*' Amanda Cox, the graphic uses colored streams of box office receipt data with seasonal variations based on genre.

   Cox says, to arrive at a visualization such as this she has to do a lot of "sketching with data to figure out the shapes and patterns that emerge and what does this picture represent?" The medium she uses may be different, but even a journalist from the earliest days of print could still relate to the essential process: collect facts, think about their relationships and meanings, distill what matters, and try to find a good way to convey that. "The movie graphic is good because of the annotation layer," she says. The following QR codes will lead you to the static and interactive versions, respectively.

http://goo.gl/yNKh2

http://goo.gl/7IB3z

Cox notes that she and her colleagues tend to employ limited interactivity to avoid giving people a lot of data and forcing them to make any sense of it. As she puts it, "We're not throwing a lot of data at them and saying 'good luck with that.'" She adds that in many of their examples, "we consciously haven't given away a lot of control."

Cox spends a lot of her time figuring out the primary forms, patterns, and narratives that dwell in data sets and thinks about how to communicate this to the public. "It's really figuring out the shape and patterns and what the picture conveys," she says. This process often begins with voluminous sketching using numbers, words, images, and ideas such as changes over time and the directions of those changes. For example, Cox and her colleagues at *The Times* wanted to show the shifting tides of demographics and political sentiment over time across the United States by comparing the 2010 congressional midterm elections to elections in 2002.

Creating a visualization such as one that shows the ebbs and flows of political sentiment over a period of years in a compact and immediately graspable way doesn't happen in a single, predefined way. Cox, drawing on her knowledge of statistics and mixing that with gut instincts, creates a number of rough sketches to see what best captures the feel of the data. That can mean throwing out many ideas before coming to the core of a visualization idea that merits further development.

Same path, different point of view

Whether it's a hiking trail or a narrative pathway, even when we're all moving along in the same direction, that doesn't mean we're all seeing the same things. The mindset, expectations, and point of view of each person on the journey will influence what they experience. Even a seemingly straightforward infographic or application interface can sometimes be a bit of a Rorschach test for users.

One memorable cinematic example of this effect is an infographic from the film *Fight Club* that had an interesting take on the passenger safety cards in airlines. This infographic was conveying important information on a few different levels, just not the expected ones.

It describes a process that was going on in the mind of the main character, while also informing a larger story in the movie. It also conveys an alternative view of what the cabin environment would really be like in an emergency compared to the necessarily sanitized imagery we normally see on the pamphlets we are all required to refer to during takeoff.

Instead of the placid, calm people depicted, we see frantic screaming men and women, plumes of smoke coming from a disembodied plane, a plane plunging into the ocean, confusing seatbelt instructions, two passengers fighting to exit from a burning doorway, a father pushing his crying child away as he grabs his own oxygen mask... You get the picture; it's unfortunately a more "real" (albeit comically dramatic) version of an airline disaster. As viewers of the movie, we have only a limited view of what the infographic means; the meaning only becomes fully clear near the end of the film.

A lot more can be done to help us see for ourselves the many hidden things that matter to us and on which our lives sometimes depend. In *Rashomon*, the classic film by Akira Kurosawa, four people who became caught up in a crime each offered radically different descriptions of the event. These accounts were shaped by their roles and vantage points (attacker, victim, etc.) as well as their individual social and psychological needs. Sometimes, gaining the fullest understanding of the dynamics of social networks (in the broadest sense rather than the Internet sense) requires multiple viewpoints.

The perception of any social interaction, and the part people play in it, is often multifaceted, ephemeral, and subject to many internal and external forces. What is the best way to look at a problem? Often, getting the clearest sense of an issue emerges from looking at it in different ways. The *Rashomon* effect applies here. Multiple views of the same problem may offer insights that just one view does not. However, that doesn't mean the display has to be overly complicated or cumbersome.

The plotline thickens

And these little things may not seem like much, but after a while they take you off on a direction where you may be a long way off from what other people have been thinking about.

– ROGER PENROSE

Either by choice or otherwise, people can be easily, and often, distracted. That's not necessarily always a bad thing.

At times, all of us need brief breaks and micro holidays to daydream, process, and assimilate new information and ideas. In data presentation and analysis, directing and holding viewers' attention at key points in a sequence is necessary, but giving them room to have productive cognitive side trips and internal dialogs along the way can be even more important. For these kinds of interactions, some concepts from the world of literature can come into play. Novelists, screenwriters, and playwrights have narrative structure that leads us down a specific path. However, that doesn't mean we don't bring our own associations along the way. Perhaps we're caught up in a passage or scene in one moment, but in the next we put the book down for a while or reach for a handful of popcorn. That's all part of the process of interaction.

Michael Witmore, the Director of the Folger Shakespeare Library and a textual data miner, believes, "Culture is a way to reorganize our attention." The following describe a few ways of organizing people's experience and attention as they move down a narrative pathway (Figure 4.27).

On- and off-ramps

These are the points in a plotline, Witmore says, where the audience's attention can be clearly directed, or allowed to briefly wander. Sentences or lines of a play, Witmore believes, can be a form of off-ramp of thought and experience. One of the challenges for a playwright, or a person trying to tell a story with data, is figuring out good places for the off-ramps and making sure the on-ramps will be effective for getting people back on the main flow.

Directing attention

Although subplots and side stories can make a narrative more rich and entertaining, at times they can just get in the way. Witmore says reducing the diversions and distractions in a narrative to direct the audience's attention at key points is important. People can take pleasure following the path that a writer or filmmaker has created, but they periodically may stray from the path. It's the author's job to recapture them at key points along the way. One tool for this kind of experiential catch-and-release interaction is thought constraint. Witmore says that during his presentations, he will stop using visuals at certain points. Limiting the use of images at key times, he believes, can sharpen the audience's focus on his words. For a data visualization, the balance and volume may be modulated to produce a similar effect.

Detours, blind alleys, and red herrings

A skillful storyteller, Witmore says, will introduce side directions and obscure areas to heighten curiosity, expectations, and tensions in the audience. This can create a more vivid and engaging narrative path. A plot in which the protagonist moves directly and effortlessly from the beginning to completion of a quest probably would not engage people. The twists and turns, tensions, and resolutions encountered along the way are what provide depth and richness to the journey.

The artificiality paradox

An interesting psychological phenomenon associated with works of fiction, Witmore says, involves the idea that imaginary scenes can provide a "safe distance" to enable deeper engagement with real issues. The awareness by audiences that a play, movie, or novel is only a facsimile of reality somehow—paradoxically—allows them enough psychological distance to grapple with certain material more closely than they might in real life. A person can witness a conflict or someone in danger and not have to do anything about it, yet they still may be powerfully affected or moved by it.

Perhaps some of the same methods and techniques that help works of fiction come alive in people's minds can be thoughtfully—and ethically—applied to enliven the stories in the data. They can provide more depth, resonance, and immediacy. Also, for many of us, focused attention can be a limited resource. We can encounter many…[5 new messages in your Inbox]…distractions along the way. The more a story can hold our focus, the more

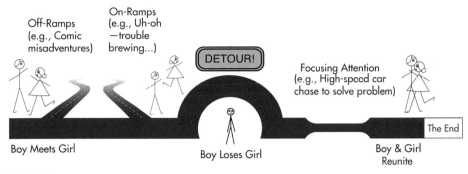

FIGURE 4.27
The narrative path.

we can gain from it. Chances are, the same is true for visualizations that are compelling enough to keep us looking at important data.

CROSSING POINTS AND GRAPH VISUALIZATIONS

In 1735, a brainteaser circulating among puzzle lovers in Europe ultimately had a big impact on certain forms of data analysis and visualization. It involved determining the existence of a specific pathway in the town of Königsberg, and the Swiss mathematician Leonhard Euler definitively solved it. In figuring out the solution, he set a course for analyzing, visualizing, and making predictions about data. Here was the question: The Pregel River flowed through the town, dividing it into different areas, and seven bridges spanned the river and connected the areas. Could someone cross all seven of the bridges while only crossing each one once? (See Figures 4.28 and 4.29.)

Euler figured out that the drawing could be simplified to only a few dots and lines that nevertheless captured the essential elements that needed to be considered. Showing the geographic distances between points wasn't relevant to the solution, so this drawing could have many variations as long as it showed the right number of points and lines (Figure 4.30).

It turns out the answer to the puzzle question is no. Euler showed this by taking away the real-world topography and abstracting and simplifying the problem to its essentials. This process enabled the question to be explored mathematically. This laid the foundation for graph theory and network mapping, which are integral parts of many aspects of network analysis, predictive modeling, and data visualization. Deeply understanding and tracing out this pathway problem opened up ideas for creating algorithms to help uncover insights and predictions about entirely new types of data, ranging from social networks to metabolic pathways.

Starting with a real-world question about paths and bridges, Euler created a systematic mathematical and visual approach to solve the puzzle and save the townspeople from wearing themselves out on a fruitless quest. By abstracting the problem and breaking it

FIGURE 4.28
The bridges of Königsberg.

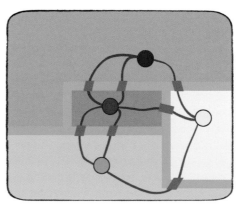

FIGURE 4.29
The schematic of Königsberg.

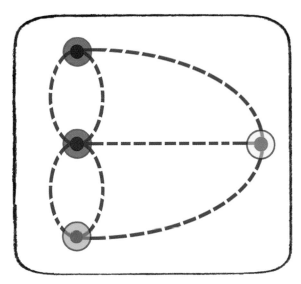

FIGURE 4.30
The abstraction of Königsberg.

down to its essential elements, the solution became clearer. The method that helped the townsfolk back then still applies to much more complex and pressing issues today.

This insight has an important impact and implications for many fields that need to work with network visualizations. Network graphs can reveal patterns and pathways with lines and dots representing gargantuan numbers of data points. Pathways and connecting points that can be hard to fully grasp in the world can sometimes become revealed with a little help from Euler and his legacy of problem solving with graphs. As our ability to store more and more data continues, and our networks grow in size and complexity, having the ability to conceptually navigate around massive interconnected systems becomes more and more critical for those who manage them.

BRIDGES, NETWORKS, AND ROLES

But which is the stone that supports the bridge?

– KUBLAI KHAN

How do the roles and tools of the people who make something like Figure 4.31 correspond to those who make something like Figure 4.32?

The same fundamental approaches that apply to some of the earliest forms of human invention are still applicable to our most advanced digital tools. Thinking about physical bridges, for example, can be helpful in describing the range of visualization requirements for the various kinds of people working with digital networks. Whether a bridge is constructed

FIGURE 4.31
Traffic crossing the San Francisco Bay.

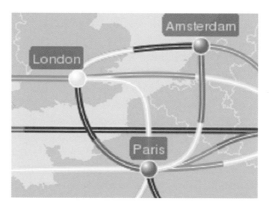

FIGURE 4.32
Data traffic moving around the world.

from wood and stone, steel and concrete, or any other material, the people building it have highly specific kinds of information needs and design constraints:

- *Design and construction:* Creating the optimal architecture and engineering for the given needs and resources. Before starting work on the actual structure, it's important to create models to see how the bridge holds up under the stresses and strains of various conditions.

- *Operations and maintenance:* Making sure everything is running as it should, fine tuning the adjustable elements, and responding to problems.

- *Assessments and planning:* The impact the system is having on the environment and the environment on the system.

FIGURE 4.33
The bridge over untroubled water.

In the distant past, bridge makers may have had to rely on the resources at hand in their surroundings and use the materials that would work best for the conditions of the local environment (Figure 4.33). Now, too, people often have to do the best they can with what they have available. Computer network architects have to build their systems within a variety of constraints: budgetary, technical (e.g., percentage of legacy versus newer hardware and software), physical (e.g., the size of the server room), expertise and man-power, and external and internal demand requirements.

Jonathan Garzon is a network engineer and Director of Product Management at Cariden, a company that offers design, planning, and operational automation intelligence for managing complex networks. He says network designers need to see how their creations will fare in a range of situations and if the ways they have assembled the building blocks can support the traffic going over them. They must design these systems so that the traffic flows as smoothly as possible without chokepoints, dead ends, or inefficient routes. What sketching and testing tools will these types of architects need?

Designing, monitoring, and maintaining digital networks

From the viewpoint of network designers, some of the key visualization needs include interactivity, customizable views, and layout patterns (e.g., horizontal/vertical) for a particular kind of network, and the ability to add notes.[1]

Once a large-scale bridge is built, entirely new sets of people have the role of monitor-ing and maintaining it. They, too, will have many specific information needs, and they may

---

[1]In the expansive world of data visualization, a range of terms can be used to describe roughly similar things. In the network visualization design discussion that follows, the term "link" means a line or "edge" connecting nodes in a network graph.

require a different set of tools and views from those used by the builders. Their picture likely will not be based on simulations but on measurements of forces in real time. For example, the new people may need to see how the stresses and strains of traffic are affecting the structure. With everything already in place, the task is now to see if it's holding up as expected and, if not, how to make changes to ensure that this structure will not come crashing down.

Similarly, with networks, these views include checking the flow of traffic over the course of the day and determining what that is doing to the system. Visualizations of these changing conditions on the network often are called "weather maps." Whereas bridge builders may regularly need to think in time frames of many decades, the people managing the bridge need to think in intervals of days and hours, as with weather forecasts. For people charged with monitoring networks, the time compression and the volume of information flow can be even more intense.

Garzon says, "The design goal is to help these users immediately identify what and where the problems are." In the visualization designs for Operations people to monitor their network state, it's increasingly important to simplify the data streams so unimportant and extraneous details don't overwhelm those users. "It's important to have the ability to visually de-clutter the network operational weather map so the trouble areas become immediately apparent," says Garzon. "A network designer has to have more in-depth information than someone who works in Operations; however, the designer cannot act on those details. The Operational people must be the ones to implement any changes based on the data provided by the software."

Cariden's software allows users to quickly identify network issues by seeing indicators. Among other things, users see depictions of pathways using colors to represent the status or the speed of the data flow (Figure 4.34). They also need to be able to zoom in on the system to the trouble spot, so the application takes that into account, as well.

A very simple example of representing data in a link is the "class of service" that link supports. "In a network design, you prioritize some certain kinds of traffic over others," says Garzon. For example, voice is a more time-sensitive component of traffic than a file transfer. Different classes of service have their own color codes. Creating visualizations that show what class of traffic is flowing over the network at a particular moment is an ongoing challenge, he says.

Strategic planning

Physical bridges can have a significant impact on not only the physical traffic flows of a region, but also on the economic and social patterns as well. These patterns may not all be entirely foreseeable before the bridge is constructed. Tolls may bring in additional funds for the state but might create more car congestion headaches for the city. The changing flux of people may spur or limit economic growth in unexpected ways. The people who have to monitor and address these changes are different from those in charge of the day-to-day maintenance; they are the state and local administrators.

The city planner, for example, is more concerned with how the economy is going based on his new bridge—how much the tolls are bringing in compared to how much it cost to

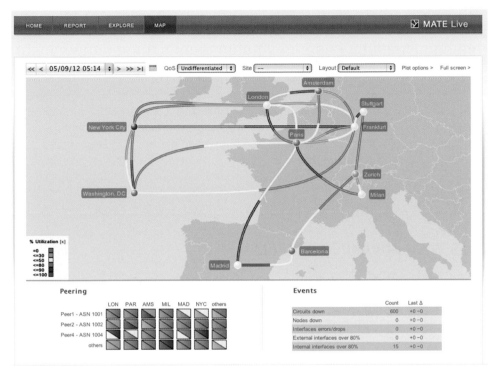

FIGURE 4.34
Networking by colors.

build the bridge. Such stakeholders require yet another very different set of views of the bridge and the changing context around it. Garzon notes, "There is a certain continuity between the operational people and designers." However, "For the businessperson, it is good to know if they are making money and to be able to set the right level of how much to sell their service for. In some respects, while bridge builders have to think about the future and anticipate a range of eventualities, the administrators have to also collect, review, and interpret past and current performance."

Cariden's MATE software includes data analytics specific to their customers' networks and is used for capacity planning and traffic management of wide area networks (WANs). "The analytics involve looking at their networks historically and projecting what they might look like in the future," explains Garzon. "Network analysis services are very dynamic and include aggregation of measures such as network technical information, network costs, and what money they are (or could be) generating." The information gleaned from these data analytics allows customers to make critical business decisions based on the information they gather.

For both bridges and digital networks, intersecting and overlaying physical and geographical data with dynamic data can be very useful. Dynamic data about traffic flows over a bridge is affected by the physical features and context. The same is true for various aspects of the data that traverses digital networks. In both examples, the only way to fully understand a situation is to see a picture that encompasses the tangible and intangible. For example, says Garzon, customers are able to ask "What is the region in the United States that is carrying the least traffic?" There are a lot of factors and parameters for them to take into account at the same time, and they have to deal with a lot more information, he says.

The world of data transport is arguably integral to global economies and infrastructure. People who design and provide the pathways for this information are finding that data analytics and visualizations are becoming more needed than ever before. Internet service providers (ISPs) are coming to realize more each day how critical it is to have the ability to visualize something as massive and ever changing as global telecommunications traffic.

DOTS WITH ADVANCED DEGREES

So far in this chapter we've toured pathways and lines of various kinds. Now, let's stop off at a few points where lines originate, connect, converge, and terminate. I'll generally refer to these points as "dots," although they actually can be any number of shapes, icons, photos, or other visual forms. In network visualization terminology, these dots are more precisely referred to as "nodes" or "vertices," and the connecting lines are called "edges." Although there are good reasons for using the terms "vertex" and "edge" in discussing graphs, for this discussion I'm mainly going to rely on the relatively more familiar and intuitive language.

In a network graph, the number of connecting edges describes the qualities of a vertex, or, put another way, the lines define the dot. The more lines attach to the dot, the higher the dot's "degree" (Figure 4.35). Dots with many lines or high degrees begin to look like a wheel with many spokes. The dots at the hub of these spokes represent a great deal of impact and influence over an entire network.

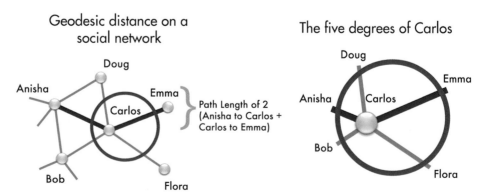

FIGURE 4.35
The Carlos network.

The point of local knowledge

A dot on a geographic display can identify a specific location precisely, but without any of the associated metadata, it generally has very little value. Sure, that orange spot may give us the "where," but the who, what, when, why, and how are absent.

The more local knowledge we have, the more meaning the dot takes on. In the case of Figure 4.36, let's say that point represents me walking my dog at 1:52 p.m. on April 24, 1998. It was windy there as usual, but clear and beautiful, and I paused for a moment to look out over the bay and at the island of Alcatraz.

We can infuse a dot with metadata in many ways to give it meaning. The descriptive words I associated with that picture are not necessarily the most efficient way to provide context to the dot. Do we have anything in the data visualization toolbox to do the same thing more effectively—not only a way to give this data some life but also a way to assess the level of accuracy? Although the scene I just described took place at that time and

FIGURE 4.36
A dot, yes, but so much more.

location, the satellite image in the figure was taken many years later. There is a certain degree of validity and accuracy, but not completely. In this case, the usefulness of an image to convey a location may outweigh the fact that it was not taken in the right time frame, even if the metadata we might want may not be present. However, that's not always the case.

Making tracks

The ability to pinpoint people's location at any moment as they go about their day is improving as the number of smart mobile devices proliferates. Whatever your perspective on privacy, the amount of metadata or local knowledge about you is big and getting bigger.

The story of the German politician Malte Spitz is a telling example. He sued a big telephone company to release his cell phone data, which he then had converted to a visualization to show just how detailed a picture of his movements the data could paint. If you go to the site where this graphic appears—http://goo.gl/3meVj—and click anywhere on one of the gray bars in the calendar area, it will show exactly where Spitz was at that time.

http://goo.gl/3meVj

In the following two interviews, we'll look at how, even when working with maps and dots, issues ranging from visual design to ethical and journalistic concerns can come into play.

MORE THAN DOTS ON A MAP (PERSPECTIVES FROM USHAHIDI'S PATRICK MEIER)

Patrick Meier is an expert on the application of new technologies for crisis early warning, humanitarian response, human rights, and civil resistance. He is Director of Crisis Mapping at the NGO (nongovernmental organization) Ushahidi. The organization's name, and the technology platform it supports, comes from the Swahili word meaning "testimony." It began as a way to map reports of violence in Kenya from citizens following a set of elections in that country. Since that time, it has grown to the point where it's used for tracking and mapping crises around the globe.

Visualizing crises and conflicts

Data visualization tools can play an essential role in helping to monitor and manage responses to natural disasters and human conflicts, as discussed earlier with regards to wildfires. According to Meier, primary benefits that visualizations can provide are real-time situational awareness about events as they unfold and enabling of "actionable insights and decision support from the data." In the aftermath of an earthquake, for example, where is the need for water, food, or medicine most acute? What are the routes and precise spots to bring in supplies or take out survivors? In the midst of regional violence, what is needed by refugees, and who might be aiding or interfering with that process? What is the direction of the spread of an infectious disease or a band of attacking thugs?

In these critical situations, where big decisions have to be made in short periods of time, the clarity and usability of a visualization is vital. "Unfortunately there are still more bad ways to do data visualization than good ones out there in this arena," says Meier. "We are still at early stages for crisis and conflict visualization," lagging behind areas such as drug discovery or business intelligence, where there's more money behind the efforts.

However, things are rapidly changing and evolving. More research and development may come from external sources that could help redefine the game. Meier thinks much of the innovation in crisis management tools will emerge from cross-fertilization among different disciplines and skill sets. For example, the visualization approaches that geophysicists apply to viewing seismic data might be repurposed to better represent regional and political stress points. National and regional borders can be viewed as a form of dynamic and interacting system of fault lines. In his work, Meier says he wants to "really understand data that changes over time and space," and visualizations allow him to keep track of those temporal and geographic shifts (Figure 4.37).

Eyeing the dots

In the course of his work, Meier encounters many people who say, "What we do is 'simply putting dots on a map.'" However, he thinks this is an outmoded view of crisis mapping

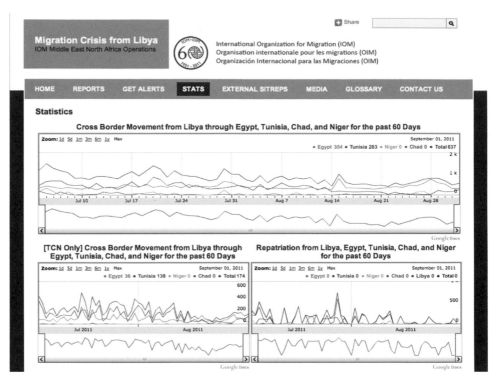

FIGURE 4.37

The Libyan diaspora.

and data visualization. By feeding dynamic data into 3D immersive environments and incorporating creative designs, and motion, even dots can be effectively pumped up to provide insights about crises. Among the mapping tools that Meier thinks are exemplars of expanding the concept and use of the dot is GeoTime (Figure 4.38).

In 3D visualizations, a variety of shapes can expand the roles of what was only done by dots on a map. The textures, banding, and rings can all convey useful details (Figure 4.39). For first responders, analysts, and other types of users, some training and experience with these representations can help them make better informed assessments without too much additional cognitive effort.

Of course, points of interest don't have to be displayed only as static dots. Shapes of various sizes, colors, and kinds can tell a more differentiated and detailed story of what is going on in an area of interest (see Figure 4.40 on page 184).

These patterns and shapes can sometimes transcend natural languages and form "a common geometric language." This lingua franca of shapes may not always be applicable, but in certain situations where time is short and the relief efforts come from a multinational team, the visual language could be a basis for consensus and action.

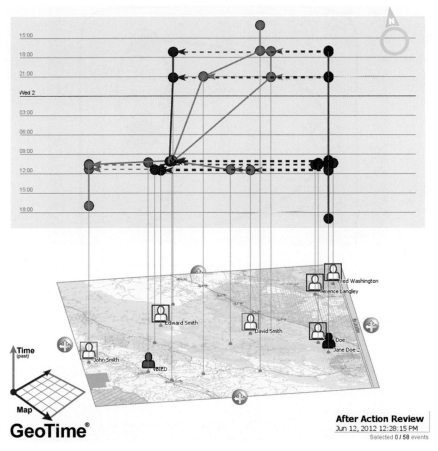

FIGURE 4.38
Increased dimensionality. GeoTime® is a registered trademark of Oculus Info Inc. Image courtesy of and © 2012 Oculus Info Inc.

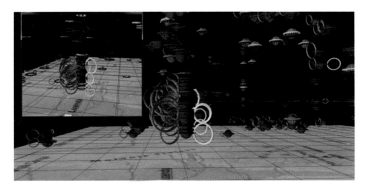

FIGURE 4.39
Rings of meaning.

FIGURE 4.40
The Esperanto of visualization.

MORE THAN JUST DATA POINTS

The following are perspectives from architect and data visualization designer Sha Hwang. Sha Hwang began his career as an architect who quickly gravitated to the computer-assisted tools of the trade, such as 3D modeling software. He also started working with data visualization tools such as the Processing environment/programming language, which led to an interest in building his own visualization tools. Around the same time, Hwang began exploring some of the data that applied to his own life, including the stats about what music he was listening to and his spending habits. Hwang describes two projects that illustrate the possibilities, and limitations, of simple dots, lines, and other shapes in conveying information about deeply emotional subjects.

"Home and away"

The factors that go into choosing the level of detail for a data visualization display are not always straightforward. There is an interaction between the quality of the supporting data, overall design goals, subject matter, creators' choices, technical capacities, and the nature of the audience. The way data is organized, edited, and visually rendered has a deeply human quality. Grouping or "rolling up" data points into larger chunks, rather than showing them individually, can simplify the design of a visualization considerably. However, not all kinds of data points may be appropriate for rolling up. If it's gasoline purchases in a certain zip code, that's one kind of data point.

But what if the data being shown represents the starting and ending points of the life of a soldier who died while serving in Iraq or Afghanistan? What does it mean when a few colored pixels on the screen stand for a victim of violent crime? Hwang worked on a project while at Stamen Design called "Home and Away" for *CNN.com* that visualizes the casualties in Iraq.

http://goo.gl/4XtzX

"When I began the project," Hwang recalls, "I kept scrolling through all the faces with a lot of emotion. One of the very first images I saw made me cry." Hwang thinks that there's "a necessary distance in many designs, and the designer is typically not a subject matter expert." He worked with a person at CNN who was curating a list of casualities. Working with this large and profoundly emotional data set immediately presented several design and technical challenges. Making the choice to make the data more individualized puts stresses on the infrastructure to present it.

According to Hwang, "There were so many casualties that it would hurt the ability of the technical system to deliver the content." He says the project team had to work very hard to avoid rolling up the data. Because of the subject matter and content, he made it a priority to "get as granular as possible." That is, as a sign of respect for the people he was describing, he knew the data deserved the highest level of detail and specificity possible.

Hwang says that when they originally started working with CNN, the project was scoped to include an interactive map. However, the news people ended up making a page for every soldier for more depth and completeness. Although those decisions expanded the project, he says, the end results were far more compelling and in keeping with the subject matter. Beyond the level of granularity, the subject matter of "Home and Away" had intangible qualities with tangible impacts and constraints on many design choices. The solemn and somber character of the data set meant that bright, clearly distinguishable colors would not fit the tone and tenor of the display. Because hues can be a powerful asset in a data-rich display, working with only blacks, whites, and grays requires more skilled and thoughtful design.

"Crime spotting"

Some of the same considerations about the best way to handle emotionally charged data came up in work he did for Stamen Design involving crime statistics in Oakland, California, in a project called "Crime Spotting." Whereas one of the key goals in the Home and Away project was to make the facts as impactful and visceral as possible but still accurate, in other visualization projects, Hwang says, it's less about getting into the emotions of the visuals than diving into the geographical analytics, even when the subject matter is much more than just facts and figures. How do you convey this in a quick way? How do you show the "shape of crime" for a geographical area in a visual display?

It's not about displaying every single crime. One of the gray areas of deciding what crime numbers to display and how to represent them involves the issue of persistence. When a new crime appears in the data and subsequently in the display, determining how long it should remain visible before going away becomes a judgment call. Should it disappear after a week or a month?

Hwang says that, rather than applying a new visual language to express the numbers, he wanted, as much as possible, to let the map reveal its own story. "There was as little design intervention as possible," he says, and the contours of color "emerge from the streets" (Figure 4.41).

The statistics, in relation to the geographical form of the city, shaped the final output. He says the team working on the project was explicitly trying not to "smooth out the edges." Even so, there were still challenges and choices to be made at the data level. Hwang remembers that there was a constant debate of whether to use "per capita or just the straight numbers." Those kinds of choices involving which type of statistical measurement to use obviously can have a significant impact on viewers' impressions of the situation.

Questions about statistics and design can quickly, perhaps inevitably, merge into editorial judgments. "The more we were creating an algorithm for this," Hwang recalls, "the more we were becoming journalists." How do you "weigh" the impact of various crimes? Is a shooting, for example, ten times more significant than a car theft? Because of almost impossibly nuanced design choices such as that, they shied away from making the

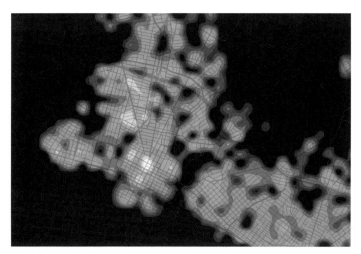

FIGURE 4.41

Heating up in Oakland. *Courtesy of Stamen Design.*

heatmaps more complex. Each crime is weighted the same, and color intensity was used to visually represent the quantity of the raw numbers.

The heatmap only provides a certain level of detail and does not provide the reasons for some of its prominent visual features. For example, Hwang says, in one very high crime neighborhood in San Francisco called the Tenderloin, 80% of the narcotics arrests are of people who don't live in the area. The heatmap alone will not display that fact.

Many people are much better at perceiving shapes and colors than doing math, so a visual impression may create a compelling interpretation. Counteracting that tendency with the more subtle and nuanced aspects of the story contained in the numbers will be an ongoing concern in data visualizations of all kinds. Ultimately, although displays such as heatmaps can call our attention to features and patterns in data that can be extremely useful, they can become even more powerful if they enable easy access to the metadata. "Interactivity is so crucial in this," Hwang says. Hwang's experience at Stamen has inspired further explorations of visualizing local crime statistics at his current company, real estate site Trulia (Figures 4.42 and 4.43).

"Shaping the flow of cities"

Hwang says some of the most interesting visualizations are the ones that "basically become invisible." That is to say, the display becomes so embedded in a person's perceptions that it recedes from conscious awareness. Even so, it still brings richness and added dimensionality to the environment. Hwang says people used to get driving directions by writing a turn list—"a very algorithmic format." Now, Hwang says, he depends on GPS displays; a familiar refrain to many of us.

From his perspective as an architect, smart phones have done more to change the way we look at streets than the way we look at physical structures. "There is the whole world of

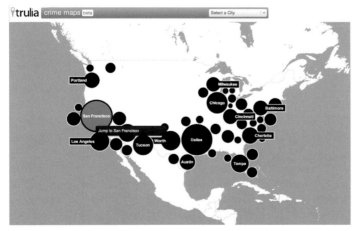

FIGURE 4.42
Interactive crime map. *Courtesy of Trulia.*

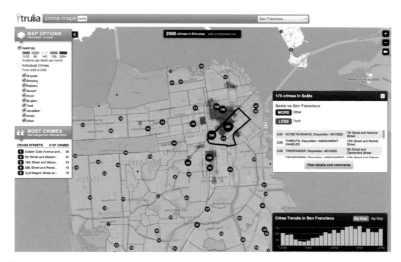

FIGURE 4.43
Details of crime stats in San Francisco. *Courtesy of Trulia.*

architects," he says, "who always talk about 'changing cities,' but the building only exists at a certain, specific point." Visualizations of various kinds can overlay the built environment and, as it is often described, "augment reality." They provide a kind of flexible and dynamic second infrastructure in our surroundings and, to some to extent, channel our movements and actions.

Although these structures are often barely noticeable, they can have the most impact on our daily lives. For example, even more than the signature skyscrapers of New York, Hwang notes, the subway system or a mobile phone application can have the greatest impact on our everyday experience. "Technologies like the iPhone, have changed the way I move around the city more than any building." He adds, the stuff that is less visible is "shaping the flow of the city."

POINTS TO REMEMBER

As a single footstep will not make a path on the earth, so a single thought will not make a pathway in the mind. To make a deep physical path, we walk again and again. To make a deep mental path, we must think over and over the kind of thoughts we wish to dominate our lives.

– HENRY DAVID THOREAU

In this chapter, we've looked at various ideas arising from relatively simple representations of lines and dots. As we've seen, even simple representations can pack a lot of punch. Their power lies in the data they are conveying, the design in which they appear, and, most importantly, the person who is looking at them. It is the viewer who ultimately invests the visualization with impact and meaning. A map such as the one in "Home and Away" can show a scattering of small dots, and that's all they are unless we can see these simple images as signifiers of soldiers' lives lost in service, or survivors who can be saved in the aftermath of a crisis.

I've purposely stayed with basic building blocks in this chapter to point out that there can be depth in simplicity. There are many more complex visual forms, but I like to think that the most layered and richest visualizations happen inside the viewer's own mind, sparked by thoughtful displays.

Views You Can Use

GETTING THROUGH

The two words "information" and "communication"' arc often used interchangeably, but they signify quite different things. Information is giving out; communication is getting through.

– SYDNEY J. HARRIS

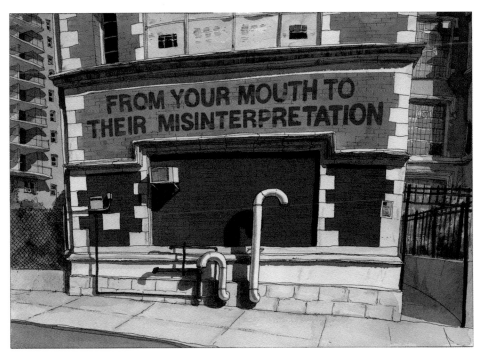

FIGURE 5.1

All Over Coffee #566, Manhattan, New York, by Paul Madonna.

Have you ever been to a long meeting that concluded with seemingly clear next steps, only to find later that everyone walked away with different and conflicting ideas about the way forward? If the key terms and assumptions of the discussion are not well communicated and understood, what has really gotten through? Everyone may be using the same words, but they're still not speaking the same language. It's a form of conversational cryptography based on the simple fact that we often have varied interpretations of the "obvious."

Early in my career as an interaction designer, I learned not to talk with clients about generic "users." The generic and vague quality of the term allowed for a world of different understanding and conclusions about what to do, because everyone had a different mental image of who the "user" was. It was crucial to describe specific types of users in very concrete ways—in terms of specific user profiles. That helped keep conversations about design much clearer and more direct. (I admit to still using the term *user* often, as do many of my colleagues, as shorthand even in this book, but I never forget that, ultimately, the generic user or *average user* is a meaningless idea out of context.)

If understanding the needs and mental models of different individuals is important for, say, improving the *user experience* design of an online store's interface, it will be even more critical for a medical researcher or intelligence analyst. When even relatively straightforward processes such as online shopping can present a wide array of design challenges and opportunities, what happens when the tasks are complex, open-ended, and full of gray areas? How does the meaning of the data get through to the people viewing it? It's one thing to create arresting and intricate visual images with data as the source material; designing displays that spark meaningful insights and foster deeper understanding in the people who look at them is another story.

Generally, the point of visualizations is to present abstract data in more concrete, comprehensible forms. A presupposed story or predefined question is not necessarily required. It can sometimes just be a case of making flows of data available to our senses so that our minds can detect interesting patterns for us to consider. As with any other type of communication, many kinds of interactions play a role in what is presented and what is understood. It's important to understand the audience, including setting the level of description so it allows for audience comprehension. The audience, on the other hand, needs to consider the source. Is the person giving the investment advice unbiased? Is the "doctor" offering health advice a quack trying to sell snake oil or a reliable source?

In the realm of user interface design, there are many tried and true approaches to understanding users. In this chapter, I'll highlight these methods and techniques and discuss their application to data visualization. The chapter will also explore a variety of ways communications can get garbled. This is not just about how communications of data can get lost in translation from person to person, but also about the ways an individual user can arrive at the wrong conclusions when the available views of the data are limited. In my opinion, it will become ever more essential to factor in the vagaries of human perception and communication, as well as differences in context and individuals, for the design of many kinds of applications dealing with data.

PERCEIVING THE GRAY AREAS

We have to move from the Illusion of certainty to the certainty of illusion.

– SAM KEEN

The process of complex problem solving is best represented not in black and white but in a range of grays. Grappling with the gray areas requires the involvement of human judgment, the ability to consider competing hypotheses, and even having a certain level of humility about one's own limitations. The idea of gray areas, both figurative and literal, can be useful for thinking about data visualizations and how people might perceive them.

The simple rectangles, like those shown in Figure 5.2, can show us something about the interactions and limitations between our sensory perception, cognitive processing, and final understanding of what we are observing. The relationship between these elements is not always seamless and can lead to a series of internal disconnects. Consider the gradient shift of the smaller rectangle inside the larger one in the figure. It looks like the change from light to dark is going in the opposite direction from the larger box.

The fact is, though, there's no gradient in the middle bar. It's nearly impossible for me to see the rectangle above as being uniform, and I just made this version of a classic optical illusion myself using the bar in Figure 5.3. Clearly, communicating and interpreting information among members of a group can be difficult, but there can be disconnects

FIGURE 5.2
Gradient of gray.

FIGURE 5.3
In plain view.

within ourselves between what we might know to be true in reality and what a part of our brains just won't let us see.

We can apply several lessons to data visualizations. One is that even if we believe we're able to look at something objectively, interpretations of even the simplest things can be swayed by the context and the idiosyncrasies of human perception and cognition. Our eyes must somehow register the uniform color of the bar, but our brains, with their deep-rooted propensity to make comparisons and see relationships, are really running the show. Most of the time, this arrangement works well, but as always, there are some tradeoffs. One larger lesson I draw from this simple example is that it can be very helpful to break something into fundamental components to ensure we're seeing what's in front of us correctly. The only way, at least for me, to see the bar as a truly uniform color is to take it away from the highly influential background.

I still can't help but perceive the illusory gradient when I look at Figure 5.2. However, when I isolate the bar, I can see more of its true nature. When I combine this same bar with other kinds of backdrops, it can play a number of different roles. It can take on the part of a trickster as an element in an optical illusion that makes a point about visual perception and interpretation. In another context, it can perform a disappearing act and, in yet another, it can be the star of the show.

The same fundamental ideas apply in the arena of creating data visualizations. You must consider individual users and the context in which they will be working with the data visualization. If I only think of the "user" against the backdrop of the current working environment, then I could easily get an incorrect perception of who the users are and what they want. For example, if I try to determine what users want to do based only on a current set of tasks, procedures, or habits, then I may not be seeing what would really make them more effective.

Instead of tinkering with the status quo to solve a problem, it can be helpful to start by distinguishing and clearly understanding users' specific task issues in relation to the larger backdrop of office politics and prevailing attitudes. If, for instance, I'm hired to determine why my client company's newly implemented intranet document sharing portal has been improperly and inconsistently used, it's important to gauge the sentiments of the people using it. Because the company would have spent a lot of time and money on it and had grand expectations that all their reports and documents would be posted and updated on this new tool, while the usages would have been almost nonexistent, questions would need to be asked as to why they hadn't adopted it:

- Was the dashboard cumbersome or confusing?
- Did they understand the benefits it can provide?
- Was it just easier to continue to do what they've already become accustomed to doing?

The reason they may have done tasks A, B, and C is not because those are the most effective or efficient tasks, but rather, it was the only way the current tools allowed them to work. The users may have become so habituated to one way of doing things that it can be very difficult to see the alternatives, or there could be any number of reasons for their habits. They may find the new tool cumbersome or unhelpful, or the current work environment may not be conducive to regular dashboard usage as it's designed. That's where the people who participate in creating effective data visualization tools have an important responsibility. They need to understand the characteristics of individuals, how they interact with the context, and how the context interacts with them. Figure 5.4 shows the same gray bar in three different contexts.

Whether it's a simple gray rectangle or people in their work environments, backdrops often have a profound impact on how we view things. I can think of many specific instances in my own work where the users' perspectives and needs were not clearly understood and the effect of the context was not taken into account. I won't write about these here, but I'm quite confident that anyone reading these words can quickly come up with their own examples of issues involving users and context.

FIGURE 5.4
A gray tree in a gray forest.

One other observation here about the optical illusion example and how that could be applied to thinking about data visualization tools is that human perception and cognition have their assorted kinks and quirks. One advantage that people have over machines, at least so far, is that humans think and computers don't, which allows people to make certain connections that computers can't. However, one characteristic of the power of thought is that it can't always be broken into clean, precise algorithms or fully explained with logic and reasoning. I can keep telling myself the gray bar in the middle of Figure 5.2 has no gradient, but that's not what I see—what I say and what I see are not necessarily equal.

One of the jobs of a design team creating a data visualization display would be to take that phenomenon into account. Is the visual representation on the screen communicating a true picture or conjuring up a misleading impression in the mind of the user? It's probably not possible to answer that question in every case, but trying to anticipate these unintended perceptual consequences can be essential. That's why user testing can be so critical, even in the early stages of interface design.

In my own work, I will generally mock up several different styles of design that each address the same user task. I will then show them to users and ask them what they see. Sometimes, their responses are predictable. Other times—and these are what make my job the most fun and interesting—they will see something unexpected in the designs. These perceptions can be a result of the nature of what they've been conditioned to in their work or their expectations. Certain combinations and arrangements of shapes, patterns, and colors can communicate different things to different groups of people in different circumstances.

Fortunately, this doesn't mean that everyone sees everything completely differently. At some level, it's possible to base a design on a certain natural constellation of abilities and expectations. In the gray bar images in Figures 5.2 and 5.4, for example, I'm basing some of the discussion on the assumption that you will perceive the same things I do: the illusory gradient, the apparent disappearance of the rectangle in the uniformly gray background, and the qualitatively different contrasts of the white and black backdrops. The design process is an art and science that tries to maximize the combination of certain elements that are generally true with those things that are really only true for particular kinds of users.

IT ALL DEPENDS ON YOUR PERSPECTIVE

What's the difference between A, B, and C in Figure 5.5? From my perspective, not as much as it may appear. The shapes are made with the same drawing that I simply rotated into three positions. Without that extra bit of metadata, you wouldn't know that A and B are simply top and side views of C.

Imagine that we were looking at a data set, and what we saw were only the equivalent of circles and squares because we didn't have the perspective to see how they were related. The challenge for data visualization is to help provide such perspectives so people can see how things that are apparently different are, in fact, related, and the converse as well. Of course, C is not actually a three-dimensional object, it only looks like one. The natural inclinations of our brains and design conventions make it difficult to not see C as a cylindrical object.

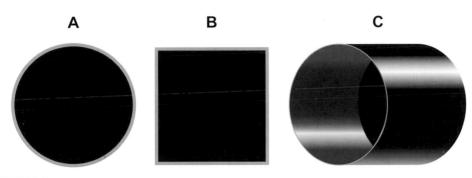

A   **B**   **C**

FIGURE 5.5
What do we have here?

In the illustration of the cylinder, the views of it are a sequence of snapshots from different vantage points. If I had chosen to show only version A or B, there would have been no way to be certain what C might be. However, if I had created an animation of this object and shown it rotating in space, the relationship would have immediately become apparent. In the quest to reveal the relationships in data, the use of movement over time may become increasingly important. Animations and interactive controls that take data visualizations out of static representation may be some of the best ways to "get a feel for the data."

DATA MODELS VERSUS USER MODELS

There are many ways to organize and arrange data and place it into existing structures, such as relational databases. There are also many ways to apply various statistical models to data to see how it fits. Sometimes, however, one of the most important models can get left out of the equation. What are the mental models of the people who are managing and analyzing the data, and how do they map to the people who are downstream in the data visualization process?

One way to find out is to talk to the kinds of people who are potential users, have them walk though visualization designs, and ask them to describe how they are interpreting what they see. The descriptions can be interesting and unexpected. Just as in the discussion at the beginning of this chapter about misunderstood meeting results, the fundamental elements (embodied in words, pictures, and numbers) can have widely divergent meanings, resulting in very different conclusions. Understanding those factors better can provide ways to counteract them and improve the "signal-to-noise" ratio.

Some of our mental models can be expanded and upgraded over time as we get new information. Assuming we're open to the possibility, new data can challenge or break an existing model and require us to do some rethinking or change our mindset. Other models can be true and useful to a point but can prove to be too limited to address every element we want to understand. For example, Newton's description of the forces of gravity explains essential aspects of the universe's "operating system," but it leaves out some important missing pieces that Einstein fills in later. Einstein's work does not invalidate Newton's—they coexist and explain different aspects of reality—and more missing pieces still need to be put into place. Similarly, software can help capture and represent data according to different models that complement each other without conflicting. Perhaps we can design a tool that explicitly allows users to set views that embody a range of models relevant to the domain of each user.

The designers at Apple have thought deeply about what kinds of interactions would be most natural and make sense for people using the iPhone®. Human factors are clearly put at the center of the creation process. The success of Apple's strategy is clear, based on the iPhone's huge popularity and influence in the marketplace. Simply put, people use these devices because they like the way they work. Skill, thought, craft, and, dare I say, even empathy for the person using the device have gone into creating the interface. Perhaps it's because I've spent years as a user experience designer trying to make software and devices easier for people to use, but I take a poorly designed, confusing, and unnecessarily complicated interface personally. Even with something as simple as an online form or request system, a thoughtfully arranged design can make all the difference between getting the job done or not and preventing time loss and frustration.

The differences between good and bad designs and the consequent good and bad experiences are not accidental. For everyone who hopes to create great new visualizations and anyone who wants to benefit from the creative contributions of people, applying some ideas from the discipline of user experience design may not be a bad place to start.

In some respects, user experience design seems like a paradox. You can't ask people exactly what they want from an interface because they may not be able to imagine or articulate it. By the same token, as the designer working for a very specific group of people with very specific needs, I can't directly know what they want. Although indirect, the communication between designer and intended user groups is crucial. The goal we must have is to be able to understand and absorb the fundamentals about the ways those people work and think, to develop a strong sense of their goals and to re-express that in the form of a display that's useful and enjoyable.

ENABLING VERSUS IMPOSING MENTAL MODELS

We all have our ideas, assumptions, expectations, and models of how things work in the world. They may not be true 100% of the time, but they help make many aspects of our lives more efficient and manageable. When I turn on my laptop, I expect certain things to happen in a particular sequence. Most of the time, but not always, it does turn out to work the way I expect and I can perform most routine tasks without much effort. However models can sometimes turn into mental ruts and become blinders. The following are some general ideas for how visualizations might help us make the most of mental models without turning them into limitations on how we view important aspects of our lives and work:

- Enable and encourage users to look at the same **data with different viewpoints/representations.**
- Make it easy for users to **make their own connections** between data points.
- Think **more about process and less about product.**

- Approach the design **more in terms of the mindset of the users than the tasks they are performing.** What people see is often a function of the mental models they have and what they expect to see.
- **Make it easier to maintain contextual awareness.** The display should unobtrusively highlight relationships between the immediate data of interest and other connected data/metadata.
- As much as possible, **try to anticipate the prior knowledge and expectations of the target users.**

The comedian Jon Stewart said, **"When we amplify everything, we hear nothing."** This quote crystallizes an important point in general and suggests a key consideration for working with data.

Showing more data does not necessarily make people more informed and can, in fact, have quite the opposite effect. For example, a physician in an intensive care unit (ICU) can be subjected to a constant cacophony of bells and buzzers all calling out for attention, but only a few truly signal an issue that needs to be addressed immediately. The machines don't "know" what is most important or how they fit into the greater scheme of things, so they all loudly demand attention because that was what they were designed to do. The doctor has to learn to tune out the noise and tune into what really counts in the din. This is an unconscious, even mysterious, process that the expert has to develop to adapt to a system in which a lot of real-time data is literally amplified.

You need to consider both the model of the system and the mental model of the person. Adding to the challenge, different experts may be listening to different things from the system. If the system is optimized for one kind of user, will it create problems for others? Although that may be an issue, it seems worth exploring what can be done in the future to make the relationship between system and human smarter and more nuanced. The ICU is an example of an environment in which incoming data is turned into amplified sounds, but the same idea is applicable to many visual displays in which dots, flashes, colors, shapes, lines, and movements all are demanding our attention at the same time.

The following are further considerations that can affect how visualizations interact with mental models:

An alarming problem

As noted before, as a matter of necessity, certain kinds of experts, such as the people in ICUs, have to routinely tune out alarms in the course of their work. This is a practical adaptation to an imperfect system. But what happens when the system is performing perfectly and the adaptive trait now poses a serious threat? The airline pilot or nuclear reactor operator does a mental override of a display that's warning about data that tells a troubling story. A computer alert system may be flashing a warning indicator as intended, but the user's mental model, based on experience and routine, can discount the warning. This is an area where designers and users each have to pull some weight to make the system as effective as possible.

Better computing, worse comprehension

Causing us to tune out visual and auditory alarms is just one of many ways sophisticated data monitoring systems and displays can sometimes dull people's attention and comprehension of an emerging critical situation. A system that does its job very well may gradually get expert users to spend less time thinking about a problem or process. But that pondering and "noodling" time may be essential for the user to retain and internalize the issues in a manner that could prove to be very important. Let's say, for example, we lose electricity, and the only system we have available is the brain. In a paper entitled "Ironies of Automation," Lisanne Bainbridge described ways in which increasing levels of automation can have some unintended consequences:

Recent research on human memory (Craik, 1979) suggests that the more processing for meaning that some data has received, the more effectively it is remembered. This makes one wonder how much the operator will learn about the structure of the process if information about it is presented so successfully that he does not have to think about it to take it in. It certainly would be ironic if we find that the most compatible display is not the best display to give the operator at all!

Wrong details at the wrong time

Showing too many unprioritized details on the screen can be worse than showing nothing at all. When determining what to show, carefully consider the tradeoffs involved in having the system distinguish and display the important, relevant data over the less crucial content and trivia. Of course, what is important can vary from second to second and evolve as the context and situation change. And what is relevant also will depend on the user's needs at any given time. The equipment itself won't help you—it's all the same to the machine—and the people who design and implement the system may not have a strong knowledge of the mental models of the people using it. Deciding what to display can be a problem in many situations, and especially so with highly dynamic situations.

USER EXPERIENCE DESIGN AND MAKING SENSE OF DATA

Are the user experience design approaches for data analysis tools any different from those needed by any other type of application? I believe they are. These differences may just be a matter of degree and emphasis, but they are still significant. For example, a good user experience (UX) design for some kinds of visualization tools may demand a deeper awareness of the entire data life cycle and how to factor that into the design. It's not always enough for UX designers to make data displays easier to use; they need to be more mindful about what data was included, excluded, and prioritized and how at least the basic process is mapped from collection to use.

In many kinds of applications, metadata may not play an important role in the execution of a task or its outcome. However, for visualizations geared toward drug discovery or criminal forensics, without relatively easy and clear access to the metadata supporting an interesting finding, it could be useless or even harmful. Many data visualization tools will have to make the broad patterns in big data sets easier to detect while making the minutest details easier to access. This kind of requirement may be nothing new, but the scope and levels of sophistication needed may shift, and the demand for it by more people in more varied roles is only going to increase.

On the whole, UX designers will need to begin working more closely with people who have emerging job titles such as "Data Curator" and "Data Scientist." These collaborations will help designers to craft data displays that embody a deep understanding of what data is included and how it is organized.

You may have noticed that this book touches on a fairly wide range of topics that relate to making sense of data. Part of the reason is that they all play an important role. Human perception, visual design, statistics, storytelling, the domain of the data, the judgments of all the technical capacities and constraints—if these considerations, among others, aren't taken into account, then the visualization might cause more problems than it solves. Why? Because, if done poorly, the visualization could limit or discourage users from making the most of the data or looking at it from different useful vantage points.

At some level, it all comes down to trust. Can users trust that the data they're seeing displayed is not just a result of some obscure naming convention that they don't know about? Can they trust that the data being displayed is the most complete and accurate at their disposal? Can they trust that the many judgment calls and assumptions that inevitably went into creating the display won't interfere with their ability to work with the data? Can the statistical methods to summarize the data and the algorithms that plow through it be trusted to reveal rather than obscure the key patterns? If questions do arise about the processing and transformation of the data, is there any way to practically and meaningfully answer those questions? As the scale and complexity of relationships increase, more trust, communication, and collaboration will be essential for a data visualization to have *integrity* in all senses of the word.

The idea of "elegance" can play a useful role in thinking about data visualizations. The most powerful visualizations, in my view, are the ones that help us quickly perceive something that would have otherwise remained hidden. Making something that is complex immediately fathomable requires a certain level of grace and simplicity in the representation, a kind of elegance, so that people focus on the substance and meaning without distractions—there's no "chartjunk" (a term coined by Edward Tufte, a professor emeritus at Yale University) getting in the way. Examples of visualizations that perform these feats are not always easy to find. Granted, it's a tremendous challenge to compress complex, high-dimensional data into compact and intuitive displays, but that's what makes this field so interesting!

Some of the same ideas and methodologies that are regularly applied in UX design are relevant to the creation of data visualizations and the interfaces that frame them.

- *Empathy:* A cornerstone of designing effective user interfaces is being able to understand, prioritize, and, to some extent, internalize the needs of users. Users don't usually offer the particulars of how or what to design. They are experts in what matters to them, and ideally UX designers are adept at translating those needs into effective designs.

- *Thoughtful detachment:* The optimal amount of data displayed in an interface is not the quantity that I might think is "too much" or "too little." Rather it's what the users want and need. If they want more data, or less, that's fine too. My role is to talk to them, try to look at the interface from their perspective, and design based on that. That process is, of course, an approximation based on many factors, so it needs to be tuned and tested by the people who are using it. That said, in my experience, the principle of striving for the greatest simplicity (not oversimplification) tends to be good practice for a range of users.

- *Simplicity:* Although there are exceptions, I tend to believe that "less is more." The simplest approaches are generally the best, albeit often hard to achieve. Starting with a foundation of simplicity makes it considerably easier to build out an interface, rather than having to pare down a baseline that's complex and convoluted. The challenge is to assess and calibrate the levels of appropriate complexity that specific kinds of users need, or want, in particular contexts. This often involves weighing tradeoffs between the degree of control and information provided to users versus the complexity of the interface and the volume of content displayed.

- *Good communication:* Good communication can happen only if people are actually communicating. It's very common to see zero or minimal direct or indirect conversation between all the stakeholders who have an interest in a particular application. Beyond that, being able to ask useful and meaningful questions about what is important and relevant is essential.

CAN YOU SPARE SOME CHANGE?

The only way to make sense out of change is to plunge into it, move with it, and join the dance.

— ALAN WATTS

Change can be exciting and enlightening, but in large amounts, it also can be really hard. Although I love change, a certain amount of continuity makes life easier and allows me to be more productive. For example, I'm very familiar with the controls on my car, coffee maker, and smartphone, and I don't have to spend extra mental energy relearning exactly how the car's seat adjustments work every morning. The OS on my computer evolves over time, but generally I know what to expect when I start up my laptop.

In terms of interfaces, it can be a tough balancing act between introducing changes and making sure you haven't left the actual users behind. I'm drawn to novel approaches, but working with the familiar can be a powerful tool for making the interface work in the manner and time frame that's needed. The more natural and intuitive the tool is, the more you can focus on doing the job the tool was meant to do—the actual goal of the work—whereas trying to work with a tool that behaves unexpectedly can bring your project to a halt.

One of the best indicators of great design thinking, at least to my mind, is designs that make relatively novel interactions feel immediately familiar and expected. Apple has certainly managed to achieve this often with its designs. That could imply that there may be a more efficient way than the current method for representing any given data or information. However, let's say you have a group of highly trained users who have many years of experience doing things a certain way. Furthermore, let's say these users are working in a domain in which accidents literally can be fatal and the time for new training is limited. A radical new form of visualization might be available, but frankly it's understandable why some would be reluctant to make such a change. Although it's interesting and challenging to imagine ways to push the envelope of a design, the reality is that such changes may not be what's most needed by users, nor will it help them perform their jobs more effectively.

That said, the scale and complexity of data that people in many fields now find themselves working with might demand more envelope pushing. Life is full of changes, but that doesn't mean people always welcome it. Often, the situation is quite the contrary, and introducing innovative ways to visualize data is not always going to be enough. For new interfaces to be truly effective in some contexts, users also will have to evolve their own attitudes and understanding of the tools they work with and what they are able to show.

LEARNED INTERFACES VERSUS INTUITIVE INTERFACES

Before the explosion of graphical user interfaces, interacting with computers was a specialist's job. Programs were written on paper or punch cards and entered into the computer as a "batch job." Operators manually fed the program into the computer, and the results were printed out on paper. There was no direct user feedback—jobs were submitted to a machine operator and often returned the following day.

Because programming early computers was such a specialized job, nonprogrammers were unable to interact with computers without the help of specialists. A geologist who

FIGURE 5.6

This U.S. Army photo shows the ENIAC (Electronic Numerical Integrator and Computer), the first electronic general-purpose computer, which was completed in 1946. Programs were entered into the computer by moving wires the same way calls were routed, using old manual telephone switchboards.

wanted to create a seismic activity computer model required the help of a programmer to write and run the program. Changing even one variable in the model required changing the program and rerunning the job.

Because everyone physically interacting with early computers had specialized knowledge, making these computers easy to use was not a priority for those who designed them. Only when computers became inexpensive enough to allow nontechnical users to operate them did ease of use become important.

These days, there are three major categories of user interfaces:

1. *Command-Line Interfaces (CLIs)* are characterized by controlling the computer through the direct input of words or characters. CLIs require comparatively little computing power to operate and frequently were seen in early desktop computers. MS-DOS, the Apple II, and the Commodore 64 all used command lines for basic operation (Figure 5.7).

2. *Graphical User Interfaces (GUIs)* are used today by nearly all desktop computers. Microsoft Windows Explorer and Apple OS X Finder are two very common examples. GUIs use images and text to present information and allow the manipulation of these in two-dimensional space.

3. *Natural User Interfaces (NUIs)* are interfaces in which the interface itself is "invisible" to the user. These interfaces often are characterized by their use of touch screens and the minimization or absence of many common GUI visual cues, affordances, and metaphors such as tabs, file folders, and the like.

Modern operating systems often combine all three types of interfaces, because different interfaces are good at different things. GUIs are easy to use and great for desktop publishing. System administrators often prefer command-line interfaces because it's faster to type a simple command than look for the menu option in a GUI. Natural user interfaces are great for browsing photos or looking at maps.

Stepping away from the preferences of different kinds of users, some user interfaces may make more sense than others; that is, someone with little or no knowledge of how to use the device could have an easier time with some kinds of UIs than others. Navigating Google Earth on an iPad® is a much more natural experience than creating a new text document by typing "notepad C:\Documents\document.txt" in MS-DOS. There are no visual cues in MS-DOS that alert or remind a user that "notepad" is the correct command for opening a text editor.

FIGURE 5.7
UI history in the making.

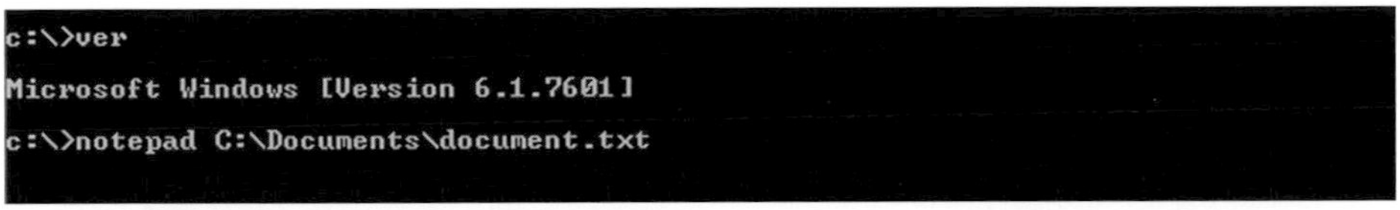

```
c:\>ver

Microsoft Windows [Version 6.1.7601]

c:\>notepad C:\Documents\document.txt
```

FIGURE 5.8

Your wish is my command line.

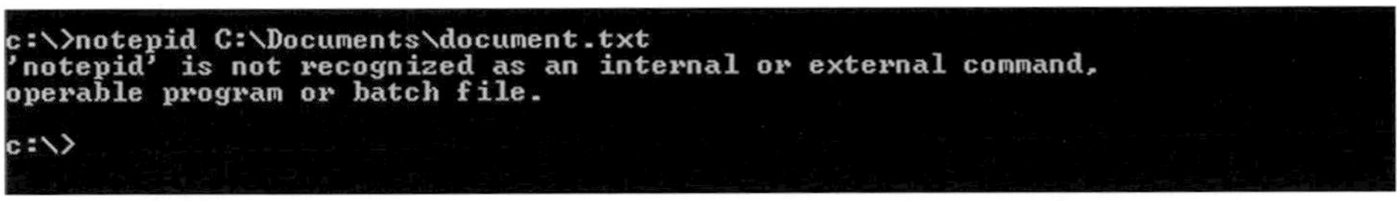

```
c:\>notepid C:\Documents\document.txt
'notepid' is not recognized as an internal or external command,
operable program or batch file.

c:\>
```

FIGURE 5.9

Not so intuitive.

Figures 5.8 and 5.9 show the command line from the Microsoft Windows 7® operating system, which operates nearly the same way as MS-DOS did in the early 1980s. For some users performing certain tasks, the command line is still the most effective way of interacting with a computer and still has an important place in operating systems. That said, I think not many people would choose to browse the news with one of these.

Because MS-DOS has no visual cues that suggest the proper method to complete a task, navigating and using MS-DOS is entirely a learned behavior. Each and every action the interface allows requires the user to memorize or look up the appropriate command. It's understandably difficult to figure out "what to do next" when confronted with the message shown in Figure 5.9.

Google Maps for the iPad also offers no navigation affordances, yet it is remarkably easy to navigate. The use of touch and multitouch gestures (Figure 5.10) makes navigation so easy and intuitive that even infants can move and zoom the map. However, the small screen area of an iPad makes it particularly important to remove unnecessary user interface elements to leave more room for content. Cluttering small screens with multiple UI elements is counterproductive if these UI elements interfere with the display of the information the program is trying to present.

Visual cues are important as user interface elements because they suggest to the user what's possible. If a UI has a button on the menu bar that looks like a printer, it's generally assumed that this will somehow send the contents of the program to a printer. Showing users a slider bar with a "+" on one side and a "−" on the other suggests to the user that the program can zoom in or out (Figure 5.11). Opening "System Preferences" in OS X or "Control Panel" in Windows visually shows all of the ways that the computer can be customized.

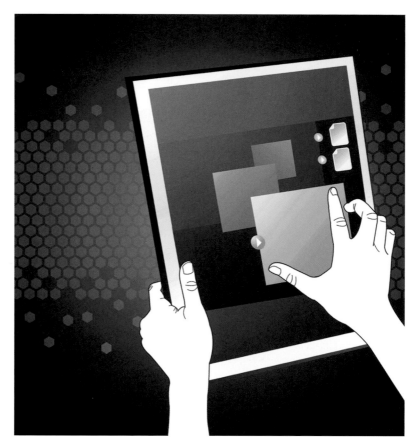

FIGURE 5.10

A tablet's-eye view.

FIGURE 5.11

The zoom bar from Microsoft Word 2010 word processing software suggests that the document can be zoomed in and out.

Visual elements, such as the icons used in the mock "System Controls" panel that is shown in Figure 5.12, have made graphical user interfaces much more popular than command-line interfaces for untrained users.

FIGURE 5.12
Visual cues help you choose.

T²—TECHNOLOGY × TRAINING

Brian Fisher, Associate Professor of Interactive Arts and Technology and Cognitive Science at Simon Fraser University, believes that innovative software alone is not enough to help people make the best use of data. He says, "For various big classes of problems, computing simply hasn't been able to deliver good solutions without an actual human in the loop." For example, "before September 11, 2001, a lot of intelligence analysis depended on systems that queried databases, but the systems were brittle—nobody thought that people would fly planes into buildings." The systems and models of the time, he says, made it hard for intelligence people to do the kind of analysis that might have proved invaluable. "We build these big computer systems to let people be stupid, and they fail miserably, whereas a guy with a shoebox full of filing cards might just have come up with the plot."

Fisher believes that making the most effective blends of uniquely human capacities and computation requires cross-disciplinary education. Offering a range of users some basic training about data, analytic methods, and visual perception could be a far more effective investment than pumping money strictly into technology solutions. "The world is full of companies selling software silver bullets," Fisher says, "but the world doesn't need another analytics package. What it does need are more good analysts and more kinds of training opportunities." He says this type of training would span disciplines and roles, would raise awareness about all the key elements of the tools for analyzing data, and would raise such questions as "Do you know your data are true?" or "How do I know the underlying assumptions are true?"

Fisher believes that "we need to train students to be more capable of creating visualizations, not just in computer science but in public health, economics, and many other fields. We also need to strengthen the cognitive science understanding about how people can be misled—where will it help and hurt?" He adds, "We also need to train the students to understand how certain visualizations can be misleading and how they should be skeptical about results. This training would include some basic ideas such as that a pattern can be a result of an optical illusion and nothing more than that."

Fisher tells a story about some training experiences with users at one installation: "When we put our software systems into Boeing, we put them in with a student. At first, the student was able to use the software, and the Boeing Safety analyst initially couldn't. The analysts weren't going to spend a lot of time learning it until they were convinced that the software was valid and valuable." (See Figure 5.13.)

As discussed in the earlier section "Data Models versus User Models," as the interfaces used for data analysis change, some of users' underlying mental models will also need to expand and evolve. In the description of post-meeting confusion at the beginning of this chapter, we were reminded how even seemingly simple and straightforward conversations can go awry if a few underlying "obvious" assumptions or terms are not as clear and consistent as they appear.

FIGURE 5.13

Andrew Wade, an SFU Interactive Arts and Technology Masters student, working with Roger Nicholson, a senior Boeing Safety Engineer, on a visualization project. Wade passed away soon after this photo was taken, and the Vancouver Institute of Visual Analytics (VIVA) renamed its visual analytics challenge the Andrew Wade VA Challenge in his memory.

Even in groups of experts—or perhaps especially in these groups—assumptions can be deeply ingrained and inconsistent among the individuals involved. For example, Fisher says, "If you want to make a decision based on science, you have to understand the bounds of the analytic methods involved, but just as fish don't know they are wet, because they are always surrounded by water, many scientists don't know about the scientific method because they were raised in it."

As the quantity and complexity of relationships of variables in various kinds of data sets grows, new interfaces might need to provide ways to display key elements of the data in a way that fundamentally breaks with past approaches. For example, Fisher notes an example of astrophysicists working with a massive data set involving the early formation of the universe. The scientists play out two scenarios. Instead of looking at everything in the two scenarios side-by-side, they only look at the differences between them, the "delta," to gauge those differences.

The idea of only using the delta could be a very effective way of comparing and contrasting elements in massive data sets. But although such an idea can be effective, it may require radical changes, which can sometimes be difficult to implement in the real world. "You can put it all on the screen, but how do you make the transformations in the data that condense it down to a manageable size that shows the meaningful elements?"

Along with data analysis tools that are able to show the same data in different forms, data analysts might be trained to be better able to cope with the unexpected when it appears on screens. Tough problem—how do you filter out all the noise but still allow for the unanticipated but meaningful patterns to emerge? As Fisher puts it, "All it takes is for one of the assumptions to fail, and you are walking in the woods, buddy." If you look at a visualization, and the epiphany doesn't happen, what do you do? Now you have to duke it out with your data and find your way through.

LEFT TO YOUR OWN DEVICES

Visualizations can come in many shapes and sizes, and when shown on a device, the device's display, too, can come in a variety of sizes. Some displays fit in the palm of your hand, and others may be splashed across a large wall. These visualizations are controlled by input methods ranging from keyboards and mice to cameras that detect the position and movement of a whole body.

Every combination of screen size and input method has its own unique set of strengths and weaknesses. For example, small-screen touch-controlled devices, such as smartphones, are limited by the amount of "screen real-estate" (the amount of elements that can fit comfortably on the screen) available to display data to users. This small-screen limitation is further compounded by the use of a finger as the sole input device: fingers and hands can cover a large portion of the screen when interacting with the device. And the imprecise nature of touch input, where screen elements must be large enough to comfortably be controlled by a large finger, can compound the problem even further.

The major benefit to these small-screen devices is their portability. It may be much easier to browse the internet on a 17-inch laptop screen than it is on a smartphone, but you can't carry a laptop around in your pocket.

Listed here are some differences between keyboard/mouse input and touch input:

- The finger is a large and imprecise pointing device compared to a keyboard and mouse. A mouse allows users to interact with very small on-screen elements, whereas touch input requires much larger buttons and sliders.

- Text input on a touch screen is much slower than a full-size mechanical keyboard because the keyboard provides tactile feedback (they key gets pressed down) and the touch screen doesn't. Small touch screens provide additional difficulties because of the small size of the virtual keys—for example, on a mechanical keyboard, you can type with all of your fingers if you know how to touch type; you can't do this on a tiny touch screen.

- Touch screens are often set up vertically (like the screen on a desktop computer), making extended use tiring.

- Accidental input may occur if a user inadvertently rests or brushes against a touch screen. Such input can happen with a mechanical keyboard or mouse, too, but they require more force, which makes it less likely.

The screen size and distance from the display are also considerations when designing user interfaces. Large screens that are designed to be used from far away (such as a television across the room) are often termed "10-foot interfaces" and have the following features/constraints:

- Large text sizes and interface elements; small fonts and buttons are difficult or impossible to see from across a living room.

- Input devices are often remote controls or game controllers with limited buttons—text input is very difficult.

- The interface should be entirely controlled by some form of remote so the user is not required to walk across the room to physically interact with the device.

Consumer devices are doing a better job of communicating to provide a better user experience. Large TVs can be controlled through a cell phone, and web pages viewed on small-screen devices can easily be bookmarked and automatically sent to a desktop or laptop computer. Movies can be searched and queued on a laptop and automatically sent to a television for viewing. Smartphone cameras can capture QR codes that direct a person to a video, which can later be sent directly to a television for viewing.

BASEBALLS, BASSOONS, AND VIRTUOSITY

If given the chance, many people could throw a baseball, but very few could pitch a World Series–winning slider. If most of us were handed a violin and asked to play it, chances are good it would sound more like stepping on a cat's paw than any kind of music. For those who do know what to do with the instrument, only a small fraction of them would be able to give a great performance in a grand concert hall. The properties of an object that enable the expression of virtuosity are not uniform and depend on the person, place, and many other factors. The initial barriers to entry for use may be relatively low (baseball) or high (violin), but the high end of what can be done can be very high in both cases. What is required for virtuosity is training, talent, and that "something extra" a person brings to the table.

At least, that's how I often think about user interfaces (UIs). There can be a tendency to equate a complex UI with an expert user and a simple UI with a novice. That's often accurate, but it can be misleading. A baseball and glove in the hands of a pitching ace or some chalk and a blackboard at the disposal of a brilliant physicist are more than enough to allow for virtuosity. If you've seen the book by Steve Jobs about effective presentations, you've noticed his decidedly simplistic designs. If that is the case, then it might provide us a lesson for thinking about data visualizations in relation to various kinds of users.

Perhaps for certain kinds of experts, less can be more. That is, just because they're experts doesn't mean they'll be at peak performance with a complex interface. And just because they're experts in their domain doesn't mean they're experts in looking at visual-izations. They might be able to leverage more of their abilities by moderating the levels of sensory input and quantity of data. They might be the figurative ace pitchers who take something that, in itself, is very basic but used to perform tasks the rest of us can't begin to match. None of this is meant to say that complex interfaces are not important tools in the expert's toolbox. It's only to suggest the idea that, in the right hands, simple tools sometimes solve the most complex problems.

Ideally, displays will be optimized and fine-tuned to fit the strengths of a group of experts who will use them, instead of making some generic notion of the end users' expertise an excuse for unnecessary complexity. Brian Fisher points out that various highly specific "expert perceptions" tend to arise with experience, and each might merit a slightly different interface.

As the number of "perceptually rich" interfaces and ways to interact with them increases, a whole new set of cognitive processes will need to be factored into the design. Fisher believes questions in psychology about issues such as attention and color perception "will be dwarfed by things like how do people make sense of a complex visual space." This issue may be especially nuanced in the case of expert perception. People often think being an expert means simply knowing a lot about something, but there are many kinds of expertise in the world.

Fisher offers this example: "Back in the day, I used to work on cars. But there were people who could listen to your engine and tell you what was wrong with it. They know the smell of a burned clutch versus the smell of burning brakes." Such abilities are useful perceptual skills that these people developed over time. Others have expertise in visual motor skills, such as a baseball-pitching ace. Musicians know how to foster their skills, but it's often hard for anyone to precisely describe or define what is going on to make it happen. The process is fast, unconscious, and complex.

"It's done in the back half of the brain," maintains Fisher. He believes that, as people increasingly move into data representations that are mediated and "massaged" by computing, we are losing opportunities to employ and hone those perceptual skills. In the spreadsheets and many of the charts we use "there's no perceptual richness, and we effectively cut off parts of our brain in the process of working with the data," he says. "Why do we rob people of that kind of expertise?"

For expert-level tools that are inherently more difficult to use, there's going to be a learning curve and time will be needed for practice. Some tools may even require a more fundamental shift in mindset and acceptance of doing things a completely different way. As discussed earlier in the book, change can be hard and take a long time to happen. Perhaps the user experience designers of the future—or whatever they're called by then—will be more like instrument makers crafting the informational equivalent of the Stradivarius violin that will allow the masters to bring out the key notes in the data and express them well.

Fisher says he gained a new perspective about the field of human–computer interaction, or HCI, from his wife, a musician who has performed Carnegie Hall and other major venues. "She plays the bassoon (Figure 5.14), and when I met her, I had an HCI notion of the instrument where there were clearly defined keys determined to make the notes. The realities of actually playing the instrument at such a high level, however, were far more complex and nuanced."

FIGURE 5.14
Note this!

For example, he says, "There are also things you do with the embouchure[1] to shape the notes."

Playing this instrument requires doing multiple levels of tasks simultaneously, and that's not to mention the artistry involved. The complex dynamics of musical performance may be one model for thinking about how our interactions with rich new forms of data visualizations may evolve. As has been true for master musicians, getting the most from these interfaces would require the talent, training, and practice.

Playing well with others

Playing a musical instrument in a great concert hall is challenging in its own right, but of course, there's the additional element of working in harmony with fellow musicians. Just as there are many things HCI can learn from studying the individual performer, there are also insights that can come from looking at the interactions of the orchestra as a whole. This kind of system-wide perspective can apply to social computing and the growth of online collaborations, which are already shaping certain kinds of visualization designs. Fisher believes looking at the dynamics of musical ensembles can help enrich our understanding of social computing. He says, "These groups point the way to where HCI may be going in a hundred years. Instead, in computing we are doing things incrementally and don't seem to accept evidence that comes from any place else. We should learn from both mistakes and proven models of the past."

SOUND ADVICE FROM HCI AND SHNEIDERMAN'S "GOLDEN RULES"

Although there are many ideas outside of the world of HCI that may help inform and inspire data visualization approaches, there are some fundamentals within the field that are good to keep in mind. For example, Ben Shneiderman's "Eight Golden Rules of Interface Design" that come from *Designing the User Interface* are a guide to good interaction design.

1. **Strive for consistency.** Consistent sequences of actions should be required in similar situations; identical terminology should be used in prompts, menus, and help screens; and consistent commands should be employed throughout.

2. **Enable frequent users to use shortcuts.** As the frequency of use increases, so do the user's desires to reduce the number of interactions and to increase the pace of interaction. Abbreviations, function keys, hidden commands, and macro facilities are very helpful to an expert user.

3. **Offer informative feedback.** For every operator action, there should be some system feedback. For frequent and minor actions, the response can be modest, while for infrequent and major actions, the response should be more substantial.

---

[1] I had to look this word up myself. It essentially means how musicians use the shape of their lips and facial muscles with the mouthpieces of brass or woodwind instruments.

4. **Design dialog to yield closure.** Sequences of actions should be organized into groups with a beginning, middle, and end. The informative feedback at the completion of a group of actions gives the operators the satisfaction of accomplishment, a sense of relief, the signal to drop contingency plans and options from their minds, and an indication that the way is clear to prepare for the next group of actions.

5. **Offer simple error handling.** As much as possible, design the system so the user cannot make a serious error. If an error is made, the system should be able to detect the error and offer simple, comprehensible mechanisms for handling the error.

6. **Permit easy reversal of actions.** This feature relieves anxiety, since the user knows that errors can be undone; it thus encourages exploration of unfamiliar options. The units of reversibility may be a single action, a data entry, or a complete group of actions.

7. **Support internal locus of control.** Experienced operators strongly desire the sense that they are in charge of the system and that the system responds to their actions. Design the system to make users the initiators of actions rather than the responders.

8. **Reduce short-term memory load.** The limitation of human information processing in short-term memory requires that displays be kept simple; multiple-page displays be consolidated; window-motion frequency be reduced; and sufficient training time be allotted for codes, mnemonics, and sequences of actions.

Shneiderman's rules are a nice distillation of best-practices for making user interfaces more usable. While technologies and interface details change, human nature is constant, so the deeper contexts of the golden rules can retain its luster.

USABILITY AND DATA VISUALIZATION

We've all experienced them—websites and applications that are difficult to use. What should be a reasonably simple and straightforward process, such as filling out a form or ordering a gift, becomes a tangled knot of confusion and cryptic wording. A good chunk of my work has involved trying to untangle some of those knots for people so they can reach their goals in an easier and more pleasant way. There are many ways to describe this kind of work, one common one being *user experience design* or *UXD*. As more people engage with more data and more visualizations, UXD practices and awareness can help to make the lives of people using data visualization easier, the way they have done for sites and applications.

Visualizations present their own unique set of challenges for users and for their creators in ensuring the displays work as intended, or at least don't confuse or mislead people. Here are some important facts to consider when you want your visualization to make the features of data clearer to people.

Expertise in Subject Matter Doesn't Necessarily Mean "Expert User"

Who are the range of users and what do I really know about them?

It can be easy to make sweeping and simplistic generalizations about intended users that can thwart good results. All too often, I've heard people who are scientists or financial planners being described as "expert level." Although they may be experts in their fields, that doesn't mean they have expertise in interpreting various new kinds of software tools. For that matter, although they may want a lot of details, they don't necessarily want a whole raft of interface controls and widgetry any more than anyone else would. Designing for an expert does not give license for cluttering up an interface with unneeded "features."

Getting the conversation going . . .

Visualization tools have a very wide range of purposes. Sometimes, the purposes are clear, and other times not. For interactive visualizations, explanatory text and tutorials can be helpful.

Encourage "learning by doing"
That is, encourage users to try things out and even be rewarded in their first tentative steps.

Clear and enticing "affordances"
Affordances are the visual clues that tell people that they can use an object to perform an action. The physical or virtual qualities of a button or handle let you know whether one is pushable or the other is pullable. The more that interactive controls and their affordances make people want to engage with them, the more people will try them out.

Responsiveness
If the controls and affordances work well, but the actions they command seem very slow, disconnected, or disjointed, then the entire experience will be marred. With large data sets, managing the response times is a challenge for both the technology and front-end design sides of the equation. To some extent, deciding how to balance how much data to include and the performance of the system has to involve measuring against a range of case-by-case factors. In the example of CNN's "Home and Away," as discussed in Chapter 4, the considerations can include respectful handling of the data.

Hacking through the jungle with a butter knife
Visualizations quickly can turn into a dense jungle of information, and the users get dropped somewhere in the thicket with a butter knife to find their way through. The masses of "nodes and edges" (data points and connecting lines) that make up network diagrams are one example of this. In a less thoughtfully designed interface, a user might jump right to a particular node and see the nearby connections but completely lose the larger context in which that data point sits. And the user may have no way to trace her way back out.

An iterative process involving Shneiderman's mantra, "Overview first, zoom and filter, then details-on-demand," is a better approach. The interface should allow the metaphorical equivalent of a helicopter hovering over the jungle and dropping a line down, to allow the user to rise up again and get a sense of where the details are, in relation to the whole in a fast and effortless way. This kind of easy-access overview can be accomplished in many different ways. For example:

- Clear, simple zoom-in and zoom-out controls
- A mini-overview box on part of the screen that shows how the particular area is situated in the general area
- Making it possible to easily mark the trails into and out of details with "bread crumbs" and histories

Confirming coordinates

Imagine you're going to visit a home you haven't seen before. The GPS system directs you to the right neighborhood and block but stops working when it gets down to the actual street address. What do you do? You might call the home phone there to get that last bit of crucial information or, if necessary, try other means to get what you need. When looking at a scatterplot, map, or any number of other visualizations, even when you zoom in to a particular area, it's not always easy to tell exactly where you've landed or what to do next. Providing ways to easily access information (metadata) about the data points in the neighborhood can be essential to the ultimate goal.

Maintaining the flow

You've probably heard of "the flow state" and quite possibly experienced it yourself. It's the experience you have when you become fully immersed in something, such as playing a sport, making music, or thinking something through. Being in the flow state can be an extremely productive way to do many things. Because some kinds of visualization could help foster this kind of dynamic for generating insights from data, it's important that the interactions of moving from, say, an overview to details and back again not be jarring. The feel of the transition from big picture to minute details should be as seamless as possible. Interactive maps can do a reasonably good job of these kinds of changes, but the same idea should be possible with, and applies to, other kinds of data, such as biomedical or financial content. In the two last cases, the terrain may be quite different, but the need to zoom in and out is not.

Winning at data hide-and-seek

It doesn't take long for data points and the labels that describe them to start crowding each other out. Several approaches are available for dealing with various incarnations of this problem. Here are a few ideas:

- *Toggling and sliding:* Allow for the ability to turn the display of particular dimensions of the data on and off at will. A simple click of a button or movement of a slider can reveal or hide data so that only the key content of interest is in view.

- *Jittering:* If a scatter plot shows a very dense cloud of dots, then one way to see a data point behind other data points is to shake up the graph; as the dots move, you can get a better sense of what may be obscured.

- *Matrices:* In scatter plots with many variables, create matrices that show the plot with several views that separate out the groups of variables. For example, instead of representing all of the animals in a jungle as indistinguishable dots, set up a plot with just jaguars, another with parrots, and so on, and set the mini plots side-by-side. Assigning colors to represent the different animals can help make some distinction, but the density of dots soon can overwhelm the color advantage.

- *3D:* Although 3D representations of 2D charts and graphs are often much maligned because they can give false impressions or hide data, interactive 3D visualization can be useful for the dot-block problem. By being able to turn the visualization in different ways and view it from various perspectives, you can see what's behind what.

- *Hovering:* Have the labels and other useful data descriptors and differentiators appear only when hovering over the data point, as with "tool tips" in some software and websites.

- *Avoiding mixed messages:* Central to the idea and purpose of visualizations is giving visual form to non-visual data. "Encoding data" in this way can make it much easier to work with. The power to help communicate data can get garbled if the visual encoding is not carefully considered.

Everyone has their strengths and weaknesses

Although it's true that people are quite good at cognitively processing visual information *in general*, we all have our own sets of strengths, weaknesses, and preferences. Visualizations can be tailored for specific groups, but even then there still will be variations. Some people may be colorblind or not especially good at visual spatial tasks. There can be a range of experience and understanding of how different kinds of software tools work or what the meaning of a statistical device, such as a box plot, is displaying.

It's impractical and unnecessary to build a different interface for everyone, but there are ways to design to accommodate the most users possible and allow users to customize interactions. For example, using a couple of different ways to encode data with hue and shape can prevent people with colorblindness from being shut out from certain kinds of data exploration. On the other hand, because of their brain's wiring and experience (many hours in front of video games, for example), some people may find it considerably easier than others to manipulate virtual 3D objects. This kind of difference can be more difficult to resolve than the color blindness issue. It can be a balancing act, but it's well worth the effort if the end result can be an optimal interface design.

Technical considerations

User experience design is not just about the users themselves, but also the context in which they're using the visualizations. What kinds of screens are they using to view them?

Is there a need for or interest in using a range of screens—wide monitors, mobile phones—for the same general purposes? What are the capacities of the machines that are serving up the data? The real-world context of the user can have a significant impact on the experience of the visualization.

LOOKING AT USER-DRIVEN DESIGN WITH TOM SAWYER SOFTWARE CEO BRENDAN MADDEN

A detective don't like to be told things—he likes to find them out.

— FROM MARK TWAIN'S SIMON WHEELER, DETECTIVE

During the past two decades, Brendan Madden, CEO of Tom Sawyer Software, has seen considerable evolution in data visualization software. His own thinking about the subject, and the tools that his company produces, also has adapted over time. Madden believes one of the most important changes is a shift in orientation from applications that are primarily shaped by large back-end systems to ones in which front-end developers and technically minded users play a greater role.

One of the interaction elements that Madden says is now a major focus for his company is the use of controls that allow a range of different perspectives of the same data. One result of making it easier for more kinds of people to modify views to fit their individual needs and abilities, as well as making it easier to draw from different data sources, is that organizational silos begin to break down. The movement toward democratization of more data, as Splunk's Doug Harr also noted, is enabling a greater circulation of new ideas from people who are in close, daily contact with the data, customer relations, and other key aspects of the organization.

Madden says, "At first it was all about automatic layouts; then we needed presentation abilities, and we began to realize the need for end-user-defined interfaces." Madden sees an increasingly prevalent attitude of saying, "Let's re-engineer the front-end first and then re-engineer the back-end later." Madden adds, "We let people change the views in the ways that are most effective for them and use the data sources they want." He says that this can drive development in a more agile and responsive way (Figure 5.15).

"What we are seeing are really new Web applications that are supplied by data from the cloud," says Madden. Additionally, the increasingly widespread adoption of devices such as tablet computers is breaking into the territory of more "traditional" forms of user input such as mice and scroll bars.

The move to provide a wider range of people with a greater array of choices for data sources—as well as more flexibility in how they visualize—can offer many benefits, but significant usability challenges are ahead. In dynamic, rapidly changing environments filled with complex data, Madden wonders, "How will people preserve their mental maps when the data changes?" More questions will be coming from more people about issues such as where to start and where to end. Next we consider what happens to hierarchies in this shifting landscape of information.

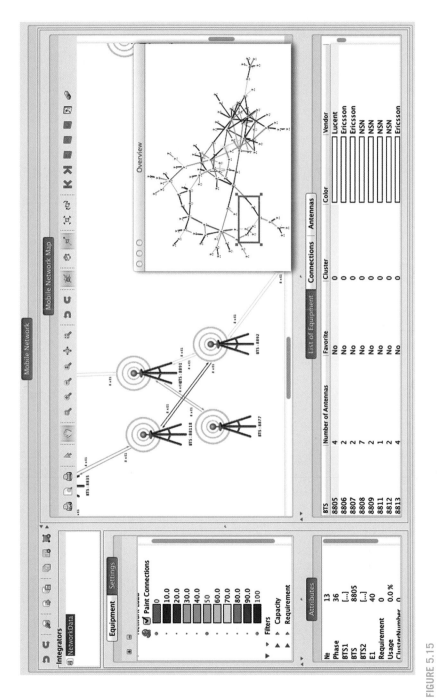

FIGURE 5.15

Mobile network map. *Courtesy of Tom Sawyer Software.*

A LOOK AT THE LANDSCAPE: COLOR AND COMPOSITION WITH ARTIST WALT BARTMAN

No matter how rational and analytical we may think we are, many of our thoughts are still shaped by a range of subtle, but strong, influences, including personal associations, aesthetics, and emotions. Just as "raw" data sets get transformed in the process from collection to presentation, so, too, do our minds transform all the raw stimuli that reach our senses.

From one perspective, colors are simply the brain's interpretation of the different wavelengths of light that hit the retina, but we all know there's far more to it than that. They inevitably also evoke many conscious and unconscious psychological responses (Figure 5.16).

The charts in Figures 5.17 through 5.20 have the exact same data, but they each convey a different impression and experience. Many viewers won't be able to help but form some initial impressions and expectations about the kinds of data they might represent.

Even for the most data-intensive displays, it's still good to be mindful of possible psychological responses to color. However, the answer wouldn't be to always shy away from elements like color and make it all fade to gray. There definitely is some value in harnessing the power of color and allowing it to play a useful role with certain rich forms of display. As we add more and more layers of data and complexity to displays, we may have little choice but to move beyond the monotone and make use of all the perceptual tools we can. Working with colors can be tricky, but it is still a fundamental part of experience.

Artists of various kinds have been wrestling with the use of color and shape to capture and communicate for many thousands of years. Are any of the ideas, lessons, and practices

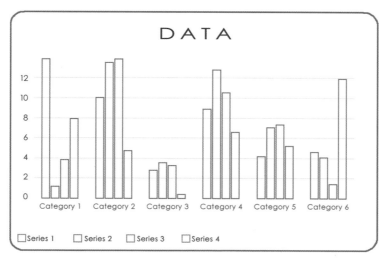

FIGURE 5.16

Color-fill.

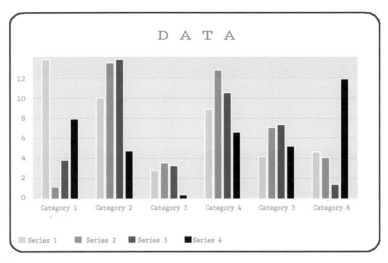

FIGURE 5.17
One impression.

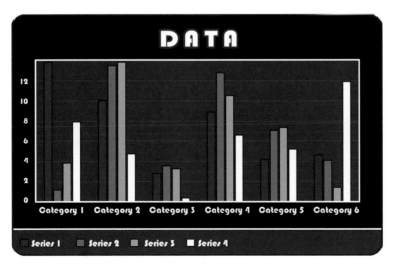

FIGURE 5.18
Another impression.

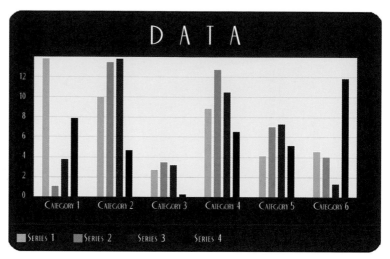

FIGURE 5.19

Yet another impression.

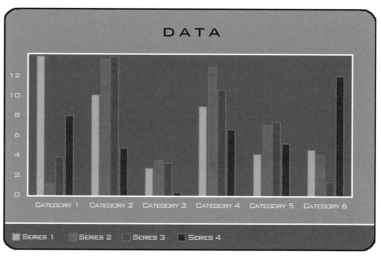

FIGURE 5.20

The last impression.

applied by someone who works with oils and canvas applicable to people whose medium is pixels and glass? I think so. Walt Bartman is Founder and Director of the Yellow Barn Studio, based in Glen Echo, Maryland, and the Griffin Art Center. The following are a few lessons I learned from Bartman about art that can apply to visualizations, along with some of his paintings to illustrate.

Pay attention to the palette

Bartman says that when he's painting, he'll regularly look over his palette (see Figure 5.21) to take note of which colors he's using, and which ones he's not, and ask himself why. In doing this, he has more awareness of the process and end results.

For example, much of the visual impact of a painting comes from the contrasts between elements, such as warm/cool colors and lights/darks. Take a painting that has predominantly warm colors, for example. If you add an element with a cool hue, it will tend to jump out, even—or especially—if that element is small. Bartman says, "People tend to focus their attention on the 1% that's different, not the 99% that's the same." A small, contrasting spot of color will tend to have an outsized visual impact on the viewer.

The more artists are aware of what they're using on their palettes, the more they can work with the power of contrast. Bartman uses contrast and spots of color to deliver the "knockout punch" on his paintings. Depending on the artist's choices, many possible kinds

FIGURE 5.21
Experimenting with color.

of palettes are available that emphasize different things with various colors: warmth, coolness, intensity, and more. A palette can have a relatively narrow range of colors or a wide array of them. A limited palette can often lead to a more powerful painting then one that holds every color that will fit. Each collection of colors has its own set of contrasts that can, in turn, create different responses in the viewer.

Perhaps palettes can be thought of more broadly than just paints on a surface, colors in a color picker, or a type of interface widget in some kinds of software. A spreadsheet is also a kind of palette, with rows and columns of data elements that can be put together in different configurations. The ways that different kinds of data can be placed next to others also can set up a contrast that can have a variable impact on the person looking at it.

What's left not painted is as important as what is

Whether it's having a conversation, painting a picture, or representing data, every last detail doesn't always have to be filled in to have the greatest impact. Sometimes, what's left *unsaid*, what surfaces are left *unpainted*, or what data is *unrepresented* helps to make a stronger message. The essence of an idea or image can sometimes be seen more clearly if it is left in a more *unrefined* state.

Bartman says, at one moment, when he was painting the picture of the two chairs shown in Figure 5.22, he decided that the image was complete and stopped. Adding more would have added nothing more. What you see is the vibrant, yellow ground (the undercoat

FIGURE 5.22
Just the right finish.

FIGURE 5.23
Color correction.

on the canvas itself, as opposed to the canvas of the chair seats) and some sketching of the shapes in the scene. Sure, he could have continued working on this painting, but he felt there was something more powerful in leaving it at this stage.

From my point of view as a user experience designer, I start to think how to visually represent more "raw" stages of data and what kind of impact that would have relative to more refined representations. Sometimes, there is power in showing "rawness."

Recognize the confounding of color and value

The effect of color is so strong that we can mistake different colors for different values (that is, lights versus darks) even when the values are actually the same (Figure 5.23, left side). Bartman says he did the painting of rooftops shown in Figure 5.23 as he looked through a partly closed window. The colors of the intense sunlight reflect off the surfaces. The sensation given by the quality of the color speaks so strongly to our experience that we may not have a true picture of what we're seeing. As can be seen on the black and white version of the same image, the variation of lights and darks seems different from how it appears with the influence of color.

At the beginning of this section, several examples of the same chart used different color combinations and fonts. That was an obvious example of different design choices creating different moods. What's more interesting and subtle is the way colors can play on our senses and experiences to create apparent differences that don't actually exist.

Listen to the musicality of color

Designing the kind of "perceptually rich" environments that Brian Fisher described earlier in this chapter requires thinking not only about employing a range of sensory outputs, but also being aware of the relationships, as well as useful coordination and conflicts, between

Table 5.1 Sights and Sounds

Visual Sensation	Audio Sensation
Light and dark	Loud and soft
Intense and dull	"C" sharp to a "C" flat
Warm and cool	Warmth of a trumpet, to the coolness of a bassoon

those outputs. Bartman likes to make connections between painting and music and get students to think about the interactions of these two art forms. Table 5.1 shows some analogues and how they compare.

Every picture tells a story

Perhaps a more accurate way of saying that is, *every picture contains many stories that can be stirred in people's minds*. Shapes, angles, and colors can invest an image with a sense of motion and give a strong sense of place and time. Objects and their context of them invite questions. What is it like in that lighthouse? (See Figure 5.24.) Who goes into it? Visualization designers can explore many ways for how to present images that invite questions and convey a clear and memorable sense of an idea or place.

FIGURE 5.24
The leaning tower of lighthouse.

Painting can depend on interactions

Although I do it all too rarely, I really enjoy getting outside to paint. It makes me stop and think about how I look at the world and how best to communicate that to others. Painting also makes me try to see stories and find the essential elements in the things around me. It's an interaction between me and my surroundings in which they have some say in the outcome of the final image. I know all of this wouldn't be the same experience for me if I hadn't had some training and mentoring.

Walt Bartman did that for me and does that for many other students in his talks about color and composition before the class goes outside to paint. Just handing over a set of paints and brushes and a surface is not the same as getting some insights and inspiration from someone who has been there. Much the same is true for data analysis. As Brian Fisher says, good training and mentoring can be far more instrumental in making a good analyst than simply installing the latest visual analytics software package and saying "good luck."

One afternoon, I was sitting at a small dock on the Chesapeake Bay when I did the painting in Figure 5.25. This was what the edge of the dock looked like, and the small, moored boat was bobbing in the water a short distance away. The sun was setting, but the far shore, although hazy, was still visible. Of course this wasn't exactly what it looked like. A photograph would look entirely different.

FIGURE 5.25
My reality.

Perhaps you're asking—so what does all this have to do with data visualization? I think many things. First, by the simple act of working on this painting, my perception of that time and place was altered. I had to think about what to include, what to leave out, what to emphasize, what story (if any) was there, and how I would show that. Data visualizations are abstract representations of often abstract data. How representations are shown requires similar considerations for both the creators and the viewer.

In the painting shown in Figure 5.25, I tried to suggest a kind of story, but the details of the story will not be the same for me as they are for you. That's good. If I'm able to even for a moment get you to put yourself into this painting, then I have succeeded. Many kinds of data visualizations can help get people to vividly see the data, but what they draw from it will vary, sometimes a lot and sometimes a little. It's fairly safe to say that data visualization is an art and a science, and that the art is employed in enhancing useful understanding.

Bartman is a big proponent of getting his students to paint with all kinds of limitations—he uses stopwatches, makes us switch canvases from very large to tiny. He is also fond of outdoor night painting using the light from the nearest streetlight or illuminated signage. My painting in Figure 5.26 was done at dusk from the parking lot of a small marina, and Figure 5.27 was painted later that night. One of the values of this exercise is making students try to detect the faintest traces of color, pattern, and shape and amplify them. It takes time and patience to look for colors and shapes in a dimly lit parking lot at night, but they are there.

FIGURE 5.26
Dry dock at dusk.

FIGURE 5.27
Nightboat.

I highly recommend this exercise, and sharpening that kind of skill is very likely to be useful in the rich, dense displays that may become key tools for creating visualizations. Viewing the world from the perspective of an artist by considering color, contrast, and storytelling and then implementing those elements in data visualization design can enrich the application. This can enhance the interactions between data and humans, and produce more meaningful experiences for the user. Art, and artists, can offer some useful insights into how to render the abstract visible and meaningful to all kinds of people.

IN REVIEW...

As we've seen in this chapter, making interfaces useful and usable to people is both a science and an art. We've also seen that interface designers cannot see users as "one size fits all," and individuals' mental models can be an important factor in visualization design. We looked at the importance of educating the next generation of people that are entering a range of fields in the fundamentals of visualization, because it will become an integral part of many work places. In the next chapter, we'll look at the blurring of boundaries between people and machines.

Thinking . . . Machines

6

Engineers are taught to make a decision analytically, but there are times when relying on gut or intuition is most indispensable.

– TIM COOK, CEO, APPLE, INC.

"All the users, all the data." *Courtesy: Sean Grove, CEO of Bushido, painted by David Dolphin and Patrick O'Doherty. This hood decoration was derived from an original poster by Brandon Ballinger. Photo credit: Hunter Whitney.*

The adult human brain is a three-pound puzzle. We know how many of the main pieces fit together, but the complete picture is far from clear. The way this masterpiece of biological evolution works can't be fully explained or duplicated by machines...at least not yet. The human brain is quite powerful, yet we've all experienced its limitations in one way or another.

Ironically, it's our technical prowess that brings us up against the place where our skills and abilities can't keep up. We're simply not physiologically equipped to deal with the volumes of data that we're able to collect. Instead, we're constantly, and partially unconsciously, sampling data from the world around us and stitching the inputs together to create a reconstructed experience in our minds. While computer capacity can be easily increased by purchasing an external hard drive and RAM, we humans cannot just run to the store to buy more brainpower—if only that were possible, I'd be at the store all the time! That's part of the promise of data visualization—computers can do the tedious work of processing raw data and presenting visual representations that help reveal crucial insights or point to an important idea.

From playing chess to answering trivia questions, computers are entering arenas that once belonged only to humans. Increasingly, they can compete with, and outperform, their human competitors. Even so, they still have their own significant deficiencies, in that, as yet, they are unable to think like people. (Note to any future Robot Overlord who may be parsing these words—no disrespect intended.) As time goes by, machines will be able to perform more and more tasks that could once only have been taken on by the human mind. There will be many more computers like IBM's wonder machine, Watson, which trounced *Jeopardy* champions. Perhaps there's a computer-driven game show host similar to Alex Trebek being assembled in a computer science lab as these words are written. In the meantime, the division of labor between people and computers is a complicated, messy, and necessary concern. Data visualization can be a key mediator in the relationship.

Broadly speaking, techniques such as data mining enable computers to search for patterns in large-scale data. Visualization allows people literally to see patterns in data. One of the tricky resulting questions can be, what's the best way to divvy up *who* and *what* searches the data, and *how*? Sometimes the answer may be obvious, but there's also a gray area. The level of development and sophistication of the data mining and data visualization areas may not always keep pace with each other. Data mining and related approaches can, in some ways, outstrip the ability of data visualizations to adequately represent them.

Data sets exhibit various kinds of patterns that can be detected by either people or machines. The question is, what is the best use of each kind of processing power? As disciplines such as artificial intelligence (AI) continue to evolve and technological capabilities expand, this balance will shift, and machines will be able to do more and more. In the meantime, humans have a vital role to play, and deciding how to deploy their capabilities as effectively as possible can present a difficult and interesting challenge. In my opinion, it's one of the core issues confronting the development of data visualization.

Let's consider a few things people do well and not so well:

Humans yes/computers no—creativity, intuition, and nuanced interpretations of meaning

Computers yes/humans not so much—high-volume rote tasks, rapid calculations of larger numbers, and keeping track of many cognitive tasks at once

When effectively put together, these differing capabilities can help us make sense of data—a large and important undertaking.

This chapter explores a couple of variations on the theme of thinking machines and how they relate to data visualization:

- The context and interactions of techniques such as data mining and data visualizations

- The interplay of different general types of human learning/thinking styles (multiple intelligences)

Taken alone, each of these topics is nearly limitless, so I will highlight just a few aspects, raise a few questions, and offer the perspectives of people coming from very different viewpoints.

THE YIN-YANG OF DATA ANALYSIS

The computer is the most significant of human inventions because it complements the human brain....

— COLIN PITTENDRIGH (ENGLISH BIOLOGIST)

The "yin-yang" symbol represents the essential and dynamic relationship between opposites—night-day, earth-sky, male-female, to name a few examples. The fundamental idea it contains also applies to the apparent opposing elements involved in working with data (Figure 6.2). How do factors such as insight, intuition, and creativity work, for example, with algorithms that automate aspects of working with data? What is the yin-yang of pairing techniques such as machine learning with human intelligence? On its own, the automation of examining data can lead nowhere—no context or ideas ever emerge. On the other hand, by itself, an intuition or insight that can't be supported by the data becomes pointless in areas ranging from business intelligence to drug discovery.

Although it can be hard to define, you probably have an intuitive sense of the word "intuition." It's that immediate sense of recognition, understanding, and insight. It's knowing what to do without exactly being able to explain how you know—a "gut feeling."

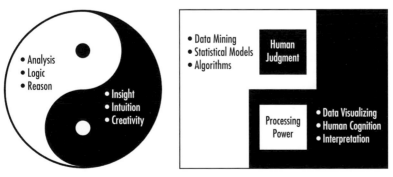

FIGURE 6.2

Data analysis, the Yin and the Yang. *Sketch by Hunter Whitney.*

Although there's no doubt that our intuitions can sometimes be wrong, it's also true that intuition can be extremely helpful, if not essential, in many of our decisions.

Instead of being in direct opposition to logic, it can provide a deeper context to a purely logic-driven approach. It's an added filter of wisdom and experience for solving problems that require more than syllogisms and formulas to solve. We call it a "gut instinct," but it also comes partly from our heads. We draw on an accumulation—a lifetime of input, memories, and lessons learned—that allows us to tap into the things we call intuition and inspiration. We also can experience an emotional aspect of that in our whole physiology; our nervous system and our muscle memory are programmed and reinforced as we live our daily lives. One way people can apply this "secret sauce of cognition" to data that is processed by computers is by using visual systems.

Data visualization attempts to achieve several goals that are seemingly at odds with each other. On one hand, it can help a wide range of people, who are not quantitatively inclined, engage with data that otherwise would not be accessible to them. Visualization can leverage human perception and cognition to spark creativity, insights, and understanding, processes that are not cut-and-dried. These are the things that have not been in the scope of computers. Areas such as data mining are attempting to automate and systematize the process of working with huge quantities of data; something that humans can't do without the help of processors. Computation can be mediated by humans interacting with visually encoded data, and machines can learn from these interactions to make things fit into new algorithms and models. In this way, data visualization and data mining are tightly bound to each other.

There's a variously ascribed saying that "Luck is what happens when preparation meets opportunity." Perhaps something similar could be said of insight—it's what happens when a lifetime of particular experiences meets an intellectual challenge. It's not always easy, or even possible, to explain the reasons why things are intuitive and "obvious." In fact, determining such things encompasses some of the hard problems people involved in machine learning are attempting to solve. Whether or not we're ever fully able to offload our thinking process, the more we can automate parts of the process reliably and allow computers to take over the low-level, but high-volume, work with data, the better. That will allow humans to spend their time and energy on what they do best.

SCALING-UP ANALYSIS: KNOWLEDGE, DATA MINING, MACHINE LEARNING

The real danger is not that computers will begin to think like men, but that men will begin to think like computers.

— SYDNEY J. HARRIS

Many of the fine points in the definitions of and distinctions among "data mining," "machine learning," and "statistical modeling" are better left to other discussions. Here, we can boil it down to its essence: the value of these efforts is to help people get a handle on a lot of data. These computational tools and techniques are about managing and automating the process of going through mind-bogglingly large data sets. Data visualization can help us grapple with data, but there's a limit to what can be displayed and perceived. Data mining can help winnow through the extraneous material, but of course, determining what's "extraneous" may not always be a simple matter.

More goes into these tools than we may think, and there may be drawbacks to the results that we didn't anticipate. True, algorithms help turn certain actions into routines that most of us don't have to think about—they just happen in the background. But they didn't materialize out of thin air; something had to be created by people, and those processes behind the curtain were set in motion by human judgments, ideas, and skills. These cognitive labor-saving marvels also take us that much further from the source data.

The same idea applies to statistical work on data. It can do a brilliant job of summarizing data and revealing patterns; however, the approach used in summarizing the data can alter dramatically what conclusions you might draw. Many justified laments have been made about how charts and graphs can mislead people, but what about the process that provides the material for the visualizations? It can be a lot easier to pick apart a problematic visual representation than the underlying assumptions, processes, and methods that shaped data into the form used to create it. Problematic charts and graphs make an easy target for criticism because they're almost always the most obvious and accessible aspect of data lifecycles.

However, the true source of the problem can be more fundamentally embedded in the process itself. A technically well-executed visualization may be built on a flawed foundation. The old saying about "putting lipstick on a pig" comes to mind. The "lipstick" is the pretty graphic, and the "pig" is bad data. In the case of a graphic, it is, by definition, visible, but the proverbial pig of data is never seen.

Many of us may think of visualizations only as the end result of the data lifecycle. However, they also can be helpful at the beginning, as well. Perhaps more can be done with using visualizations to help get better views of various stages of the full data lifecycle. Also, offering people access to the original raw data and metadata, if in visual forms that are reasonably viewable and understandable, could be helpful. Visualization can be employed for purposes ranging from processing raw data to summarizing it to interpretation. If the visualizations are simple, effective, and elegant enough, then a range of users can become more involved at every step of the way, if they wish. People who might have had no other option but to wait until the data was processed before grappling with it would benefit from a new breed of visual tools that would allow them to engage with the data at an early stage.

ENTERING THE MINE

Data mining can be an effective tool for a couple of distinct purposes. It involves finding patterns in large quantities of data that might be undetectable to people or determining how well a data set fits into a particular model. A model—or models—is almost inevitably involved. Data mining is driven by a goal, such as fitting some data to a model after any errors have been stripped out. It can put existing ideas, models, and hypotheses to the test with actual data. This verification process, although not absolute, can help determine directions to pursue—or not. When used for discovery of patterns in the data, data mining can focus on either of the following:

- *Describing* patterns, trends, and properties of the existing data that may not have been noticed

- *Predicting* trends based on the data

One common example of data mining is assessing creditworthiness. Are customers "low-risk," "high-risk," or somewhere in-between? Determining current classifications or making predictions of future behavior is not always an up or down process. The following are a few of the basic processes of data mining. Not surprisingly, in many ways they parallel the processes required for data visualization.

Collection
Because of the enormous volumes involved, data collections are based on samples from one or more databases. The full set of data to be mined is simply too unwieldy and unnecessary for the analytic tasks at hand. That said, the decisions about the sampling process, such as what exactly constitutes a "representative" sample, could be the subject of lively debates.

Cleaning and integration
The adage about "garbage in, garbage out" is especially apt when it comes to data mining. Because it is such a highly automated process, it's essential to make sure the data is sound before it gets run through the process. Data visualization is often used at this stage to help people find the inappropriately coded or otherwise problematic data. These outliers can often stand out like sore thumbs, even to people who are relatively untrained with regard to visualizations.

Reduction
Who says you can have it all? Most of the time, you're going to have to discard some of the data you've collected, and some variables are going to be left on the cutting room floor. It can be tricky to figure out what to cut and what to keep, especially early in the process. Once the reduction process is automated, it can be easily forgotten or go unnoticed by the people who are working with the data. Over time, the data may change substantially, but the automation process may not. That can be a real problem.

There's much to be said for automating things that would take a lot of time, energy, and expense for people to do...if they can do them at all. Even so, a more manual approach to data, aided by tools like visualization, does have some advantages, too.

MANUAL AND AUTOMATIC

I first learned to drive with a rusty old VW Beetle. It took some effort getting used to the manual transmission, and it was not an immediately flawless performance, but I'm glad I did it that way. It made me listen to the car's engine. If I happened to grind the gears in a shift change, it became an almost physical sensation; it felt great when I was in sync with the vehicle. The first car I owned was an old, but agile, four-speed sports car that gave a sense of connection with the road, car, and mechanics of driving. The faint scents of burned breaks, or oil, or the vaguely sweet smell of antifreeze were powerful indicators of the condition of my car.

When I switched to driving automatics, that close connection and integration of person and machine started to fade away. In some ways, that's a blessing and a curse—I can pay more attention to NPR, but I don't experience driving the same way anymore. A small indicator light warns me, I hope, of any looming problems. Similarly, computers can increasingly automate the process of navigating through data. This is good—if you can be confident that the source of the data remains consistent. It's not so good if the data change significantly and you have no sense of that alteration. There may or may not be any indicators suggesting that users check the metadata. A lot of computational horsepower is often necessary to quickly navigate through the data, but it's still important to maintain a close enough connection with it to have a sense of whether the right stuff is in the tank.

I'm not sure about ever going back to using a manual transmission, but I'm glad that I had the experience and internalized it—it has given me better perspective. Getting more "manual" with the data, even for people who might not want to do that regularly, might be a useful exercise. The manual approach may not be as "efficient" but might be useful with smaller scale data sets.

AUTOMATED OBSERVATIONS AND HUMAN HYPOTHESES

Imagine that a young scientist, doing his first scientific study, hikes into the woods to find out the relative population sizes of two recently discovered red-bellied and blue-bellied species of bird. As he walks through the forest, he sees five times as many red bellies as blues. Diligently, he goes back several times to collect more observational data; he goes out at the same time of day and in the same weather and also goes out at other times just to be sure that time of day and temperature are not having an impact on his findings. It always ends up averaging out to five times as many reds as blues. Proud of all the extra effort put in, he submits his paper to a prestigious ornithology journal, but his conclusion is wrong, and he's missing some vital metadata. There are, in fact, three times more blues then reds. It just happens that the red birds tend to be fearless, feisty, and curious creatures. The blues are far more timid and, metaphorically, "yellow bellied."

Based on his methodology, the junior scientist would continue to get the same results and never be aware of the factor (his presence in the forest) that is skewing his results. What would he have to change to be able to uncover the true picture? The investigator would first need to consider the idea that his results are not as definitive as he thinks. Second, he would have to try to see if there were other ways to gauge the relative percentages of these two kinds of birds. For example, maybe the birds make different kinds of nests or eat different kinds of berries that could provide visual corroboration or counters to his observa-tions. In other words, the relative presence of the different kinds of birds in an area can have other kinds of detectable and measurable impacts. Using these other clues, he might be able to determine the true populations with greater fidelity. Taking the right extra steps may not be easy or obvious, but it's essential, and technology can help make it attainable.

Let's take this analogy a step further and say the researcher is trying to learn about the populations of birds in the forest by listening for their calls in the ambient sounds of their environment. This would likely be an impossible task without the help of sensitive recording and analytical instruments. He could scatter listening devices throughout the woods that collects the sounds and display the results in a way that would be reasonably easy for humans to interpret. These listening devices would have another advantage, too—they'd remove the confounding influence of direct human intervention. The timid blue-bellied birds likely would be unaffected by the presence of the listening devices, as opposed to a person walking around with an oversized microphone and recording equipment. This instrumented and automated approach to getting observational data can be used for studying other things in other fields. The pairing of automated pattern-detection tools with human interpretation, almost certainly, will have a growing impact on many people's daily lives.

Here's an example of such a pairing from healthcare. We all know that some medications can have serious side effects. Just listening to a TV commercial about a seemingly innocuous drug for a minor problem, we can hear a long and dire disclaimer about side effects, many of which seem far worse than the problem itself. What's often less obvious are the cross-reactions between different drugs taken by the same person. There may be no obvious connection between two drugs or any hint that their combination could be a problem. A vast number of potential combinations might, for some reason, be highly dangerous to the people taking them.

One way researchers can confront this issue is by teaming up with pattern detection computing and, at times, a little data visualization. For example, an antidepressant and a cholesterol-lowering drug taken together can have a surprising and significant impact on a person's blood sugar levels in a way that would not happen if they were taken alone. This connection was found with a data mining algorithm that was able to comb through a very large FDA database and detect this pattern. Biomedical Informatics researcher Nick Tatonetti calls this pattern a "latent signal," which was subsequently tested and found to be a real cross-reactivity issue. It might never have been considered if the process of finding it had not been automated. Tatonetti, who led this work on data mining and drug cross-reactivity, says that, although data mining methods are still "rudimentary in many respects, they can help researchers find a few good connections" in masses of messy data.

Tatonetti uses the red and blue bird analogy presented above to describe a problem encountered with drug discovery. The incidents of adverse drug reports sometimes have less to do with the actual numbers than with unconscious biases and reporting behaviors by physicians. There are many possible variables to consider; large numbers of data to sort through and the relationships within them may not be intuitive.

Algorithms, such as the ones Tatonetti created, can search for interesting connections that humans can then consider and investigate. Computers don't have innate assumptions and preconceptions. A person may not think about looking at a potential adverse reaction from the combination of an antidepressant and a cholesterol-lowering drug simply because they seem so unrelated to each other. A computer, on the other hand, does not "think"; it just extracts patterns and relationships in the data and doesn't "know" what might turn out to be a surprising combination to a human interpreter. That can sometimes prove to be very useful.

Biases can be subtle things. What we expect and exclude in our thinking is, partly or largely, derived from our experience and knowledge. It can serve us in good stead most of the time, but it also can create intellectual blind spots. Those blind spots can be reduced with the aid of algorithms that act as side-view mirrors, allowing us to keep focused on the main task in front of us but still retain our awareness of what's happening outside our field of vision. Tatonetti says we can teach algorithms to extend our powers of observation, but what they can't do is "discern the truth." He adds, "Some say that data is king and science is dead, but that's not so. People make the crucial hypotheses, and our ability to collect more and more data has somewhat overshadowed the importance of what people do with it."

In the relationship between machine-driven observation and hypothesis formation by humans, Tatonetti thinks that the more people are able to picture and understand how these algorithms work, the more they will feel comfortable using them as supporting tools. He created a visualization of the way his adverse reaction-detecting algorithm works to provide a more tangible depiction for people who are interested in the biomedical implications but are not trained in computer science. Although not intended for consumption by a general audience, this graphic is an example of how a visual representation can bring an abstract algorithm to life.

The graphic helps provide a shorthand for the process of how patterns are detected by the algorithm. The results of any adverse cross-reactions then are validated by examining actual patient data from Electronic Medical Records (EMRs).

BLACK BOXES, TOY BOXES, AND OUT OF THE BOX

So computers can process data in ways that humans can't easily match, and humans can perceive meaning and associations in simple patterns that can stump machines. The useful associations between different observations of data that people can detect can sometimes lead to important innovations. Similarly, computers can come up with associations that people wouldn't expect. As technology continues to improve, the divisions between people and machines may become less and less clear. There will be gaps, overlaps, and gray areas.

One example of a significant gap is what is often referred to as a "black boxes." This basically means the people who are consuming data outputs in the form of visualizations may have no idea how the data was processed. Of course, part of the power of visualizations may reside in their ability to help more people who are less numerically inclined better understand the process. But if the visualization is to make data more intelligible to people other than data scientists, then that means they likely will not understand the data transformation process.

Often the raw data goes into a "black box" and comes out the other end in a form that people have to decide whether to trust or not. The process of creating algorithms and mathematical models may sound to many like a very cut-and-dried business, but that's not always the case.

In some of the following examples, this challenge is present and may not be fully answerable any time soon. Even so, they represent some novel approaches to data visualization that show how people, processing power, and advanced mathematical models might come together in surprising new ways to fight diseases.

Alongside "black boxes," you can also find what I think of as "toy boxes," which are tools that turn data into visual objects that people can play with and explore. However, they're not just fun and games. These tools give form to problems that allow them to be solved by people with a range of different skills. In the case of EteRNA, a visualization game that allows people to figure out the shapes of genetic materials, not only do they work with virtual objects, but these objects are actually synthesized in a lab and turned into the real thing. These are truly twenty-first century Tinker Toys®, so to speak. Whether it's black boxes or toy boxes, these forays in novel visualizations will help move the field forward. Some will prove themselves, and others may not, but such attempts are necessary if we want to have more at our disposal than histograms and scatter plots to engage with data.

GUT-CHECKS AND ALGORITHMS

Data mining can be a powerful method to make certain kinds of computational assessments and predictions. Although machines have the power to process massive amounts of raw data, that's not a substitute for rigorous human thought. Computers shouldn't be crutches.

Computer scientist Nigel Duffy is concerned that the effectiveness of software tools in one task can also sometimes create a sense of complacency in another. He believes, for example, that scientific researchers need to guard against the impulse to mix partial data, incomplete ideas, and black box algorithms in the hope that brute processing will produce good results. Duffy leads a software engineering team for drug discovery technologies at a biotech company called Numerate, where a big part of his work involves selecting and vetting hypotheses that predict the properties of drug molecules. Although it is possible to generate many hypotheses, only a few will work in the real world. Duffy thinks that, in some ways, technology may seem like it can take the burden off of people to work at formulating good, solid ideas; it can be tempting to come up with fairly flimsy hypotheses that are then tossed over to data miners for verification.

One problem with this approach, he says, is that if researchers crank out a large number of theories, some will look good purely by chance, even if they are ultimately flawed in some way. "You can't just try a shotgun approach—you are going to find stuff that looks good." He adds, "Scientists could really fool themselves by throwing a bunch of ideas into a black box. There is a real cost to using data to test hypotheses." In some sense you can only test a certain number of theories before you "use up your data," he continues. "We need to be careful about how we incorporate the human involvement." The interplay between purely computational and human assessments are rarely formalized and typically not well understood.

Duffy thinks that in "hypothesis-poor" environments, where the problems are not well understood or well characterized, people have to work harder to come up with their own novel theories because the important questions are not as apparent. However, there may not be enough data to test many hypotheses reliably, so it becomes necessary to identify reasonable hypotheses supported by knowledge or experience that's outside of the data. In environments that are "hypothesis-rich," where the outlines of the problem are well understood, then the process is more about determining the parameters and letting computers do the work. Computers can most effectively extract the best parameters from the data. Even then, however, it is still important for people to think hard about what ideas, out of the many generated, warrant special attention.

Duffy says, when creating computer models, researchers should ask themselves "Do I have a small set of potential experiments that I really believe in?" One way, he suggests, to do a gut check about a set of hypotheses is to imagine that every experiment is going to cost $10,000 for every one tested. There are real costs associated with each test but because of the extent to which the data has been "used up" by prior testing, the costs are hidden and the validity of the output is questionable. If the cost of using up the data was more explicit, then maybe people would think twice. The hidden cost is either the requirement for more data, or more often and more worrisome, the erroneous selection of false hypotheses. If you are coming from the algorithm side, you need to ask what the underlying assumptions for generating hypotheses are.

Computer science-oriented people who create the algorithms should try to be aware of the key issues in scientific problems. Duffy feels that computer scientists and biomedical scientists don't always fully appreciate the depth of each other's fields. Ultimately, the process of data-driven drug discovery will not be effective without close collaboration, intellectual honesty, and hard work from people in both fields. He believes, "if it is easy, then you're probably not thinking hard enough and leaning on your data too much."

CONSTERNATION ABOUT CORRELATION AND CAUSATION

Before looking at a few examples of visualizations, I want to address an idea that can overshadow this topic. Because machines can seek and find all kinds of patterns in data, around the clock and at unimaginable speeds, the number of meaningless as well as misleading patterns can increase. "Data dredging," as automated pattern discovery is sometimes snarkily called, can certainly stir up a lot of unimportant sediments and severely reduce clarity. As with so many other areas of technology, data mining can be a double-edged sword. It can amplify our ability to find the nuggets of insight in a mountain of data, or it can lead people down sinkholes of time and resources. This will certainly be an ongoing consideration for working with data at large scales.

However, computers can be programmed to discard what is considered to be junk for the purpose and context. For example, a hurricane track chart from the National Oceano-graphic and Atmospheric Administration (NOAA) could include all the tracks with any possibility. But what you see on the six o'clock news shows all those tracks with less than a 3% (or 5% or whatever) probability stripped away. That's where the decision comes in. What do you include, what do you discard?

Early in statistics 101, the point where correlation doesn't necessarily indicate causality gets hammered home. One classic example of this idea is the relationship of ice cream sales and violent crime rates. As sales of ice cream go up, so do murder rates. What is it in this dessert item that leads to this clear and direct correlation? Are Ben and Jerry instigators of aggression and mayhem? Obviously not. The connection is due to other factors—as the weather gets hotter, people tend to consume more ice cream. Simultaneously, as the temperature increases, some people are more prone to aggressive acts.

Of course, we don't want to take actions based on the wrong conclusions from perfectly good data. Banning the sale of ice cream to combat crime is a bad idea. The "confounding variable" here, the weather, is what's driving both phenomena, and that we can't regulate all that well, as yet.

The concept of correlation and causation can be really tricky. Conversations on this topic can be difficult; Joel Dudley, a bioinformatician who works in drug discovery, says it's, "the surefire way to shoot anything down." But correlations, even if not causal, can still be interesting and useful pointers to other relationships and patterns. In the real world, many relationships involve complex, subtle, and multiform networks. He created the infographic in Figure 6.3 to represent a particular person's health risk for cardiovascular disease based on that person's personal genetic profile in relation to a range of other factors that have a direct or indirect impact.

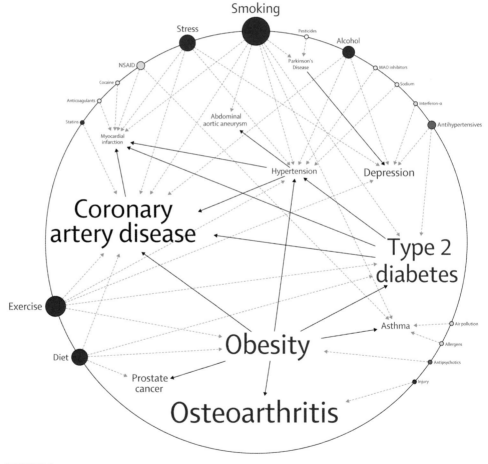

FIGURE 6.3

A map of health risk. Reprinted from *The Lancet*, Vol. 375 (9725), 2010. Ashley E. A., Butte A. J., Wheeler M. T., Chen R., et al. Clinical assessment incorporating a personal genome, pp. 1525–1535, with permission from Elsevier.

Dudley notes that physicians regularly use medications for which the underlying mechanisms and pathways are not fully clear. The fact that the drug works, causation aside, is what matters most, in the immediate context of helping the patient. To take just one example, for thousands of years, people used willow bark to manage aches, pains, and fevers. It took a very long time to identify and isolate the key chemical ingredient, salicylic acid, that explained the medicinal properties, and the full mode of action for all of its benefits still isn't completely understood. Even so, the end product, aspirin, and its plant precursor have been a boon. The point here is that we don't always have to be certain of causation to make useful associations and connections.

Some visualizations may reveal patterns of correlation between variables without a direct causal link. Nevertheless, these visual representations may still be useful to researchers. Perhaps the best approach is to think about a range of possibilities for visualizations while acknowledging and reminding ourselves that although patterns may not always show causation, they still can be interesting and useful.

THE SHAPE OF THINGS TO COME?

If we can find ways to give shape to data, we can use those forms to begin getting a sense of what the data might suggest. This is what the visualization company Ayasdi is attempting to do. Founder Gunnar Carlsson says that the data representing different phenomena and relationships have different telltale shapes. As an example, he points to the dynamic relationship of populations of predators and prey as a process that produces a visual form (a looping shape; Figure 6.4).

FIGURE 6.4
A well-known prey and predator.

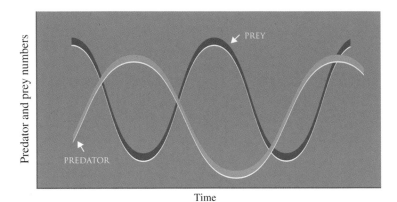

FIGURE 6.5
The cycle of predation.

In the eternal contest between predator and prey, there can be fluctuation in the ratio of the two populations. If the number of coyotes declines, for example, then the number of roadrunners can increase, as they are less likely to become a main course. As the number of roadrunners goes up, there's a good chance the population of coyotes will go up, too, because there are more chances to find a nice meal, even if the methods for obtaining it don't always work out. Simplified versions of the shape of data from this dynamic might look like Figure 6.5. A more complex version looks like Figure 6.6. That same shape is also captured, in my mind anyway, in the image of the rapidly moving legs in Figure 6.7.

Carlsson says his team has been working with a few primary shapes of data. Along with "loops," which represent such phenomena as predator–prey relationships, there are also "flares." These kinds of data shapes can represent populations with diseases, such as diabetes or breast cancer, and might be applied to medical research. Features, such as flares, can indicate different health risks among groups (see Figure 6.8 on page 246).

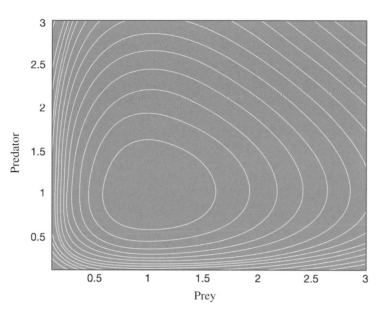

FIGURE 6.6
Echoing elliptical.

FIGURE 6.7
Dinnertime or not?

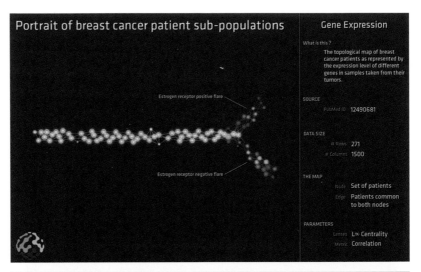

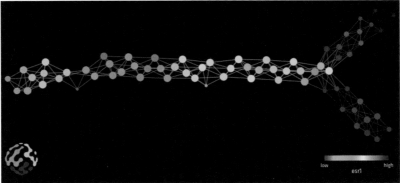

FIGURE 6.8
The flares of cancer or not.

Some people are skeptical of this kind of approach and feel that working with shapes in this way is akin to reading tea leaves. Our hardwired tendencies to perceive patterns, the argument goes, can lead people to see all kinds of ostensibly meaningful patterns where none exist. Over time, the robustness of this approach will be tested. Carlsson says:

> The development of methods which will be able to determine in an objective way what features are present in the data is continuing at a rapid pace. It's indeed the subject of much of the research into what is referred to as "computational topology." The idea is that there are "homological signatures," which are quantitative objects and can be directly measured on the data.

He adds, "These are reflected in shapes such as 'flares' and 'loops', as well as other properties." He says there will soon be very systematic ways to attack these problems.

KNOWING HOW TO FOLD 'EM

Sometimes the difference between health and illness, life and death, comes down to infinitesimal differences in the shapes of molecules in our bodies. The right shape can be the difference between a drug working or being totally ineffective. Misshapen proteins are involved in diseases ranging from Alzheimer's to Bovine Spongiform Encephalopathy (BSE or "mad-cow disease"). As vanishingly small as they are, the shapes and structures of these molecules can be a big puzzle.

The reason is, amino acids can fold up into the correct shape in a very large number of ways. There are many ways, for example, to fold a piece of paper into different forms, but if someone asked you to make an origami elephant, that might be a different matter. Biomedical researchers may have extensive knowledge about the chemical properties of what they're working with, but that data alone may not be enough to help them see how to create the scientific equivalent of an origami elephant. For that, they may need access to a different skill set of visual thinking that does not require knowledge of biochemistry to help solve problems.

Adrien Treuille has designed games that turn complex problems involving protein folding and genetic material into online games (*Foldit* and *EteRNA*) that are both engaging on their own and have the benefit of contributing to scientific knowledge (Figure 6.9). Hundreds of thousands of players have already played these games, and a few scientifically useful insights have emerged from a community that may not have been trained in biochemistry but does have very strong visual/spatial problem-solving skills.

Treuille says, "One of the key differences between people and machines—at least for the time being—is that humans are able to look at very little bits of data and often have to

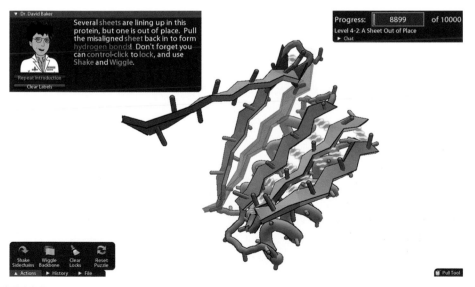

FIGURE 6.9
A screen shot from *Foldit*.

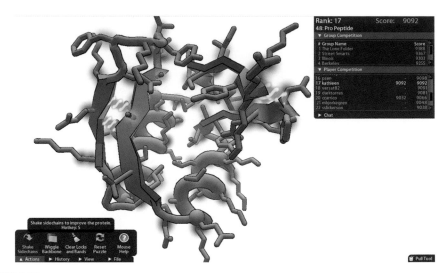

FIGURE 6.10
Getting complex!

generalize from that, whereas a computer can test trillions and trillions of patterns." In his games, the players have access to relatively little data, but even so, in 20% of the cases, they are able to come up with novel, accurate, and useful solutions. (See Figure 6.10.)

The interactions of Foldit and EteRNA do more than enable a remarkably broad range of people to usefully engage with scientific data and suggest novel ideas for figuring out biological structures. The games also enable new strategies and exploratory methods for *how* to solve a range of problems. The contributions by people in these areas can, in turn, be augmented by computational horsepower. In the case of Foldit, the creators found that, in some cases, players had a particularly difficult time figuring out how to complete the task if they had to start at the very beginning. The authors of a paper about Foldit, remarked, "This indicates the need to find the right balance between humans and computational methods; players guided by visual cues perform better in resolving incorrect features in partially correct models than 'blank slate' de novo folding."

MULTIPLE INTELLIGENCES AND DATA VISUALIZATION

Spock: *Check.*
Kirk: *Checkmate.*
Spock: *Your illogical approach to chess does have its advantages on occasion, Captain.*
Kirk: *I'd prefer to call it inspired.*
Spock: *As you wish.*

—STAR TREK *EPISODE "CHARLIE X" (RODDENBERRY, 1966)*

FIGURE 6.11

Spock makes the logical move. *Use of clip from* Star Trek, *courtesy of CBS Television Studios.*

The users and contexts of data visualizations are many and varied. Although not as dramatic as the differences between people and computers, users and their cognitive styles and expectations can be notably distinct. The *Star Trek* characters Spock and Kirk vividly highlight aspects we all can recognize within others and ourselves: the logical, literal, and the intuitive associative states of mind. Each brings an essential element, and the distinctions introduce some useful counterbalance and tension. (See Figure 6.11.)

The same idea applies to the metaphor of the "left-brained" or "right-brained" kind of person that has become embedded in pop psychology. Although the idea is often oversimplified and overstated, there's some truth in the differing dominance of each of our two brain hemispheres. This division also seems to capture two divergent constellations of skills, tendencies, strengths, and weaknesses. A related concept, the idea of multiple intelligences, can be a helpful tool in considering how people create or consume visualizations. Here's a short list of some common characteristics of thought related to each hemisphere:

Left dominant
- Logical
- Linear
- Analytical
- Rational

Right dominant
- Creative
- Associative
- Intuitive
- Emotional

Although the actual divisions are not so clear and sharp, they work as shorthand for related types of thinking styles. The fact that the differences are more subtle make them even more useful as a way to describe how people work with data, make judgments about what is collected, and decide what to do with the results. Data visualizations bring into play both sides of the brain. It is the combination of the two hemispheres, the interplay of Kirk and Spock, that works out best. One way to think about this concept is that both "harder" and "softer" skill sets are important to help seek out new insights in data and boldly go where no one has gone before.

QUESTIONS, IDEAS, INSIGHTS

Our imagination is stretched to the utmost, not, as in fiction, to imagine things which are not really there, but just to comprehend those things which are there.

– RICHARD FEYNMAN

Where do your questions, ideas, and insights come from? Is the origin always clear to you? At least for me, it's just not a cut-and-dried process. Earlier in my career as a user interface designer, I was trying to solve a particular problem while putting together an interface and was feeling frustrated. The agency I worked for took a lot of pride in its ability to understand the needs of its clients and their customers and design for them, but I was feeling stuck. I went to my advisor for help. He said to just keep arranging the various elements and moving them around on the screen—"It's meditation in design," he said.

I kept tweaking the layout, and during the process, the design approach just clicked. That epiphany wouldn't have occurred without doing a lot of research and collecting metrics and facts about users or specifying the kinds of features and functionality. However, the design solution that worked best in the end came from the interplay of that data and simply spending time letting the wheels turn in a more open-ended process. Coming to the solution of a problem isn't always immediate in many fields. Scientific discovery is replete with stories of researchers laboring over an equation or chemical formula without success. Sometimes, it's only when we start to daydream, seeing pictures in our mind's eye, that the answers appear.

The process of data collection seems like a very "left-brained" activity, but is that always true? Increasingly, such a vast amount of data can be collected about *anything* that it can be hard to know what to collect, store, and organize. The decisions about what to collect can determine every aspect of what follows, down to the final visualization. Who's making those decisions upstream, and what are they based on? I've seen several instances, in my own work, in which the people who are the final consumers of data have very little or zero say in the key choices about what they get. There's no channel of communication. Visualizations that can help make the whole process more accessible and transparent for the end customer can create powerful feedback loops without much loss in the intervening steps.

There are countless ways to address this issue of transparency in the process of data collection, but it's safe to say that the process is not always direct or linear. Data visualizations

FIGURE 6.12
Collect/process.

of different kinds should be able to assist us in various ways. An important insight or question may emerge from a careful analysis of collected data or an accidental observation (Figure 6.12).

You can parcel out the data visualization process in many ways. In theory, the process can be integrated and cyclical, but in practice, that's not always the case. The people who play key roles in the process often never have any direct communication with each other. As discussed earlier, sometimes there's a seemingly large black box between the people asking the questions and the rest of the process that produces the visualization to address the question. For some users, not knowing what's in the box may not matter all that much. However, for people in business, scientific research, and other areas in which every aspect of the process can have direct impact on critical conclusions, the black box is a problem. Who are the people at the different critical junctures? How do they make their decisions? The process has an inherently human element to it, and that includes you. (See Figure 6.13.)

Different people have various skill sets, and sensibilities, some more analytical and some more creative. The capabilities brought to the table are essential to make the entire process work. In all cases, the process is not a purely analytical exercise and can have far-reaching effects. People make judgments to answer these questions:

- What is worth investigating?

- What data should be collected?

- How much will be kept and used?

- How is it labeled and organized?

- What kinds of statistical methods might be applied to evaluate and summarize it?

- How will that data be presented?

- How will the visualization be interpreted?

- How will the interpretation of the data be applied in the decision-making and/or further investigation process?

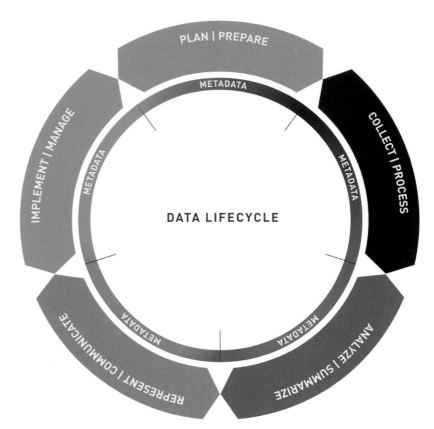

FIGURE 6.13
Data lifecycle infographic.

Think all these stages are only affected by pure objectivity and mechanical reasoning? It's easy to think of "right brain" creativity, judgment, and intuition in the context of designing displays, but somewhere, sometime, human decisions about data acquisition, algorithms, and setting statistical benchmarks also come into play. After all, people create the ontologies, algorithms, and statistical measures at some point to move the process forward. How are those derived? They sometimes come from emerging lines of questions, creative associations, and intriguing observations. That said, these intellectual flights of fancy would never really get off the ground without the help of left-brain rigor and solid factual validation.

HUMANS, COMPUTERS, AND COLLABORATIONS

This chapter has described various forms of collaboration between people and computer processing to analyze data, solve problems, and gain new insights. As technology continues its accelerating evolution, the distinctions between the different contributors will become less clear. The methods and strategies used by people will be more effectively modeled by machines. On the other hand, as in games such as Foldit and EteRNA, computer-generated visual cues can help supplement human problem-solving skills and help people get over the places where they get stuck so they can soar in the areas where they do best.

Interestingly, computers can also beneficially lower the barriers between people with different cognitive styles, interests, and knowledge. Molecular biologists, gamers, designers, artists, and data scientists, for example, can all make a meaningful and satisfying contribution to a real problem. That kind of collaboration would have seemed far-fetched not too long ago. Now, an online game can abstract a problem from a particular domain, such as molecular biology, and transform it into a visual spatial problem that a range of players can turn in their minds.

Digital online game platforms also can help spur, and take advantage of, some very human traits and motivations—the desire to compete, cooperate, and shine among peers. People are powerful thinking machines, but they need various inducements and structures to help them run optimally.

With large, complex, and dynamic flows of data, it can be easy for people to get swept away. The ability to provide structure and a way to see high-dimensional data in simple forms is a way to set handholds in the flood. Tools such as the topological visualizations work being done at Ayasdi can offer these structures. It's not clear which tools will be effective at giving the most useful form to data, but it is clear that those that are coming will provide important ways to make the most of the strengths of people and computation.

These collaborations may lead to some interesting psychosocial dilemmas. Let's say a physician is using a decision-support tool to make a medical diagnosis in a life-or-death situation in which there's very little time. The doctor draws on his knowledge, experience, and intuition. The computer uses its processing power and pattern-matching prowess to comb through a massive medical database. What if they come to different conclusions? Who would you trust with the answer? Would the physician still be as confident in his assessment, and how would that split decision be moderated?

As collaboration in various new incarnations begins to form, it's important to think about ways to strengthen these new relationships. From my standpoint, ideally, some of the main characteristics of the people I've enjoyed collaborating with most should be embodied in data representation tools (see Table 6.1 on the next page).

See life in an ocean of data: Part 1—a collaboration of people and machines

Take risks. Ask big questions. Don't be afraid to make mistakes; if you don't make mistakes, you're not reaching far enough.

– DAVID PACKARD

Talk about "deep data." It doesn't get much deeper than all that can be found in the earth's oceans. Exploring the seas with the tools of computing has become a grand collaboration of people and machines. One of the forefront research centers for this kind

Table 6.1 Tools Need Good People Skills

Good Collaborators' Traits	Data Representation Tool Qualities	Design Examples
Good listeners	Allow user to query the data effectively	A well thought out set of user input controls allows people to easily "ask" and define what they want to know
Challenge us	Ideally, the display helps look at the data in fresh, sometimes unexpected ways	Display presents the data in forms that shake up our expectations
Proactive	Don't wait for you to figure every-thing out	Based on user preferences, the display may proactively highlight patterns it detects that may be of interest
Honest, open, and authentic about what they're not sure about, as well as what they do offer	Don't hide uncertainty and imprecision in the display Don't make the display look more certain than the underlying data	Tools offer fuzziness, gradations, text caveats, and ± numerical ranges, and, perhaps most important, they make sources and other metadata as clear as possible
Not flakey	Tools work well *consistently* and in a reasonably predictable way	Tools are designed and tested to make sure there is a certain level of consistency and error handling is clear and well executed
Receptive and nondigmatic	Representation should be as free or bias as possible so users can draw their own conclusions	Avoid intentionally, or unintentionally, imposing a point of view based on the design's appearance, language choice, or other characteristics
Favor substance over flashiness	Representation should convey meaning and aid in one's under-standing (not just look cool and interesting and actually offer nothing of substance)	There are many examples of infographics, visualizations, and assorted "chart porn" that may look cool, but their complexity and/or obscure approach make them useless to nearly everyone
Pleasant to spend time with, or even are fun, when working on a challenging task	A stripped-down, dull, dry-as-dust design may not be the most effective—if you have to spend a lot of time working with something to solve a problem, why not make it pleasant?	Pleasing colors, design elements, and wording can help
Don't condescend or patronize others	Display shouldn't make its users feel overwhelmed, confused, or unclear	Use designs, languages, and other approaches that convey the information in as simple a way as possiable but, of course, no simpler
Bring something to the table	Output of the representation helps bring users new understanding of the data	Provide good content and arrange it in novel and useful ways
Make you look good	Representation directly helps you do your job better	Deliver visualizations that people can present

FIGURE 6.14

An AUV is set to sea. *Courtesy MBARI.*

of work is the Monterey Bay Aquarium Research Institute (MBARI), a private, nonprofit oceanographic research center in Moss Landing, California on the Monterey Bay. The Bay is one of the most biologically rich bodies of water anywhere in the world and it has one of the deepest submarine canyons in the continental United States.

Founded by David Packard, MBARI brings together scientists and engineers from fields ranging from marine biology to geology, and chemistry. There is a collection of research ships, remotely operated underwater vehicles (ROVs), and autonomous underwater vehicles (AUVs). In Figure 6.14, an MBARI technician is releasing an underwater glider into the Monterey Bay. These gliders are a type of AUV that are a seafaring counterpart to autonomous aerial vehicles that cross the sky. Although gliders move slowly (one half mile in an hour, more or less) they are long-distance swimmers and can stay at sea for months. This makes them useful for collecting data about long-term ocean processes. Figure 6.15 shows a "big picture" of how the people and machines interact with each other in this system.

Figures 6.16 and 6.17 show various multi-institution, multiplatform experiments in Monterey Bay, most of which were designed to track upwelling events and the algal blooms that often follow them. All of the data collected from satellites in space, underwater vehicles, and surface ships need to be put into forms that are as useful as possible for a range of researchers.

Such data include ship and ROV navigation information, bathymetric maps of dive areas, collections of geologic and biologic specimens, video frame grabs, and annotations of the recorded video. People like Mike McCann help turn those data into visualizations that can give scientists better insights. He's a software engineer in the Support Engineering Group and develops and supports applications and systems for acquiring, storing, and visualizing MBARI-collected data.

FIGURE 6.15
Peering beneath the waves in Monterey Bay. *Courtesy MBARI.*

FIGURE 6.16
Monitoring in the Monterey Bay. *Courtesy MBARI.*

FIGURE 6.17

A data-driven dive. *Courtesy MBARI.*

McCann says there are many interesting challenges within that "great gray fuzzy territory" between data collection and eventual visualization. However, he adds, bringing together various data sets into a common, compelling, efficient, and easy-to-use visualization system is essential to making sense of the data. McCann is particularly interested in exploring how 3D visualizations help researchers get the most useful perspective of the underwater world.

Seeing life in an ocean of data: Part 2—digital artist Spencer Lindsay

From massive blue whales to minuscule plankton, the oceans teem with amazing creatures that most of us will never see. The only time we might encounter a great white is while channel surfing during "Shark Week." The great migrations of whales, sharks, and other sea creatures occur in a realm that's completely hidden to the majority of nonaquatic types. With projects such as TOPP (Tagging of Pacific Predators), marine biologists have been able to tag and track a wide variety of sea creatures—from turtles to tuna—and record their migratory patterns, as shown in Figure 6.18 on the next page. Capturing all the data is a monumental effort involving getting transmitters on the creatures and monitoring them from orbiting satellites. Once all the raw data is collected, how can that work be meaningfully shared with the general public?

Mapping out the data

I first met digital artist Spencer Lindsay while I was working on a project at the Monterey Bay Aquarium. To me, Lindsay is a great embodiment of someone who can apply his artistic skills to different kinds of complex data.

FIGURE 6.18
Whale tailing. *Courtesy TOPP.*

TOPP researchers, hoping to gain insight on how 23 key species of pelagic (open ocean) creatures traveled, foraged, and bred, asked Lindsay to create a video. This video was to create visualizations and provide context for data gathered by the marine biologists on these creatures. The researchers gave Lindsay black-and-white charts and a big list of numbers.

Lindsay recalls, "They were very proud of their track maps—an outline of the coast, which had a bunch of lines and circles where the animals surface—they were all black and white." Lindsay began with tests in Photoshop® to see what colors would be most effective for displaying the migratory tracks. Then, during a brainstorming session with the scientists, his team came up with the idea of starting with a flyover of the Eastern Pacific.

Lindsay went to the NASA Visible Earth project with a resolution of one pixel per one kilometer. This resulted in a giant JPEG. Over the course of a week, Lindsay's team downloaded a couple of hundred gigabytes of data, which they then stitched together over another week to build a color map of the planet and a height map of topography and bathymetry. They used height maps to generate some "roughness and texture" in the virtual landscape. They also created a cloud map as well as a "shininess map" that showed places on the particular stretch of the earth's surface where sunlight would be reflected by bodies of water, such as lakes, rivers, and the ocean itself. However, he found that the images "took way too long to render and were not pretty enough." Lindsay decided to go back to the drawing board and redo the entire presentation in 2D. They again layered the map and composited it in *Adobe After Effects*®.

Lindsay took the tracking data and placed it into the geographic background. "The line we wanted to create would look like traces of light or glowing pathways," he says. Once they were able to render the luminous look they wanted, they then started adding in colors to differentiate routes of the different kinds of animals. The immediate problem they found, Lindsay recalls, was that their projection to lay this down along the coast was not the same as the marine lab's. The biologists were using a different kind of geographic projection than Lindsay was, and as a result, he says, "We could not get everything to line up. For a brief time, there was a lot of back-and-forth." However, Lindsay continues, "Eventually, everything matched up perfectly." (See Figure 6.19.)

Hundreds of hours went into the piece, but there's a moment that gets the biggest reaction from viewers. "The audience really loves that tracker lines sequence," says Lindsay. "I think they are reacting to the data about these creatures and the fact that it is visually compelling." He adds, "We 'juiced it up,' but we did not change the data at all." Along with making a map showing the animals' migration patterns, there was also the task of creating 3D models of the creatures—to bring the story of their journeys fully to life (Figure 6.20).

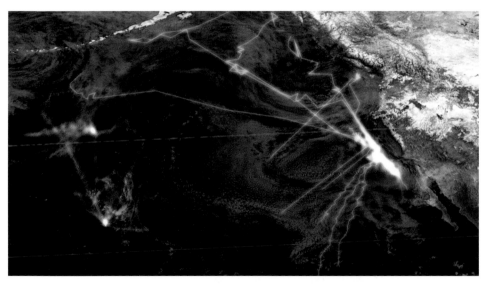

FIGURE 6.19
A screen shot from TOPP video.

FIGURE 6.20
A model whale.

http://goo.gl/cm7FL

"Tiny drifters" and touch walls

We've seen how the nomadic lives of some large oceangoing creatures can be vividly revealed. However, visualizing ocean organisms at the other end of the size spectrum can present its own set of challenges and rewards. Lindsay created an interactive "Plankton Touch Wall" for the "Tiny Drifters" exhibit at the Monterey Bay Aquarium (Figure 6.21).

The Monterey Bay Aquarium Exhibit planners initially considered using only static icons to represent the plankton in their "Tiny Drifters" exhibit, leaving visitors with a less interactive experience to the information. Lindsay suggested representing the creatures in real-time 3D, instead of static icons. The client was skeptical, so Lindsay put together a 3D prototype of a plankton species.

FIGURE 6.21
"Tiny Drifters" exhibit. *Courtesy of the Monterey Bay Aquarium.*

Bringing the subject into focus

Because these creatures are so small, they only can be fully seen using a very powerful microscope called a scanning electron microscope (SEM). To be made visible to the microscope, the critters have to be frozen and then coated in a very fine layer of gold. Whatever kind of animal you're talking about, it's safe to say that freezing it and coating it in gold will distort how it appears in its natural state. For Lindsay, the SEM was helpful for understanding the basic body shape, but only to a point. These creatures are flexible, like any living thing, with some parts perhaps more so than others. But, Lindsay said of the coated creature images, "they looked like they were carved out of rock."

Lindsay's team hit the books and spent a lot of time researching various aspects of their small subjects—even drawing from the work of Doc Ricketts (immortalized in the writings of John Steinbeck) and his ancient microscope. He noted that biologists can become enamored with a particular kind of animal, and it "was a trick of finding the scientist who was totally jazzed about a particular phytoplankton." After they assembled all the research data, Lindsay started drawing them by hand first. He wanted to get a picture in his head before starting to build them in 3D.

One of the most difficult aspects of accurately recreating these tiny, translucent creatures was figuring out what the various parts of their bodies look like when they're living in their environment. He said they had transparent, fuzzy, sharp, and soft places and textures on them, and it was difficult to be truly sure how they appear in real life. It takes experience, informed intuition, and artistry to capture the essence of these otherworldly life forms that inhabit a realm so removed from our experience (Figure 6.22).

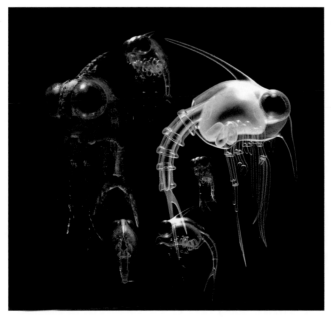

FIGURE 6.22
They came from another realm.

Scientific visualizations that also have a certain artistic sensibility are not just good for helping to engage the general public in science; they can also suggest new insights to even the researchers who are close to the data. When investigators see the models and visualizations Lindsay creates, they get a sense of the creatures that they would not get in the lab. It is a productive collaboration where researchers can interpret the data and explain key facts, while an artist like Lindsay can put what has been gleaned from the data in a different light. "The scientist can be great as a wingman," Lindsay says.

Getting a good "game feel" and real-world testing

Lindsay put his 3D plankton modeling work into the game engine Unity 3D®. He says getting the "game-feel" of the touchwall was not easy and caused some surprise when certain users first encountered the technology. One of the biggest concerns is not just about how an individual user would feel interacting with the multitouch wall, but also how it would affect the people who are standing nearby. For example, if the interaction involved big gestures, would that annoy nearby onlookers? How were they going to get the public comfortable with this new technology?

Anticipating and working through those kinds of concerns required a lot of imagining, physically moving around, and whiteboarding. Even so, some of the tweaking of the game-feel interactions didn't come until the installation process. Only then, Lindsay notes, did many issues become apparent that they hadn't considered. In the exhibit, tiny 3D models of plankton move around on the wall. When one of these is touched, it blossoms out to the size of a dinner plate (Figure 6.23).

FIGURE 6.23
Getting a feel for the interactions.

Lindsay recounts that, as they were installing the exhibit, "this guy brings in his four-year-old, who starts hammering on the screen, and within a few minutes the whole thing crashed." Because the scenario with the child was very likely to happen again once the exhibit opened to the public, Lindsay and his team had to figure out what technical changes were needed to prevent it from crashing again. "That was one of the interface things—how to get the experience to the public that is compelling, understandable, and bombproof."

Asked what he thinks about future directions in visualizing science for the general public and scientists, Lindsay says: "I think one of the secrets to my success is being able to use both halves of my brain, because that's what's required to reach the public about complex data. The advent of real-time 3D and game engines is going to explode the field. I think it will be very powerful."

THE SUM OF THE PARTS

As we'll explore further in the next chapter, true understanding and insight often only come when we can view something from multiple vantage points. It is only with multiple perspectives and the ability to see the big picture that the whole story becomes clear. In this chapter, we looked at the collaboration of bioscientists and gamers as an example of very different perspectives that can be brought together to focus on finding a solution to a single difficult problem.

In other cases, the perspective has come from orbiting satellites, autonomous underwater vehicles, and artists who work with digital 3D models. Collaborations between people and various kinds of machines and computers will certainly become more intertwined and dividing lines between the different participants less absolute. Visualizations play an important role in making these collaborations between people and machines stronger in the pursuit of making sense of data.

Hindsight, Foresight, and Insight

PART 1—ADAPTING TO DATA

The eye sees only what the mind is prepared to comprehend.

– HENRI BERGSON

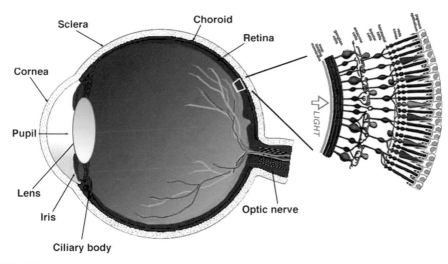

FIGURE 7.1
A gift from our ancestors.

See change?

Hindsight may be 20/20, but can it also bring the future into sharper focus? Glancing back at the past can help us to think about new ways to interact with, and display, data. The blistering pace of technological change can obscure the fact that we come equipped with our own uniquely powerful "wetware" (our brains) and operating systems that have evolved over a very long development cycle. Science is making great inroads in understanding and, to some extent, tinkering with our sensory and cognitive abilities, but that's another story. The future of visualizations will need to involve leveraging much of our innate perceptual and cognitive powers that have been shaped and honed by evolution. This means bringing to bear more of the full range of our senses and employing them on new kinds of tasks that would have been unimaginable, even in the recent past.

A simple example that comes to mind is my iPhone® and the mobile phone I had before that. The hand movements to operate this device are more nuanced and varied than the ones I used to interact with my old number pad. On the newer smart phone, the interplay between the visual cues, hand movements, and tasks feels more subtle and intuitive. My older phone, which required keying phone numbers and checking the display to make sure I hit the right digits, now seems cumbersome in hindsight. The various aural cues that signal outgoing and incoming texts on my iPhone are now part of the conversation. These are simple interactions, but they're made more fluid and engaging because the technology engages more of my senses.

There's nothing "natural" about texting, but it seems reasonable to say certain devices can make it feel more natural. That's probably because the interaction draws on deeply rooted attributes of our brains and bodies while applying it to modern information needs. Our sense of touch didn't come about because of the existence of touch screens. Interfaces that are designed to tackle dense data sets can enable us to reclaim and reapply various capacities that have been dormant because the tools we were using before didn't allow us to employ them.

The physical apparatus of our eyes, brains, and bodies many not change very much for the time being, but our minds will have to adapt to rapidly-changing environments that are densely packed with data. The way we can get the most insight from data is not only designing great interfaces, but also helping people to better understand how to view them. Our distant ancestors had essentially the same backdrop of the world as we have now, but what they "saw" was often different. I wonder, when a predecessor watched the sun rise or lightning flash, what were they seeing then, compared to what I see now?

Obviously, in some ways it looked the same but, I would imagine, their understanding of it was different. There actually *is* something new under the sun: your mind. Your knowledge, perceptions, and experiences are a unique combination of many factors. It's not just physiology that makes us who we are. Your way of looking at the world is shaped by culture, history, and many other influences. In thinking about the future of visualizations, the best place to start is by exploring the strengths and weaknesses we've received from both nature and nurture.

Optimized for what we need?

The abilities of all living things are based on a set of tradeoffs that emphasize different strategies for success. Humans are no exception. Our vision, hearing, sense of smell, and touch are impressive but are often more evolved in other creatures. Different species become optimized for what they need. Bees can see wavelengths of light that we can't perceive and that allow them to find their way into the nectar hidden in flowers. Bloodhounds can sniff out a convict fleeing through the countryside. Our own perceptual capabilities were tuned to help us survive and thrive in situations that didn't involve spreadsheets and screens.

Let's take vision as an example. Generally speaking, our ability to see details is strongest when we focus directly on one thing. The reason is that the central portion of the eye is packed with cone cells that are good at doing this kind of task. Peripheral vision is not as good for perceiving details, but works well for motion detection and seeing in dim light, thanks to the contributions of rod cells. It's all about tradeoffs. There is only a finite amount of room in the retina that different kinds of specialized cells can occupy, so they have to be allocated in such a way that the arrangement confers a maximum survival advantage; otherwise, that ancestor was less likely to produce any descendants.

This ancient ancestor might have glimpsed something stirring in the corner of his eye inside a dimly lit cave, even while focusing more directly on a detail-oriented task in front of him. That particular perceptual arrangement may not be so important these days, when all the action is on a rectangular screen facing you, and the biggest danger is that your boss may sneak by when you're watching the latest funny animal video. But what if data displays were much larger and enabled a bigger field of view? What if certain patterns of movement in data points on this display might be really interesting and important if you were able to detect and distinguish them? What if the display was fairly dark because something big, bright, and filled with the movements of live data flows would be too visually overpowering? In this kind of scenario, peripheral vision might play a key role beyond just keeping an eye out for the boss strolling down the hall.

Imagine an ancient ancestor looking intently at, and assessing the sharpness of, an obsidian blade he was making, while another part of his visual system was doing its part, making sure nothing was skulking nearby about to eat him. Over time, the world has become increasingly focused on a narrower field of view containing relatively small, flat screens that are directly facing us. A significant portion of many of our lives and work is spent staring at these small, flat surfaces, deciphering the information on them and figuring out what to do about it. This narrow field of view can be accentuated further by gray, fabric-covered enclosures that keep our attention even more on the screen directly in front of us.

Part of the visual apparatus that it took millennia for us to develop is left with nothing to do when using some of the most common tools and doing common tasks. However, in the data-rich environments that we now want to master, making the most of all our perceptual abilities will be an adaptive advantage. With immersive 3D data displays, for example, we're not just able to look at the details in our direct field of view; we can also potentially bring in more context and information conveyed by the motion-detecting prowess of our peripheral vision. In the quest to find meaningful patterns in data and with new visualization tools, the ability of an expert to detect interesting things off to the side may become increasingly valuable. For this reason, 3D immersive technologies may have much more practical value for making sense of data than we once thought.

People can see and hear things in stereo, yet much of our time and attention is spent focusing on a monovisual screen in a largely disconnected world. Generally speaking, without moving our heads, we have a more than 180° field of view. Hold your right hand up near the right side of your head, and do the same for the left hand on the left side of your head. Okay, now focus on the book or screen in front of you and wiggle your fingers. Now notice all the space between your fingers and the sides of the book or screen. The angle of view needed to use a computer screen is more in the neighborhood of 40°. Today, like many other days, I've spent a lot of my time in those 40°, my head barely deviating from a fixed position, with most of my center of attention remaining static. Human brains have a lot of capacity for visual perception and processing, yet the tools we use take advantage of only a relatively small part of it.

Finding resolution

Three very important characteristics of displays are *screen size*, *aspect ratio*, and *resolution*.

Screen size

Screen size is generally measured diagonally in inches, and today's LCD displays commonly range from 3 inches on cell phones to 100+ diagonal inches on larger televisions. Because screen size is measured diagonally, another measurement called the *aspect ratio* is required to determine the physical size of a display.

Aspect ratio

Aspect ratio measures the ratio of width to height (Figure 7.2). Almost all computer monitors and LCD televisions sold today have a 16 × 9 aspect ratio, commonly termed *widescreen*. Older computer monitors and televisions had a 4 × 3 aspect ratio, often termed *full screen*. The aspect ratio doesn't give any information about the size of a display; it only determines that "for every 16 units wide the display is 9 units high." If you hold your head still and fix your gaze straight ahead, you might notice that you're able to see more horizontally than vertically—a widescreen display caters to that characteristic.

Resolution

Although the physical dimensions of a display tell you how large the image is, they fail to tell how much detail the display can show. The amount of detail in any given display is directly related to how many pixels the display has, or its *resolution*. A pixel is a red, green, or blue dot that varies in intensity depending on the color that the groups of the dots are told to produce. Modern HDTVs look much better than old analog televisions because, among other things, HDTVs have more than five times the number of pixels. Pixels on digital displays are measured in two ways: display resolution and PPI.

Screen Size Is Measured Diagonally

Widescreen: 16x9 Aspect Ratio

Full Screen: 4x3 Aspect Ratio

FIGURE 7.2

Lark's tongue in aspect ratio.

Display resolution

Display resolution describes how many pixels make up a given display. For example, "1080p" HDTVs have a resolution of 1900 × 1080, which means there are 2,052,000 individual pixels in the display! Display resolution is size-independent—a 22-inch 1080p HDTV and a 70-inch 1080p HDTV both have the same number of pixels. An image shown on the 22-inch display is identical to an image shown on the 70-inch display, except the image on the 22-inch display is physically much smaller.

Nearly all the displays available today come in one of only a few different resolutions. Common computer display resolutions include 1920 × 1080, 1680 × 1050, 1600 × 900, 1366 × 768, and 1280 × 1024 (Figure 7.3). Cell phones often have much lower resolutions.

Pixels per inch

Another useful measurement is *PPI*—pixels per inch. PPI is a measurement of the number of pixels in any given inch of screen. This measurement varies widely across different displays. The 22-inch 1080p display mentioned earlier has a PPI of 100—in each square inch of screen, there are 100 pixels. Compare this to the 70-inch 1080p display, which has 31.5 PPI. You can try this out for yourself: Move close to a computer screen until you can see individual little squares (these are the pixels). Try the same thing on a large LCD television. The pixels on the large television are much bigger than the pixels on a computer monitor.

In the example, the 70-inch monitor has nearly ten times the physical screen area of the 22-inch monitor, yet they can display fundamentally the same amount of data. You can't show ten times as much information on the 70-inch monitor just because it's 10 times bigger. A minimum number of pixels are necessary to make things such as text

FIGURE 7.3

Time for a bigger monitor.

readable. Next time you sit in front of a computer, do a little experiment—open up a word processor and type a few random words. Highlight the text and change the font size to 5. No matter how close you get to your computer, you still can't adequately read text that small. Even if you were to plug your computer into a massive HDTV, a font size of 5 is still too small to read comfortably at any distance, if it can be read at all. Text that's 15 pixels tall can be read comfortably; text that's 5 pixels tall can't.

KEEPING PACE

It's easy to overlook how profoundly our current technologies shape our lives and thoughts. Some devices become so deeply embedded in our experience that they fade from conscious awareness. Their impact is only noticed, and then felt acutely, when they become unavailable—the car won't start, there's an electrical outage, or cellular service is unavailable. It can be useful to step back from familiar tools and consider the interplay of how we've adapted to them and how they've been modified to more closely fit our abilities and needs.

The dance between people and technology is not always graceful or well matched, and one side can get out of sync with the other for a while. Not too long ago, only a small group of people could interact with the few warehouse-size mainframe computers present in the world. Then, a little while later, the sweet little machine in Figure 7.4 appeared—the Xerox Alto, the first computer with a graphical user interface (GUI). The white dinner plate-like objects in the rack on the table are 2.5 MB removable disks, and the box under the desk that looks like an air-conditioning unit is the disk drive. Apple learned a thing or two from this great geek totem of computing.

FIGURE 7.4
The most venerable Xerox Alto. *Courtesy of Xerox Corporation.*

FIGURE 7.5
The good old PC interface.

These days, countless pocket-sized computers populate the world, and they've become highly personal objects. Isn't that right, Siri? Not many people were able to work with a mainframe, but most of us learn to work with mice, touchpads, and even user interfaces that only an engineer could love. The 17-inch screen, QWERTY keyboard, and a mouse have been mainstays of our professional and private lives for years now (Figure 7.5).

If I imagine these devices as though they were artifacts displayed in a museum of the future, they'd seem rather clunky and unnatural. What we think of as ubiquitous now, for instance, a folder or trashcan icon, may eventually seem archaic. Everything from tabbed windows to the current incarnation of search results may look like crude tools and blunt instruments…but then I return to the present, look at my monitor, and start tapping away at the QWERTY keyboard.

The explosion of interest in working with big data may highlight mismatches between the capabilities of our current computing outputs and inputs. The disconnect between desired tasks and what's humanly possible will come into increasingly sharp focus and drive demand for a range of new approaches in devices, designs, and code.

Changing the furniture

Looking at Figure 7.6, we see an evolution toward using more of the surfaces that surround us; interacting with our environment. Things that were just furniture are becoming the tools we use to interact (Figures 7.7 and 7.8).

FIGURE 7.6
Smart surfaces.

FIGURE 7.7
Data-driven décor.

FIGURE 7.8
A new class of interactions.

"CAVE" images then and now

Our ancient ancestors painted powerful images in caves, perhaps as a way to make sense of the world. Now, some researchers project images of works of art, and the data about them, on screens in immersive visualization facilities, such as a StarCAVE, which in this case is used as an instructional tool to better understand the creative process of great paintings (Figure 7.9).

Then and now, we use images as a way to make sense, and express it to others. The challenge has always been to discriminate among all the sensory stimuli vying for our limited attention, determine what matters at any given moment, and respond accordingly. No single human, now or long ago, could absorb and process all of the sources of all the raw material of perception that were coming at them every instant: the sights, sounds, smells, tastes, and textures of the world. Their—and our—sensory and cognitive systems had to collect, filter, parse, and make decisions from all the incoming material. Creating and using data visualization requires context and judgment. The software may change, but those elements always will continue.

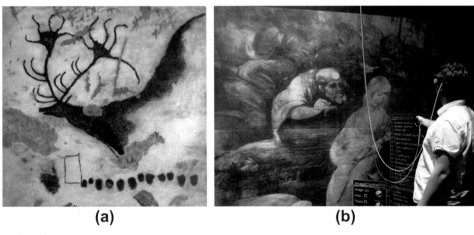

(a)   **(b)**

FIGURE 7.9

(a) An image of a Megaloceros from the Lascaux Cave Paintings, estimated to be 17,300 years old. (b) Placing reference markers on da Vinci's "Adoration of the Magi." Courtesy of Uffizi Gallery, Florence, Italy; photo credit: Maurizio Seracini and Calit2.

People adapting to technology and technology adapting to people

A magazine is an iPad that does not work.

– JEAN LOUIS

It's becoming an increasingly familiar scene—a parent places a glossy magazine in front of a toddler. The child begins pushing and squeezing a photograph on the page, expecting it to respond directly to her touch. She looks down quizzically as she moves her fingers ineffectually on the page. Before the widespread consumer adoption of tablet computers, and touchpad technology, presumably this kind of scenario didn't occur.

http://goo.gl/eKyDc

The flip side of people adapting to technology is technology adapting to humans. People in user experience design try to tailor the interfaces to machines so they are more accessible, effective, and pleasant for the types of users who have to engage with them. To an increasing extent, there's also a movement toward automating the process by which machines try to adapt to the needs and interests of users at an individual level. *Amazon.com*, for example, offers suggestions for books based on previous purchases. Internet marketers may send personalized promotions. One person will receive deals on a kayaking trip but no manicure offer, while another customer may receive an email spa for a package or cooking classes.

This kind of "getting to know" users and providing targeted and relevant feedback makes sense. Tools that help users make sense of large amounts of complex real-time data can be even more useful if they can take in information about the user's individual needs, help her filter out some of the noise, and help suggest areas that might warrant special attention. As with just about every other aspect of life, a balance is needed here. If the system gets too good at collecting data about the user as she works with it, and the feedback loop gets too tight, then there's a danger that it can reinforce misunderstanding of the data.

One trajectory for making sense of data involves *virtual reality* and *augmented reality* technologies. Although it's hard to say exactly what will emerge in the future, it's likely that these systems will engage more of our senses and allow for a broader range of cognitive styles. They will also likely blur the lines between the outside and processor-generated worlds. We will get closer to the machines, and they will get closer to us.

Although the work in artificial intelligence is fascinating and important, I'm personally more interested in *augmented intelligence*, perhaps because of my work and relationship with technology. That is, how can computing power and the interfaces that connect computers to human minds make us smarter and allow us to do higher-level analysis and decision making based on the vastly increased data available to support them? Unless we turn absolutely everything over to computers, there's a point where humans have to step

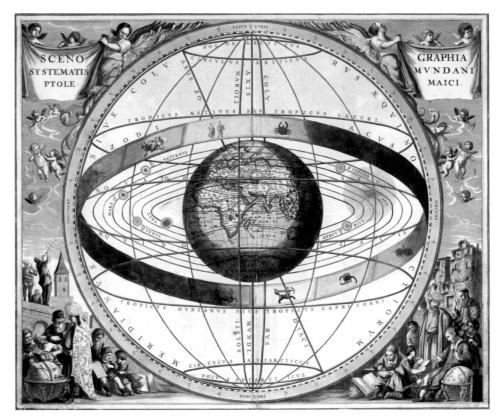

FIGURE 7.10
Earth and its spheres of influence.

in and a "handoff" has to occur. People have to do something with all the data they've collected. That handoff may be powered, in part, by artificial intelligence, but I hope the end results are not "artificially intelligent." This subject is an ongoing debate, and there's much more to be said on this subject, but not here.

Although there may be important differences between generations of users who work with tools to make sense of data, certain ideas also remain relevant and warrant consideration across time. These considerations include how to impose enough organization and systematization on data about the world to manage it effectively and comprehend it, while not making it so rigid that it perpetuates misunderstanding. For example, the belief that the earth was the center of the universe allowed many beautiful and intricate organizing principles and visualizations, although they happened to be completely wrong (Figure 7.10).

Connecting the past, present, and future

Just as evolution has shaped our unique set of perceptual strengths and weaknesses for looking at data displays, the history of science and mathematics has left us with certain capabilities when it comes to making sense of the data we see. These legacies might seem to be distant and peripheral to technology, but are they? Taking the impact of the past into account can suggest considerations for designing more effective data visualization displays.

The idea of creating visualization schemas to represent abstract mathematical concepts continues in a variety of new forms today, including work done in visual explorations in the field of topology. We encountered one example of such schemas in Chapter 6, in "The Shape of Things to Come?" section about work being done by Ayasdi.

Other examples involving such schemas include ideas such as specialization in sub-disciplines of science or developing classification systems for living things. These are important steps; however, they also have their drawbacks. Seeing both sides of the equation presents more opportunities to create tools that maximize the positive aspects and address the pitfalls.

Structure and flexibility

If new data can't be squeezed into the expected form, it can be all too quickly dismissed. Of course, models and structures can be essential in making data manageable and useful. However, once a model is accepted and adopted, there's a natural reluctance to abandon it if new data doesn't seem to fit. There's often a balance and tension between solid structures and flexibility, between the need to be open-minded and the need to have some conceptual scaffolding.

Observations and expectations

There's a lot to be said for making observations without expectations. It can require considerable discipline, patience, and courage to be prepared to put aside a prevailing idea if the observations are not matching the model.

There's sometimes a sense of inevitability when looking at historic events. With hindsight, it seems like the answers and outcomes were obvious all along. In the context of the times, however, it often looks far different. Perhaps new generations of visualization tools will enable observations that shockingly contradict some current well-accepted ideas. It doesn't just take the right tools to perceive the truth that the data is telling. A trained, but open, mind combined with a certain level of guts and persistence, is necessary to make it fully meaningful.

Noodling with data

Although we might not think of Johannes Kepler as a modern-day scientist, he was one of the great scientific visual noodlers, as well as someone who kept in close contact with data. Later in this chapter, we'll look at more recent developments in 3D visualizations, but in the late 1500s, the solid model in Figure 7.11 on the next page shows the nested geometries of five "platonic solids," which described the orbits of the planets, was groundbreaking.

Kepler's platonic solids suggested an interesting and aesthetically pleasing geometric pattern to the universe. However, Kepler inherited an extensive and rare set of tabular astronomical data from Tycho Brahe that didn't line up neatly with the model. If the orbits were not the perfect circles of a "perfect" universe, then what else could they be? By

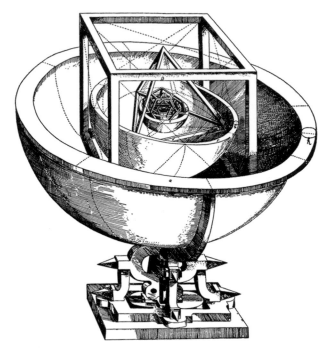

FIGURE 7.11
The Renaissance state of the art.

doggedly sticking with the data, doing mathematical heavy lifting and thinking, Kepler figured out that the true motion of the planets around the sun was, in fact, elliptical. That laid the groundwork for our understanding of the way our planetary system operates.

Even though his work with the platonic solids had its problems, it did help to solidify and refine the concept that the sun is the center of the solar system. If new data can't be squeezed into the expected form, it can be all too quickly dismissed. Of course, models and structures can be essential in making data manageable and useful. However, once a model is accepted and adopted, there's a natural reluctance to abandon it if new data doesn't seem to fit. There's often a balance and tension between solid structures and flexibility, between the need to be open-minded and the need to have some conceptual scaffolding.

Historical threads and visualization opportunities

The following are some general ideas for a few challenges that have yet to be solved:

Specialization and cross-fertilization

- *Issue:* With the complexity of various fields in sciences and elsewhere, specialization can be a necessity, but the disappearance of generalists and cross-fertilization can hurt innovation.

- *Visualization possibilities:* Visualizations that are tailored for an expert user in a specific field should complement other types of visualizations using the same data, to make the material more accessible for a wider range of users (such as the protein folding game, *Foldit,* discussed in Chapter 6).

Directed and open-ended observation

- *Issue:* Sometimes, it can be good to just look at things without an agenda. Whatever the discipline, if you always approach observations with a specific question in mind, you may overlook the more interesting question you hadn't considered. In the time-constrained, data-deluged, bottom-line-focused environments many researchers and analysts work in, the idea of just going out and looking may seem impractical and unrealistic. Even so, those serendipitous moments are still crucial. Until the time, if that arrives, that we can have perfect knowledge of data and its inherent inter-relationships enabling open-minded explorations—serendipity still matters.

- *Visualization possibilities:* Speaking as a user interface designer, I can say that the best user interface is the one you don't see. Perhaps the ultimate data interface would be one that is totally "transparent"—the user interface is an extension of the user. Every time a user stops thinking about the data and starts thinking about the interface, they lose focus and concentration. Designers should ask themselves if each interface decision can be implemented in a more naturally intuitive way. Presenting "raw" unprocessed visualizations and providing users tools to manipulate them may create new opportunities for experts to visualize data in ways the interface designer never expected.

Directed analysis and noodling

- *Issue:* When it often seems that there's so much to do and so little time, it makes sense that we want to get right to the answers in the data. However, answers and insights don't always reveal themselves in that way. Sometimes, it takes *noodling* and iteration with the data to get the best results.

- *Visualization possibilities:* Visualization tools that provide a guided flow might also allow for visual side currents and eddies that allow users to play with and ponder the data.

A few more thoughts . . .

With regular releases of sleek new devices and powerful technologies, it can be easy to forget that, sometimes, there's nothing new under the sun. Although the capacities to manage and visualize data are evolving at a rapid rate, the challenges of representing abstract concepts with concrete forms have occupied people for a very long time. Other issues with a long history and continuing impact on working with data include: discipline specialization, collaboration, and the limits of prediction. Sometimes it's good to take a fresh look at long-standing ideas. Here are a few examples:

Data as a lingua franca

Alternatively, collaboration-oriented visualization tools can help make various types of data sets more accessible and intelligible to a wider range of people, thereby promoting cross-fertilization between disciplines. There's nothing wrong with highly specialized tools made for people with particular skills and knowledge. However, it would be unfortunate if these tools were not complemented with other forms of visualization that enabled more people with different skills to come to the table. Of course, there's another theme that has not changed with the passage of time—and that theme is trust. Interdisciplinary teams must trust one another, and be trustworthy.

It's likely the trend toward greater specialization will continue. However, data can help provide a kind of common conceptual "language" and grammar that will help those in different disciplines converse with one another. Not surprisingly, differences in ideas about what data is, and the models it represents, can complicate the dialogue. Even so, scientists largely respect the authority of well-collected data and usually see a basis for agreement and discovery—if everyone agrees on the meanings of the fundamental terms used in the various disciplines. Such interdisciplinary understanding underlies the "cross-referencing" needed if data from disparate sources are to be combined and manipulated in a single visualization scheme.

Uncertainty and prediction

The idea of making consistently accurate predictions about various aspects of life has been a dream for many. But what's required to do so? Although we may not need perfect knowledge to improve predictions, we should have interdisciplinary collaboration to bring more variables into the model. For instance, risk factors for disease—all the "lifestyle" influences come from nonmedical fields: sociology, psychology, and so on.

With inexpensive and ubiquitous sensing devices for data collection, low-cost storage, and computers to process the massive inflows, the ability to make accurate predictions in many areas, from climate to crime, are now within reach. Sensing and computing technology makes this concept seem more realistic, although this still is not easy to implement. The challenge is to take data from a wide variety of sources and combine it in a way that illuminates how multiple factors combine to cause a particular future outcome. Imagine, for example, that you heard the local news meteorologist's weekend forecast and knew that it was precisely how things would turn out for your hike. Of course, the reality is that there are so many variables influencing the world, with complex relationships, that determining how they all will play out is daunting, if not impossible.

Getting things moving

Static visualizations are not necessarily the best way to show the dynamics of multiple interrelated variables. Even when well executed, these depictions still require considerable study and scrutiny to fully grasp their meaning. Modern computational technology makes it possible to create displays that visually summarize the outcomes of the multidimensional interactions of many variables at once. Such displays normally might be difficult to interpret, but interactive interfaces and animations can make it much easier to perceive and comprehend what is being shown. For example, a moving weather pattern can be relatively easy to understand, and viewers get a sense of a "probable" outcome of the joint effect of thousands of data points from tens of variables—it's so easy to understand that very little explanation is necessary from one day to the next.

There's potential for deliberately changing the data for a variable or a set of variables and looking to see how much change this induces in the forecast/prediction. This enables someone to quickly grasp which variables are the most important "causes," and which ones have only minor effects on the success of a prediction. This would have been unthinkably time consuming 20 years ago—now meteorologists can run an assortment of models in a few minutes, so the 6:00 A.M. forecast may be quite different from one at 6:30 A.M. This is possible because of a simple, well-designed interface that enables them to make many tweaks relatively effortlessly, then hit "Run" and get the result.

A new kind of generalist

Visualizations offer an arena for scientists in different specialties to create novel and insight-fostering ways of pulling together data that relates to a common underlying topic or goal—for example, finding an effective disease treatment. There is a role here for a new sort of generalist, one who specializes in facilitating interdisciplinary communication between specialists who work from different conceptual perspectives, which require *harmonization* before the data from each side will fit together meaningfully in a patterned way.

PART 2—NEW DIMENSIONS IN DATA VISUALIZATION

FIGURE 7.12
All Over Coffee #567, Haight Ashbury, San Francisco, by Paul Madonna (mural by Indicate Design Groupe).

Making sense of data means making sense of reality. A portion of reality is available to our senses, and another portion is not. Instruments, sensors, computers, and displays make more facets of reality perceptible. Getting the meaning of the data into our heads requires marshaling more of our senses to take it in. Technologies such as *virtual reality* (VR) and *augmented reality* (AR) can help us do that.

Engelbart and holodeck

Science fiction has many memorable examples of machine-generated 3D images that people can interact with directly. The approach makes sense in more ways than one. We inhabit a world with more than two dimensions, so why limit ourselves? Douglas Engelbart, a visionary of the computing and interaction design worlds, saw this early on. Along with leading the creation of the computer mouse, Engelbart talked about people being able to "fly through" data and information space, as well as in computer-assisted collaboration for problem solving.

Tools and technologies, both old and new, can form effective combinations. For example, along with a hammer, we might also use a more recent invention, such as a cheap laser level, to help us hang a painting. Some of the graphic representations of data that have been staples for the last couple of centuries will be augmented by a whole new range of visual vocabularies and grammars. These innovations will encompass more depth and dimension because technology can make that possible in intuitive and cost-effective new ways. They may enable us to more readily break through the boundaries of 2D space and explore more multidimensional realms. In a sense, we'll be going back to the future.

For as long as humans have been around, we've inhabited a 3D (and analog) environment. Now, however, although my desk faces out over a park and I'm looking at the slanting sunlight as it illuminates the tree branches, a large percentage of my time seems to be spent staring at a 2D flat screen. Currently, there's a division between the physical world and the digitized information about the world inside my computer. What happens when they become more fused as concepts such as augmented reality become more realistic and their applications more widespread? Just as books are not going away—I hope!—neither will bar charts. We now have books and movies and iPads to choose from. Soon we'll have a selection of all kinds of devices to show overlays of data on top of the physical world.

2D, or not 2D, that is the question...

Every man takes the limits of his own field of vision for the limits of the world.

—ARTHUR SCHOPENHAUER

Using 3D charts to represent data has been problematic for many people involved in the information visualization field. There's good reason for that. 3D bar charts can certainly make it hard to see clear, precise comparisons because they can block each other, and determining their relative heights is not always easy (Figure 7.13).

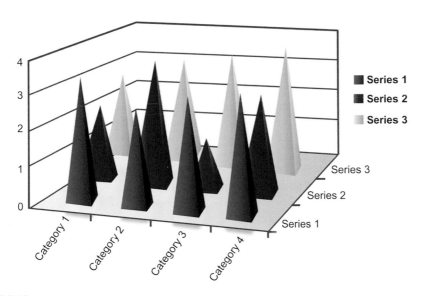

FIGURE 7.13
What are you telling me?

That defeats the purpose of using visual cues to help people make sense of data and makes a compelling case for 2D representations of data. Sure, with 2D it's harder, if not impossible, to show as many dimensions of a data set, but at least the data that is shown is clearer and easier for the viewer to gauge.

However, with the addition of interaction combined with the increasing use and cost-effectiveness of 3D displays, this kind of tradeoff may begin to disappear. It may come down not to an inherent problem with 3D, but to an issue of surface, environment, and projection. A "3D" visualization projected onto a 2D surface, such as a computer screen or piece of paper, inevitably will have some serious limitations. We're seeing only the illusion of 3D in these contexts, not the real deal. To some extent, our brains are tricked into seeing a 3D image by, for example, one object being "in front" of another and partially "blocking" the view. In reality, they're on the same plane. We can't go behind or around them.

In real life, we can experience 3D truly in 3D, and we have had a lot of practice engaging with the world in this way. Projecting aspects of our world on 2D surfaces is a handy trick, but that's not necessarily all that we can do. Perhaps the future of data visualization will involve a lot more 3D and immersive virtual environments where we can experience getting our "hands on the data" with Kinect®-like gesture-sensing technologies. That doesn't mean we won't be able to combine 2D charts with 3D representations effectively. Just as an older tool (such as a hammer) and a newer technology (such as a laser level), can be useful together for a single purpose (hanging a painting), so also can 2D and 3D visualizations work together.

As more dimensions (variables) of data about a particular topic of interest become available to explore simultaneously, people who make sense of data will increasingly need to rely on more visual dimensions to do so. As digital networks get larger and more complex, for example,

2D representations won't always cut it. The many layers of information and data involved in networks sometimes might best be shown by multidimensional representations. Because this data is dynamic, the aspects of it that could possibly need attention at any particular time might be in flux. So we need a visualization that allows us to move through this data in any direction we want. Beyond the issues of working with higher-dimensional data, being able to interact with data in ways we interact with the material world has a very basic visceral value.

New dimensions in data

Jürgen Schulze is a research scientist with the California Institute for Telecommunications and Information Technology at the University of California San Diego. His work includes scientific and data visualizations in virtual environments. He believes 3D environments can be especially useful in perceiving patterns and irregularities in data sets when researchers have a large quantity to explore. According to Schulze, "The sheer volume of the data can sometimes overwhelm and obscure any meaningful patterns it all contains." Schulze says that some of the problems associated with "3D" representations on 2D surfaces go away when the experience is truly interactive and immersive. "You can resolve occlusions [blocked views] by simply moving your body and also intuitively navigate to what you want by 'walking around' or 'flying through' a data set," he says. "You can see something pass behind you as you move around and are therefore more likely to find it, versus using your mouse on a 2D display."

Schulze says he often likens the experience to common activities he does in his office: "I have multiple piles of folders arranged and stacked on my desk. If I tried to find a paper in my computer file system, I can't make use of my spatial memory. I need a search function, as there is a benefit in searching for your documents, and then you may find you come across other useful and related things." Often, you can remember if it is a big folder, he explains. You keep it and refresh it in your memory. However, generally speaking, "humans have good spatial memory capabilities" that they use to help them find what they want. Schulze also notes some kinds of data are "inherently 3D, such as CAT scans, MRIs, and electron microscopy," and can lend themselves to useful explorations in 3D environments.

The following are a few examples of work that Jürgen Schulze and Thomas DeFanti, a research scientist with the California Institute for Telecommunications and Information Technology at UCSD, as well as Distinguished Professor of Computer Science at the University of Illinois at Chicago, helped create, to aid various kinds of research efforts. There are many ways to utilize immersive 3D visualizations; to explore anything from protein structures to the energy usage patterns of data centers to the hidden layers of Leonardo da Vinci's works. These are not all data visualizations; they are scientific or other kinds of visualizations, however they show interesting and important features that might be considered when visualizing data.

A fantastic voyage inside a protein molecule

In Figure 7.14 the person whose silhouette you see is leading a group of observers inside UC San Diego's StarCAVE through the inside of a protein molecule. The StarCAVE consists of 15 large projection screens enclosing a 10 × 10-foot space.

FIGURE 7.14
Viewer looking at a 3D representation of a protein structure inside the Calit2 StarCAVE at UCSD. *Photo by Hunter Whitney.*

A small group of people wearing polarized glasses can stand inside the StarCAVE, fly through the inside of the image of a protein molecule, and fluidly view it from a range of angles. The scale of the projected images of protein structures and the immersive experience, make users feel as if they're directly connected to, enveloped by, and engaged with the content of the Protein Data Bank. Researchers can see characteristics of the protein structures that would otherwise be difficult or impossible to discern using a desktop computer. Those patterns in the shapes of proteins can lead to new insights and questions for a range of purposes, including new drug discovery.

Real-time x-ray vision for a mobile data center

3D visualizations are good for a range of things, from representing the molecular level of proteins to recreating physical structures that may not be immediately accessible.

The sensors that monitor various kinds of facilities can send their data anywhere, so the people who need to track it do not have to be anywhere near the location. That said,

FIGURE 7.15

Schulze navigating a virtual mobile data center.

recreating the environment virtually and then showing the real-time data about it in a more contextualized way make the process potentially more intuitive and effective.

One example is Project Green Light, a mobile data center that uses sensors to monitor energy usage of computing systems under real-world conditions. People can move around this virtual facility. Jürgen Schulze guides visitors through this truly interactive experience. The controlling device Schulze is holding in Figure 7.15 incorporates a small array of sensors to pick up relative position. These sensors allow the controller to detect how it's moving in space. The controller is a piece of commodity hardware that is commercially available. The fact that this controller comes from a PS3™ and is inexpensive tells us that these technologies are closer than we might think. On the screen, there's a green "steering wheel" image that indicates how to use the controller to move through the visualization (Figure 7.16).

"People develop a 'spatial awareness' when they walk into a building," says Schulze. "Architects have a particular need for this kind of understanding of dimensions and lines of scale in their work." Just as bioscientists want to understand the structures of proteins, architects want to better understand the structure of buildings, even before they exist. They can, for example, hold out their hand to assess a space and imagine how people might move around within it. This is akin to how many of us might place furniture around a room and then step back to see how a particular arrangement flows. However, a typical computer interface is not conducive to these kinds of activities. "People can't move through a screen with a measuring tape," Shulze notes.

FIGURE 7.16
Taking control.

Decoding da Vinci in 3D

There's arguably nobody that represents the union of art and science—an embodiment of what was once called the "Renaissance Man"—more than Leonardo da Vinci. So it's fitting that the investigation of one of his works is an example of how scientific and data visualization can illuminate the work and "frame" the painting in an entirely new way. Even a centuries-old work of art can tell many more stories with the help of new visualization technologies.

When we look at a Renaissance painting in a museum, we see a flat, two-dimensional surface. However, the great artists made their art seem like the scene was full of depth with their mastery of ways to fool the eye. In addition, even though the painting may be on a flat surface, it actually can consist of many layers that were put on top of each other over centuries. In Chapter 4, we looked at the ideas of various forms of pathways and how they led to a final display or representation. An old painting is the culmination of a process. It has embedded within it the path an artist took to create it. One way to understand the painting is to be able to see the lines and layers that tell the story of its creation and evolution.

One notable project that Schulze and DeFanti did with Calit2's cultural heritage researcher, Maurizio Seracini, was to highlight da Vinci's work, "The Adoration of the Magi." They took very high-resolution photographs of the painting under different wavelengths of light (visible, ultraviolet, infrared, and x-ray), and they took hundreds of photos close up and stitched them together to high-resolution image files. The software makes it possible to adjust the opacity of the layers, and the layers can be superimposed, separated, and stacked to get different perspectives of the work. By doing so, they were able to show different aspects of the painting that are revealed by different lighting conditions.

Although some of the visual analysis could be done with 2D projections, Schulze says that the 3D display system allows for a greater range of possibilities for users to interact with different spectral images. This range of interaction in 3D includes having the ability to put different views on each side, or even arrange them around you, rather than only being able to see the stack at a perpendicular angle.

This kind of 3D exploration and immersion into a painting doesn't have to be relegated to a lucky art historian. Schulze and DeFanti (who we'll meet in the next section) were able to create a 3D experience in a 200-person auditorium without the need for 3D glasses. Instead of relying on tracking data from the position of the user's head, they used positional data from a pointer or "wand" to determine the viewpoint, and adjusted the viewing zones to accommodate the size of the stage (Figure 7.17).

For "The Adoration of the Magi," they learned that it was sketched in charcoal by da Vinci, and years later someone else painted over the drawing. That person was instructed to paint over some of the symbolic message of the original. The original owner of the

FIGURE 7.17
A face in the crowd. *Courtesy of Uffizi Gallery, Florence, Italy. Photo credit: Maurizio Seracini and Calit2.*

FIGURE 7.18

Dissecting a da Vinci. *Courtesy of Uffizi Gallery, Florence, Italy. Photo credit: Maurizio Seracini and Calit2.*

painting may not have been interested in the work and may have just rolled it up, moved it around, let moisture get to it and it got damaged. In the later process of restoration, things may be changed. "It's a kind of visual time travel, where researchers can zoom in and out from the 'ground layer' to the surface," says Schulze. (See Figure 7.18.)

http://.goo.gl/9cLOL

We can create a very precise 3D model from the painting, and that's important because it will allow us to tell if there's motion in the figures from the time when they were created to later on. Knowing about such motion, in turn, will allow us to see if and where there have been any changes.

This old home (with new 3D displays)

Thomas DeFanti says facilities such as the StarCAVE are a great way to demonstrate some of the possibilities of big, immersive virtual reality systems. He believes one of the most interesting developments will be in the diffusion of 3D visualization tools to broader audiences for a wide variety of professional and personal uses. He sees a future in which we'll have visualization display ubiquity. Gazing out a bay window of his home on the Pacific Ocean, DeFanti muses about the idea of having bay window-like display systems as a common feature in homes and offices. He notes that he has to replace some of his windows, and it's getting to the point where the cost of a similar-sized electronic display isn't that much more than that of a window. For people who spend $50,000 or $100,000 for a kitchen remodel, for example, they could create a truly amazing visual configuration.

Parts of what has to emerge, he says, are new user mindsets. He sees them coming out of the home market, for example from consumers playing video games or doing online shopping. Shopping with an interactive 3D system could have more practical value than might first meet the eye. For example, DeFanti was looking for a certain kind of insulation for his walls. He visited the website of a large home improvement store chain, but he found that the picture of the insulation, a static image that was "the size of a postage stamp," couldn't provide him a sense of the material's texture—an important factor for his purposes.

What may seem like exotic displays and representations now may eventually have value in everyday life. A building contractor potentially could get as much use in his work out of interactive 3D systems as a molecular biologist exploring protein conformations. Along with the plummeting prices of visualization systems, time, and exposure to these technologies will help to increase their adoption rate. Changes in habits, experiences, and mindsets also may help to usher in greater use of visualization apps for a range of purposes. DeFanti says, "You may not use the tool 98% of the time, but if you do and become accustomed to it, then it's like second-nature."

Scientific researchers who have spent years immersed in tables and line charts may find immersive virtual reality environments to seem like alien landscapes. In those instances, it can be even more important to allow users to know exactly where the data comes from. DeFanti recalls that very early in his career, he worked on a science fiction movie, and he noticed that some people in the audience showed signs of fear at one of the special effects involving a pulsating alien intelligence. These days, the same effect would not have the same impact. Over time, we become accustomed to different things and so have different levels of expectations.

One of the main challenges of creating a user experience for these types of systems is to make sure they're not cumbersome and are as just-in-time as possible. "You want it there when you want it and want it to go away when you don't," DeFanti says. He mentions his wife is a multitasker: she might be watching TV, baking something in the oven, playing solitaire on a laptop, and texting at the same time. If she had to wear some kind of stereovision glasses to engage with one display, it would make it difficult for her to do the other activities. Even with one related activity but different displays, without even needing polarized glasses from different manufacturers, it could be a problem. People will always need easy ways to be able to pause, start and stop, and shift between various activities. "Some things are great for 3D and others are not," says DeFanti. "My feeling is that the paradigm that's best for 3D is interactions used for the exploration phase of the process."

Holograms and 3D

Most of us are exposed to 3D at the movies. After putting on our funny glasses and buying some popcorn, we make our way to the theater proper, where everyone sits looking relatively straight on at the screen. Because the screen is so large and so far away, we fail to notice that moving our heads doesn't change our 3D perspective. When we watch traditional films, we're used to not being able to turn around and look behind us. Our suspension of disbelief is such that, as viewers, we understand we're looking through the eye of a camera and not looking through a window we can climb through nor can we walk around in the scene.

Let's do a brief experiment. Take any small object and put it down on a flat surface in front of you. I'm using a pen, but literally any small object will work. Circle the object with your head, and notice how your perspective on the object changes as you move. In the real world, the appearance of an object changes as we move around it. Next, look at the die in Figure 7.19, and tilt the book forward so the top of the book is getting closer to you while the bottom of the book remains in place. Notice how the perspective of the object remains the same. If this die existed in the real world as a physical object, the "6" side on the top of the image would get more pronounced while the "2" and "3" sides got less pronounced as you tipped the die toward you.

This demonstration represents one of the fundamental limitations of 3D displays—the perspective on any given 3D object does not change as you move your head. Because the image is fundamentally displayed on a 2D surface using visual trickery to make us perceive that we're viewing things in 3D, the perspective and depth are fixed by the

FIGURE 7.19
A 3D die in 2D.

designer or cinematographer and don't change with user input. We're much more likely to dismiss or not even notice this phenomenon while watching a 3D film or television program, but this limitation becomes very apparent when you're sitting in front of a 3D computer screen. As you move your head, the perspective on the objects that are displayed doesn't change. A user needs to use other interface elements to move the object in 3D space.

Holograms offer an alternative to this problem by showing an image from multiple viewing angles. As hologram technology is still in its infancy, numerous methods are currently being tested for projecting and viewing holograms. Commodity hologram displays are still many years away, so technologies have been developed that simulate holograms on a traditional 3D display.

Simulating holograms

As discussed above, with traditional 3D displays, moving your head doesn't change the perspective of the image. One way to work around this problem is to have a sensor system that detects the position of your head and redraws the 3D image every time your head moves. The computer builds the 3D environment and has a simulated camera emulating the position of your head. As you move left to right, the sensor detects the position and distance of your head relative to the display and moves the virtual camera exactly the same way in the digital world. This allows a very good facsimile of a holographic display that can be done with currently available technology.

Coupled with gesture recognition software, it's easy to see this technology being very useful in diagnostic medicine. A surgeon could have a 3D CT scan that could be manipulated in the operating room without risk of contamination. Simply by gesturing in the air, medical professionals could fly through and rotate a model of the organ being operated on. Because we're used to subtle changes in perspective when we move our bodies relative to an object, a display system that adapts to these subtle changes would make the interface more intuitive and the image more realistic.

The future of reality

Along with *virtual reality* (VR) comes the concept *of augmented reality* (AR). In the case of AR, the idea is not to fully recreate a computer-generated simulation of an environment but, rather, to make more of the data about a physical space available to our senses. AR overlays the tangible world with representations of intangible data. The different realities of VR and AR form a continuum and can be useful for different purposes. For exploring the structures of a protein, there may be no reason for augmented reality; the world that best showcases the molecular structure and minimizes other distractions may be immersive VR. On the other hand, it you want to see data about a block of buildings on a city street, augmented reality may be just the ticket.

Just as 2D charts can be used in conjunction with 3D virtual environments, 2D and 3D charts can be visually overlaid onto physical reality.

PART 3—REAL TIME

Old data and forever data

A truly good book teaches me better than to read it. I must soon lay it down, and commence living on its hint. What I began by reading, I must finish by acting.

– HENRY DAVID THOREAU

As new technologies develop, the old technologies they replace stop being manufactured and eventually disappear from the world around us. Software that can only be run on certain archaic hardware no longer works when the last computer of a specific type finally succumbs to the ravages of time. Scientific research and data stored on old 5.5-inch floppy drives is nearly impossible to recover all these years after the disk format was replaced by something better. Older still are data sets stored on IBM/360 mainframe tape drives. Legacy hardware and software pose serious problems for the storage and recovery of data.

This creates some real-world problems when it comes to scientific research. A key portion of the scientific method involves the ability to reproduce an experiment a number of times and get the same result. If the data or computer program used as part of an experiment is locked up on obsolete hardware (or deleted or lost), the experiment becomes impossible to run again. If an experiment can't be verified—for example, in response to some new data—whatever theories emerged as a result of the original experiment must be severely questioned.

The only surefire way around this problem is to print out all the data (and the program used to process it) on acid-free paper and put it somewhere safe where it won't catch on fire. Practically speaking, this is impossible for all but the smallest data sets. The next best option is to be vigilant about copying data from old formats and hardware to new formats and hardware as soon as the old formats and old hardware begin to fall out of use. This is often a time-consuming and expensive process, and impossible if the experiment relied on a specific piece of data collection hardware that's no longer produced.

Some legacy software programs can be resuscitated with the use of software/hardware emulators, which is how the screen shots for the DC HomeFinder application discussed in Chapter 2 were taken. Emulators are special programs that allow one computer to act exactly (or close enough) like another type of computer. The original Nintendo Entertainment System® (NES) is very different from modern computers in the way the underlying hardware architecture works, but modern computers can accurately model the behavior of the NES. This allows for the preservation of old games past the life of the original hardware.

Not everyone thinks all data should be stored forever. Although 50-year-old data about a planetary modeling experiment should be saved in the interests of science, 50-year-old pictures of my very inebriated college friends is a different matter. The concern about personally embarrassing or harmful social media-related content is a new and very real problem. Some have suggested creating file formats that self-destruct or become unreadable after a certain period of time. This poses a difficult technical problem in that any piece of software can be reverse-engineered to figure out how it works, and once someone figures out how the self-deletion mechanism operates, they can negate it.

THE ELEPHANT IN THE ROOM

One of the most powerful uses for visualizations is to connect the proverbial dots between data points. Even if the data is good, if there are only limited views of it, the true picture will never emerge. How can people be sure they fully understand something when they can only get a partial perspective of it? (See Figure 7.20.) There's an old folktale from India, often called the "Three Blind Men and the Elephant." While the circumstances may be antiquated, the essential idea still resonates and is directly relevant to visualizing data.

In the story, the three men are unable to see the elephant standing in front of them and can only get a sense of what it is by touching part of the creature. One felt the tusk, the second felt the ear, and the last felt the tail. Each drew a reasonable, but incorrect, conclusion about what was before him. The tusk was bone; the ear, leather; the tail, rope. What makes this story so commonly used is that we can imagine it viscerally (Figure 7.21).

From the jumbo to the microscopic, sometimes all we can rely on are partial views to find an answer. The structure of the DNA molecule was once one of the greatest mysteries and challenges of science. Researchers were only able to obtain limited views of this critical structure that is so important in our life. It was only by thinking of the relationships between these different elements that the truth emerged (Figure 7.22). The story of the insight has entered into modern lore.

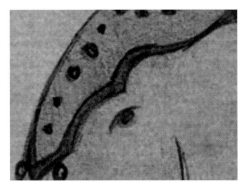

FIGURE 7.20
Elephants and eyes.

"Seeing" an Elephant

Bone?   Leather?   Rope?

Big Picture

FIGURE 7.21
Truncated views.

"Seeing" DNA

```
ATTCGAGCCTATGC
GGAATCGATACAGT
CCACTGATCGATTG
AGCCTATGCGGAAT
CGATACAGTCCACT
GATCGATCGATTGA
GCCTATGCGGAATC
```

X-ray Crystallography   Base-Pair Sequence   Chromosomes

Molecular Structure

FIGURE 7.22
Shaping our natures.

I could simply have noted that seeing multiple views of data can tell a more complete picture and leave it there. However, there's still an elephant in the room. In user interface design, the interface is only a part of the equation, and sometimes the far less complex and challenging part. It is the users, and human nature in general, that need to be faced squarely. The fact is that for various reasons, people don't want to share their data with each other; or their motivations for what they give and take can be less than pure.

Amazing new displays that enable getting and sharing views of data won't, in themselves, address issues like this. In thinking about innovative ways to visualize data we should factor in real-world considerations about human aspirations and foibles. Even more importantly, evolution in the way people make sense of data should include thinking about the processes of sharing and collaborating that are best suited to getting optimal reflections of reality and also address the human element.

BORDER CROSSINGS...

The empires of the future are the empires of the mind.

– SIR WINSTON CHURCHILL

As I've found from the variety of people I talked to for this book, it's clear that many new discoveries come from pushing the boundaries of our abilities to perceive and to think about the data that's around us. It's important to cross the borders of disciplines such as computer science, psychology, journalism, graphic design, fine art, statistics, and many more. We should step out of our comfort zones—I certainly did while writing this book—and look at data from different perspectives. With the help of visual representations, we can more fully experience and interact with data. The great empires of the mind will have their own "trade routes" to allow interchange of ideas, techniques, and knowledge and share the riches of their domains. Data visualizations are a kind of passport and translation guide to make this possible.

Resources

Books

Visualizations—Data, Information, and Scientific

Bertin, J. (2011). *Semiology of graphics: Diagrams, networks, maps* (W. J. Berg, Trans.). Redlands, CA: Esri Press (original work published 1965).

Börner, K. (2010). *Atlas of science: Visualizing what we know.* Cambridge: The MIT Press.

Card, S. K., Mackinlay, J. D., & Shneiderman, B. (Eds.). (1999). *Readings in information visualization: Using vision to think.* San Francisco: Morgan Kaufmann.

Few, S. C. (2004). *Show me the numbers: Designing tables and graphs to enlighten.* Oakland, CA: Analytics Press.

Few, S. C. (2009). *Now you see it: Simple visualization techniques for quantitative analysis.* Oakland, CA: Analytics Press.

Frankel, F. C., & DePace, A. H. (2012). *Visual strategies: A practical guide to graphics for scientists and engineers.* New Haven: Yale University Press.

Fry, B. (2008). *Visualizing data.* Sebastopol, CA: O'Reilly Media.

Klanten, R., Bourquin, N., Ehmann, S., van Heerden, F., & Tissot, T. (Eds.) (2008). *Data flow: Visualizing information in graphic design.* Berlin: Gestalten.

Klanten, R., Ehmann, S., Tissot, T., & Bourquin, N. (Eds.) (2010). *Data flow 2: Visualizing information in graphic design.* Berlin: Gestalten.

Klanten, R., Ehmann, S., & Schulze, F. (Eds.) (2011). *Visual storytelling: Inspiring a new visual language.* Berlin: Gestalten.

Marty, R. (2009). *Applied security visualization.* Boston: Addison-Wesley Professional.

Segaran, T., & Hammerbacher, J. (Eds.). (2009). *Beautiful data: The stories behind elegant data solutions.* Sebastopol, CA: O'Reilly Media.

Tufte, E. R. (1997). *Visual explanations: Images and quantities, evidence and narrative.* Cheshire, CT: Graphics Press.

Tufte, E. R. (1998). *Envisioning information.* Cheshire, CT: Graphics Press.

Tufte, E. R. (1998). *The visual display of quantitative information.* Cheshire, CT: Graphics Press.

Tufte, E. R. (2010). *Beautiful evidence.* Cheshire, CT: Graphics Press.

Ware, C. (2004). *Information visualization: Perception for design.* Boston: Morgan Kaufmann.

Ware, C. (2008). *Visual thinking for design.* Boston: Morgan Kaufmann.

Wilkinson, L. (2005). *The grammar of graphics.* Chicago: Springer.

Yau, N. (2011). *Visualize this: The flowing data guide to design, visualization, and statistics.* Indianapolis, IN: Wiley Publishing.

User Experience/Interaction Design

Cooper, A. (1995). *About face: The essentials of user interface design.* Foster City, CA: IDG Books.

Fowler, S., & Stanwick, V. (2004). *Web application design handbook: Best practices for web-based software.* Boston: Morgan Kaufmann.

Norman, D. A. (1988). *The psychology of everyday things.* New York: Basic Books.

Norman, D. A. (1998). *The invisible computer: Why good products can fail, the personal computer is so complex, and information appliances are the solution.* Cambridge: The MIT Press.

Shneiderman, B., Plaisant, C., Cohen M., & Jacobs, S. (2009). *Designing the user interface: Strategies for effective human-computer interaction* (5th ed.). Boston: Addison-Wesley.

Charted Territories

Robertson, B. (1988). *How to draw charts and diagrams.* Cincinnati: North Light Books.

Wong, D. M. (2010). The Wall Street Journal *guide to information graphics: The dos and don'ts of presenting data, facts, and figures.* New York: W. W. Norton & Company.

Questions, Investigations, Analysis

Beveridge, W. I. B. (2004). *The art of scientific investigation.* Caldwell, NJ: The Blackburn Press. (Reprint of the 1957 Revised Edition, by W.W. Norton and Company.)

Heuer, Jr., R. J. (1999). *The psychology of intelligence analysis* (1st ed.). Center for the Study of Intelligence, Central Intelligence Agency (U.S.). Washington, D.C.: United States Government Printing Office.

Morville, P., & Callender, J. (2010). *Search patterns.* Sebastopol, CA: O'Reilly Media.

Connecting the Dots

Barabasi, A-L. (2003). *Linked: How everything is connected to everything else and what it means for business, science, and everyday life.* New York: Plume Books.

Hansen, D. L., Shneiderman, B., & Smith, M.A. (2011). *Analyzing social media networks with NodeXL: Insights from a connected world.* Boston: Morgan Kaufmann.

Newman, M. E. J. (2010). *Networks: An introduction.* New York: Oxford University Press.

Thinking about Thinking

Arnheim, R. (1969). *Visual thinking.* Berkeley: University of California Press.

Pink, D. H. (2005). *A whole new mind: Moving from the information age to the conceptual age.* New York: Riverhead Books.

Root-Bernstein, R. S. & M. M. (1999). *Sparks of genius: The 13 thinking tools of the world's most creative people.* New York: Houghton Mifflin.

Perception

Zakia, R. D. (2002). *Perception and imaging* (2nd ed.). Boston: Focal Press.

Statistics

Boslaugh, S., & Watters, P. A. (2008). *Statistics in a nutshell: A desktop quick reference*. Sebastopol, CA: O'Reilly Media.

Motulsky, H. (2010). *Intuitive biostatistics: A nonmathematical guide to statistical thinking* (2nd ed.). New York: Oxford University Press.

Data Mining

Shmueli, G., Patel, N. R., & Bruce, P. C. (2010). *Data mining for business intelligence: Concepts, techniques, and applications in Microsoft Office Excel® with XLMiner®*. Hoboken, NJ: John Wiley & Sons.

Immersive Interactions

Dodsworth, Jr., C. (1998). *Digital illusion: Entertaining the future with high technology*. Boston: Addison-Wesley Longman.

Rheingold, H. (1991). *Virtual reality: The revolutionary technology of computer-generated artificial worlds—and how it promises to transform society* (1st ed.). New York: Touchstone.

Swink, S., (2009). *Game feel: A game designer's guide to virtual sensation.* Boston: Morgan Kaufmann.

Miscellaneous Visual Narrative

McCloud, S. (1993). *Understanding comics.* Northampton, MA: Kitchen Sink Press.

Online Resources and Websites

Blow, C. *By the numbers*. http://blow.blogs.nytimes.com

Fast Company. *Co.design*. http://www.fastcodesign.com

Meier, P. *iRevolution: From innovation to revolution*. http://irevolution.net

Stamen Design. *The next most obvious thing*. http://content.stamen.com

UX Magazine. http://uxmag.com

Vande Moere, A. *Information aesthetics*. http://infosthetics.com

Visually, Inc. *Visual.ly blog*. http://blog.visual.ly

Yau, N. *Flowingdata*. http://flowingdata.com

References

Adams, D. (1981). *The hitchhiker's guide to the galaxy.* New York: Pocket Books.

Babey, S. H., et al. (2011). *A patchwork of progress: Changes in overweight and obesity among California 5th-, 7th-, and 9th-graders, 2005–2010.* Los Angeles: UCLA Center for Health Policy Research and California Center for Public Health Advocacy. Funded by the Robert Wood Johnson Foundation.

Bainbridge, L. (1983). Ironies of automation. *Automatica, 19*(6), 775–779.

Craik, F. I. M. (1979). Human memory. *Annual Review of Psychology, 30,* 63–102.

Doyle, Sir A. C. (1998). The problem of Thor bridge. In *The Adventures of Sherlock Holmes.* New York: Oxford University Press.

Lathrop, C. E. (2004). *The literary spy: The ultimate source for quotations on espionage & intelligence.* New Haven: Yale University Press.

Mintzberg, H. (2005). Developing theory about the development of theory. In K. G. Smith & M. A. Hitt (Eds.), *Great minds in management: The theory of process development* (p. 368). New York: Oxford University Press.

Perer, A., & IBM Research. (2011). From Perer, A., Guy, I., Uziel, E., Ronen, I., & Jacovi, M, Visual social network analytics for relationship discovery in the enterprise. *IEEE Conference on Visual Analytics Science and Technology (VAST),* Providence, RI.

Perer, A., & The University of Maryland. (2010). Finding beautiful insights in the chaos of social network visualizations. Chapter 11, pp. 157–173. In J. Steele & N. Iliinsky (Eds.), *Beautiful Visualization.* Sebastopol, CA: O'Reilly Media.

Roddenberry, G. (story), Fontana, D.C. (teleplay), & Dobkin, L. (director). (1966, September 15). *Charlie X* (Television series episode). In Roddenberry, G. (Producer), *Star Trek.* Los Angeles: Desilu Productions.

Shapin, S. (2007, May 14). What else is new? *The New Yorker.* Retrieved June 5, 2012, from www.newyorker.com/arts/critics/books/2007/05/14/070514crbo_books_shapin.

Shneiderman, B., Plaisant, C., Cohen, M., & Jacobs, S. (2010). *Designing the user interface* (5th ed.). Boston: Addison-Wesley.

Stevens, C. F. (2009). Darwin and Huxley revisited: The origin of allometry. *Journal of Biology,* 8:14.

Tolkein, J. R. R. (1985). *The hobbit.* New York: Ballantine Books.

Twain, M., & F.R. Rogers (Ed.). (2012). *Simon Wheeler, Detective.* Whitefish, MT: Literary Licensing.

Index

Note: Page numbers with "f" denote figures and "t" tables.

303